LOVERS AND OTHER STRANGERS

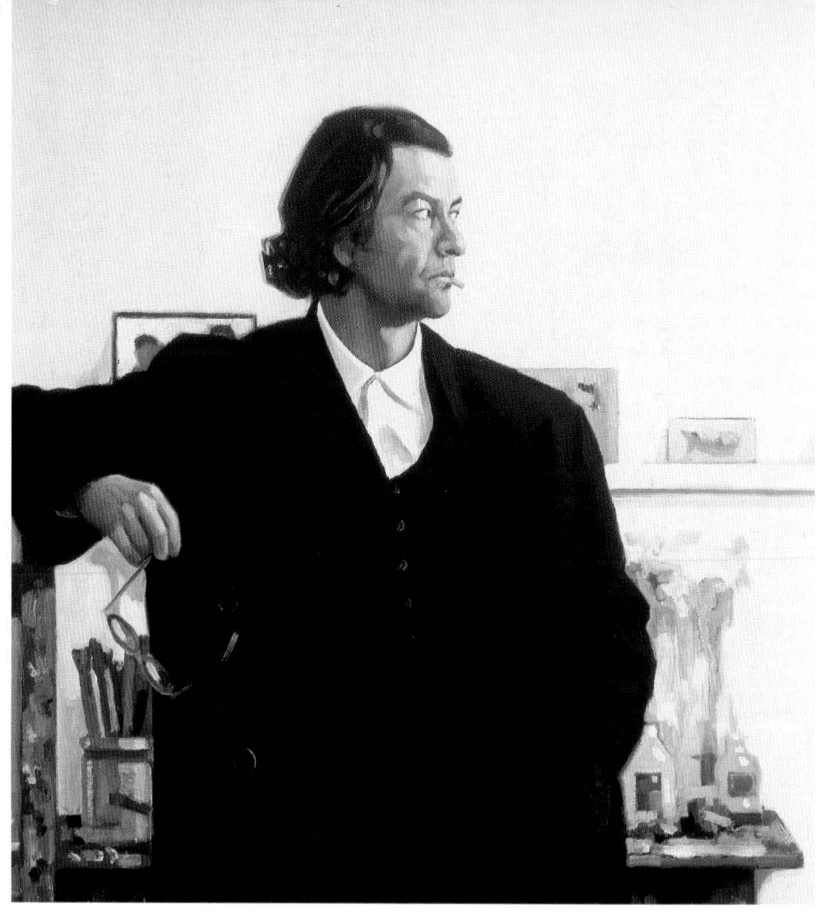

This book is dedicated to my teacher,
my pupil, my healer, my dearest friend.

J.V.

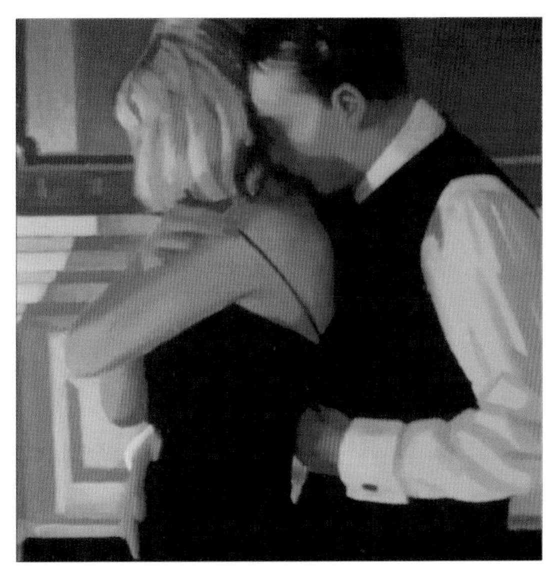

LOVERS AND OTHER STRANGERS
PAINTINGS BY JACK VETTRIANO

Text by Anthony Quinn

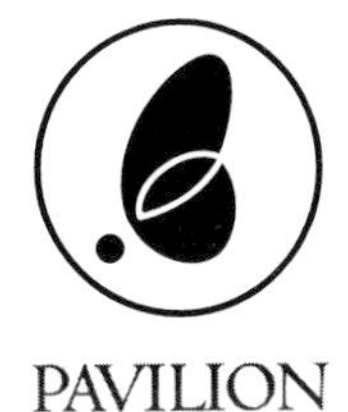

PAVILION

Hardback edition first published in Great Britain in 2000 by
Pavilion Books

Paperback edition first published in Great Britain in 2002 by
Pavilion Books

Pavilion Books
The Chrysalis Building
Bramley Road
London W10 6SP

An imprint of Chrysalis Books Group plc

Designed by Bernard Higton

A CIP catalogue record for this book is available from the British Library.

Hardback ISBN 1 86205 420 7
Paperback ISBN 1 86205 630 7

Photographic acknowledgements:

The publisher wishes to give special thanks to Hugh Kelly and to thank the following photographers for their kind permission to reproduce their photographs:

Andrew Fletcher page 8; Lesley Jones (website: www. lesleyjones.co.uk) pages 7, 13 and 157; and Robin Matthews page 36.

Jack Vettriano is represented exclusively by Portland Gallery, London

Colour origination by Articolour, Italy
Printed and bound in Spain by Just Colour Graphics

10 9 8 7 6

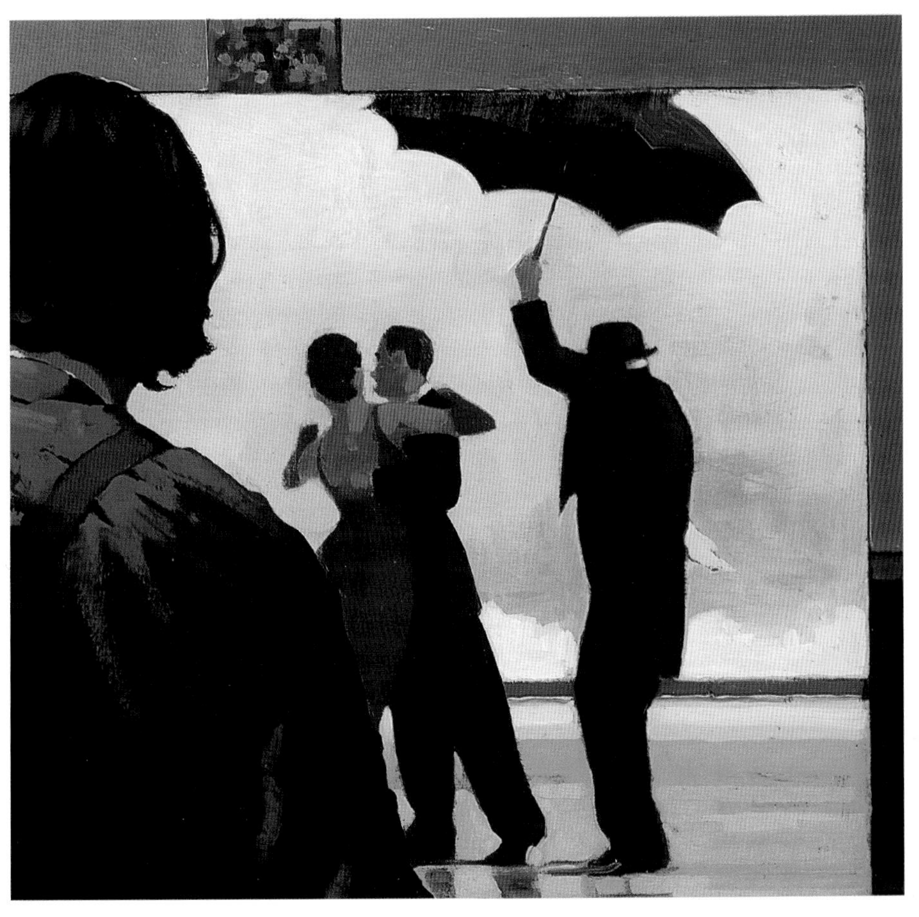

CONTENTS

Photograph of Jack Vettriano by Lesley Jones.

FOREWORD

JACK VETTRIANO has the ability to make you feel nostalgic for things you never actually experienced in the first place. He takes you to a mood and time that you know so well although you were never there. When you first look at one of his paintings you are an outsider, illicitly observing a cool, sharp world of edgy romance and sexual tension. The men are tougher than those you know, the women are unavailable. After a while you can see behind the confident poses and languid come-ons; these are people no more in control of their destinies than you are of yours. Maybe you have been where Vettriano's subjects are – it's just that the lighting and suitcases, beaches and party frocks are different. You are an insider. Maybe the time is here and now.

Jack Vettriano's paintings make you wonder what will happen next; none are static. Every picture is an episode – in a romance that is about to explode, or in a conquest that is about to be consummated, although who will conquer whom is never clear. He evokes an era of Hollywood but no film of that town's heyday was made with Vettriano's burning colour; those great movies remain of their time, these paintings are of many times – the clothes and backdrops are beautiful ornaments that could pinpoint a year, but the faces are universal, of any, or of every, of the past fifty years.

In less than ten years, Vettriano has moved into the front rank of contemporary artists. Others there (but by no means all) may match his technical skills but he has the much rarer gifts of realism and humour. Human failings and foibles are not portrayed in the easy way, through squalor and loathing of his subjects, but subtly. His men and women may win through, may come to a sticky end, but either way they will do so with glamour and style. There is hope in even his seediest settings, which is why he has accessibility without compromise.

TIM RICE

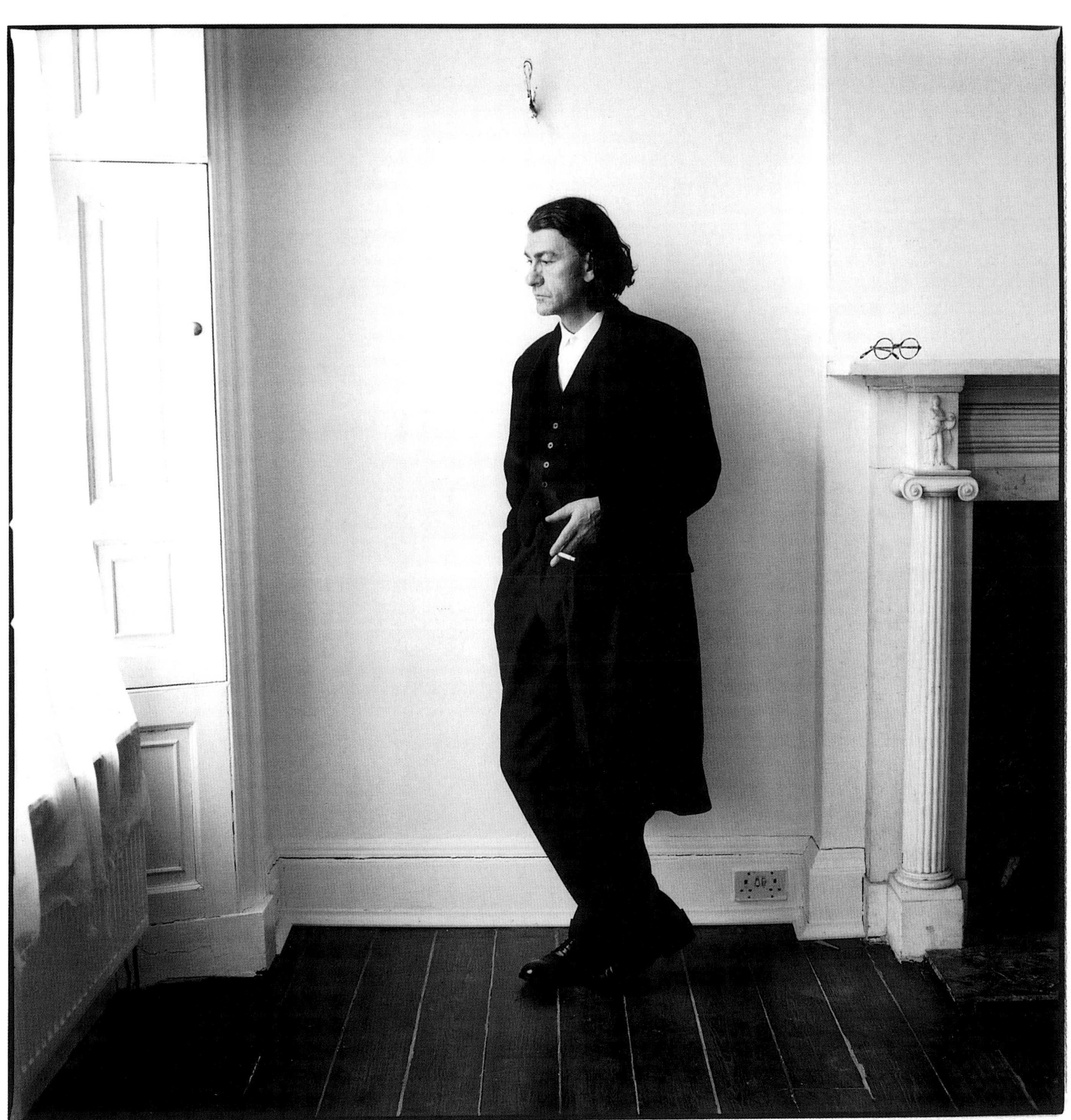

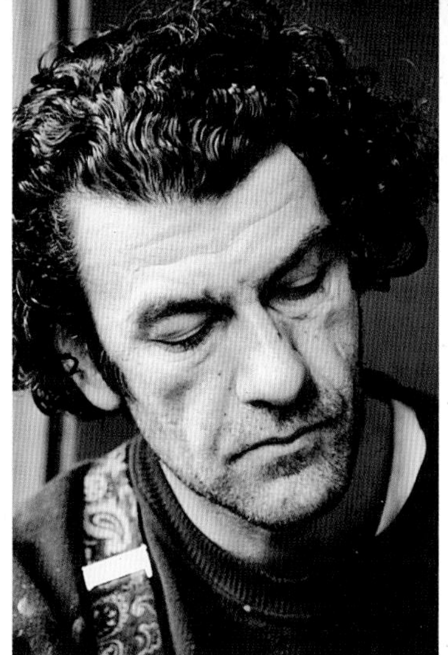

Photograph of Jack Vettriano by Andrew Fletcher.

INTRODUCTION

NIGHT-TIME. A young woman sits at a bar, her face in pensive profile, a cigarette drooping disconsolately from her hand. A waistcoated barman leans towards her, his head close enough to smell her perfume, or whisper in her ear. There's no telling exactly what he's said, but the look of quiet resignation on the woman's face is enough to suggest that it's nothing good. In the background, another man can be seen watching them in predatory expectation. Is he just a bar-room voyeur, a tourist around other people's misery – or is he in cahoots with the barman? Are we witnessing some vile transaction? The questions hang in the air.

The title of this painting is *Cocktails and Broken Hearts*. The name of the painter is, of course, Jack Vettriano. In the alluring and sinister world of his art the drama of men and women together is played out against a backdrop of bars and clubs, seasides and racetracks, ballrooms and bedrooms. The time is slightly out of joint. The characters wear clothes reminiscent of forties melodramas – a dark suit and snap-brimmed hat for him, a slash of red lipstick, silk stockings and a dress *à la* Gloria Grahame for her. Everybody smokes, stylishly. Where is this place, this retroland of glamour and sleaze? Where are these tenebrous backrooms and beachfronts vivid with bunting? Not of our time, surely, yet the details of their composition – a provocative pose, a yearning expression, a cigarette held just so – are certainly of our world, a kind of limbo where past and present elide, a dance to the music outside of time.

The keynote of Vettriano's art is atmosphere, and he likes to paint it *noir*. His work ponders the role of fate, the tragicomedy of attraction and the human potential for harm. A morbid sexual tension hums through his hothouse interiors, often rendered within a framework of horizontals and verticals that close down space and seem to imprison these highly trained social animals. We are asked to look through the peephole, to spy on these men and women as they wait and prowl, plotting seduction or betrayal or whatever it takes to forget their own loneliness. And so we too become complicit,

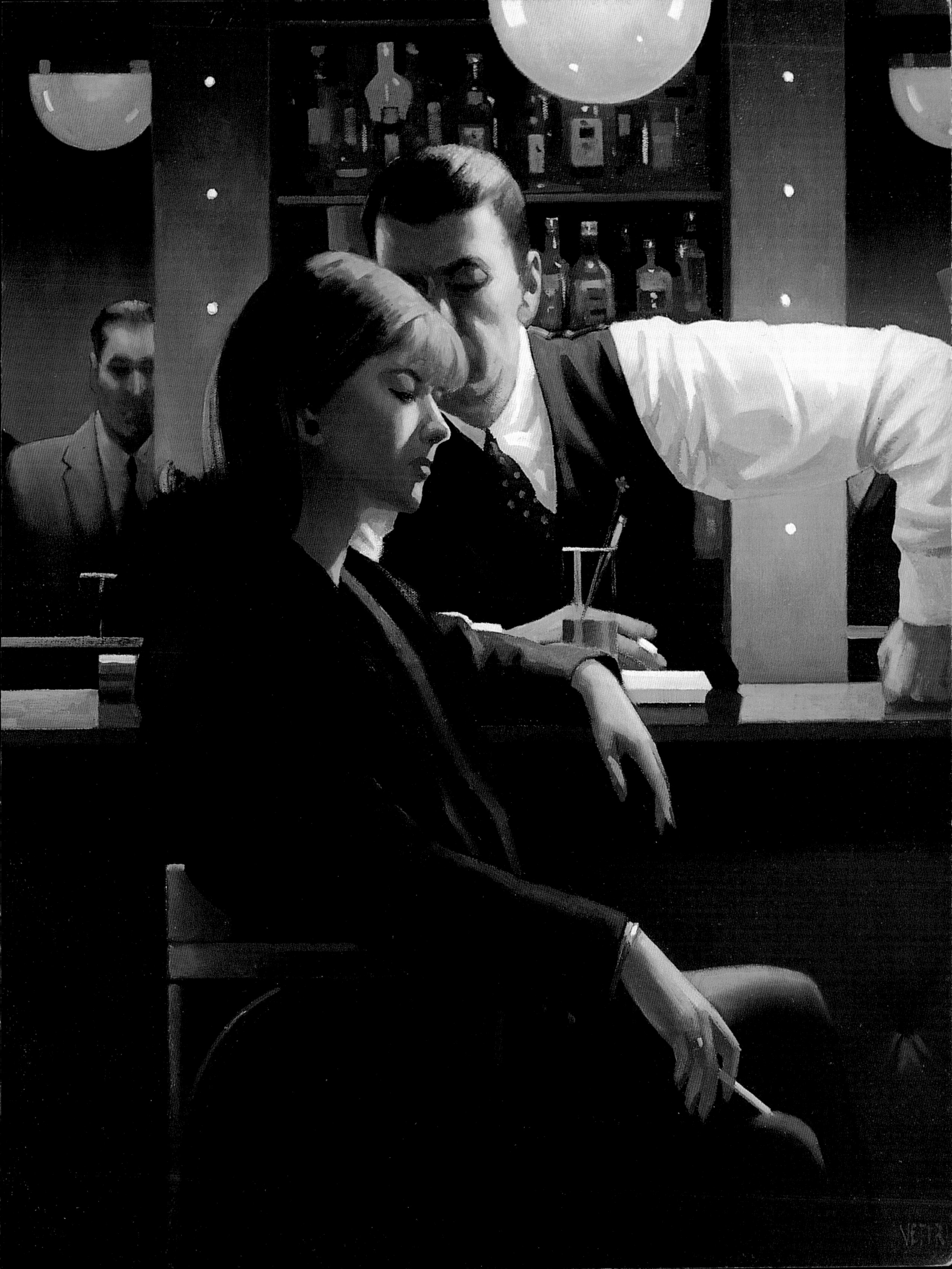

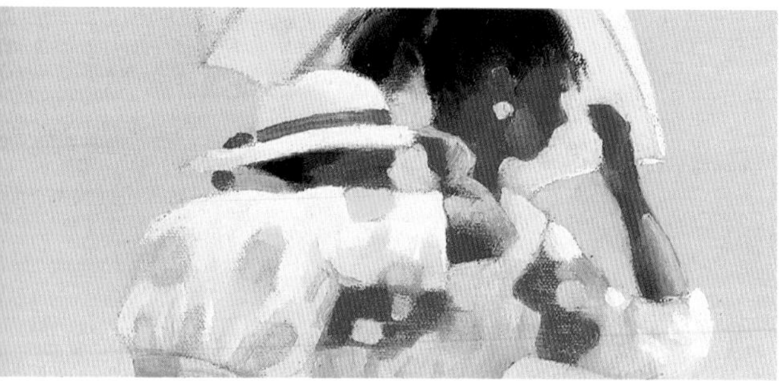

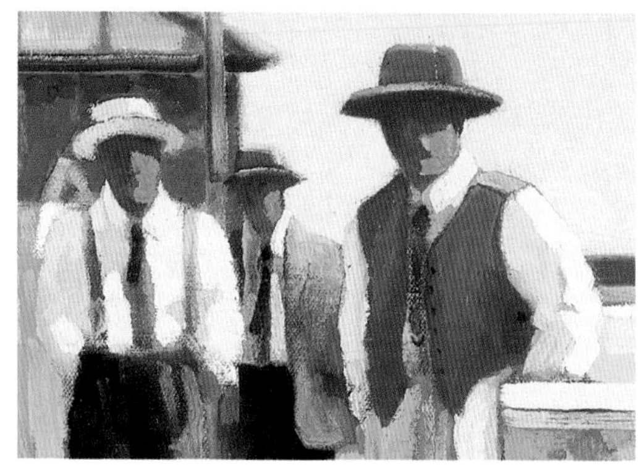

providing scenario and score to flesh out these small dramas of romantic intrigue. Why that look? Who's fooling who? How long has this been going on? *Forever* is the answer to that last question, because the torments of romance, as Vettriano believes, are eternal.

Out of doors, Vettriano's paintings seem to hold out the promise of happiness, of girls in polka-dot dresses and innocent promenades beneath azure skies. But look more closely and these summery idylls start to fray. In the foreground of *A Very Dangerous Beach* two women pause on a sand dune, shielding their eyes from the sun beneath an umbrella; in the background three men, their faces in shadow, look on appraisingly. Something about the configuration of the painting suggests that the women have taken a wrong turning, and that the men have been waiting for them. The air is heavy with an ineffable sense of menace, and recalls the horrific ending to the Raymond Carver short story, 'Tell the Women We're Going', in which the danger for two unfortunate women is not sexual but mortal. Murder may have been the last thing on the painter's mind, but so powerfully ambiguous are his dramas that the viewer can be tempted into hideous constructions.

Some have discerned in Vettriano the influence of Edward Hopper, whose vignettes of solitude became identified with a whole American look – not just in paintings but in movies and architecture. Only look at Hopper's amazing portrayal of marital disaffection, *Room in New York* or the classic *noir* enclosure of *Nighthawks* and one sees a line of descent to the theatrical tableaux of Vettriano. The critic Robert Hughes, discussing Hopper's *Summer in the City*, writes: 'It is the spaces between people that Hopper painted so well. Distance is seen as the concomitant of the act of love...Hopper's peculiar mix of voyeurism – putting our gaze in the room – and discretion – not revealing what the people are doing or thinking – is the hook in the painting. He offers slices of an insoluble life, moments in a narrative that can have no closure.' Remind you of anyone? As it turns out, Vettriano didn't know of Hopper when he began painting, but the links remain impossible to ignore.

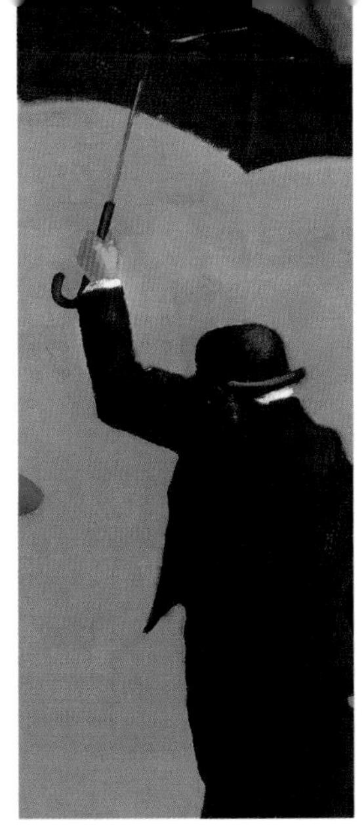

The keynote of Vettriano's art is atmosphere, and he likes to paint it *noir*.

On any reckoning Vettriano's is an idiosyncratic talent, yet what makes it extraordinary is the fact that his painting is entirely self-taught. After leaving school at fifteen he followed his father down the mine at Methilhill, Fife, working as an apprentice engineer. He later moved on to white-collar jobs in management services. Throughout his twenties and thirties he continued to paint, never quite certain of his subject but nonetheless fuelled by a belief that this was something he could do – had to do. The turning point came in 1988 when he submitted two paintings to the Royal Scottish Academy's summer exhibition. They were sold within fifteen minutes. Galleries in Edinburgh and Newcastle began to seek him out. A 1991 show at the Solstice Gallery during the Edinburgh Festival was so successful that a one-man show was planned for the following autumn. It sold out.

Since then, demand for his work has gone through the roof. His celebrity clients include Jack Nicholson, Raymond Blanc, A.L. Kennedy, Terence Conran and Tim Rice. Two of his paintings, *Mad Dogs* and *The Singing Butler*, now outsell any other picture poster in the UK, eclipsing the likes of Van Gogh and Monet. Yet Vettriano has also been in the spotlight for the antipathy he has stirred up inside the Scottish art establishment. In his recently revised *Scottish Art 1460–2000*, Professor Duncan Macmillan devotes barely a paragraph to Vettriano, and no image of his work is reproduced. His dismissal of the artist – 'He's welcome to paint, as long as no one takes it seriously' – is trotted out with wearying regularity. There has been palpable resentment of Vettriano's success, which the strictures of Professor Macmillan have inadvertently helped to consolidate. After all, notoriety isn't the worst thing you can bestow upon an artist; the worst – the thing that truly hurts and harms – is neglect.

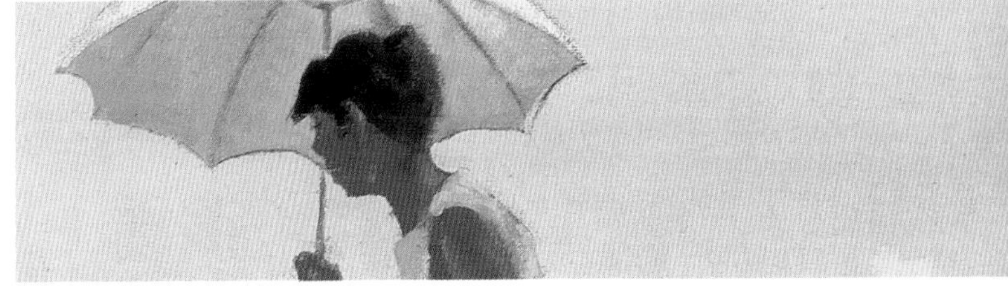

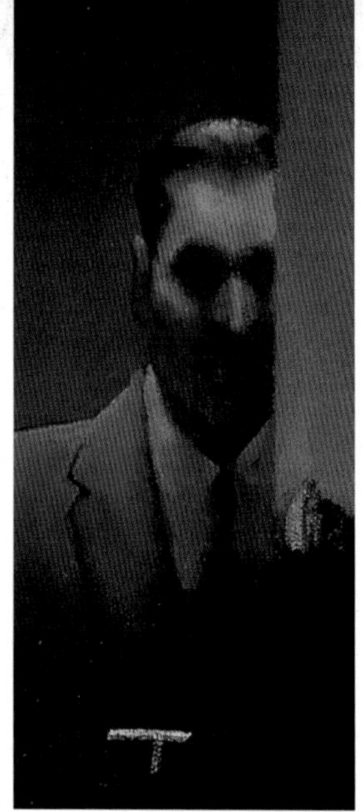

Photograph of Jack Vettriano by Lesley Jones.

Portrait of an Artist

On 17 November 1951, Catherine Hoggan (*neé* Vettriano) gave birth to a son, her second, in Craigtoun Hospital, St Andrews. She and her husband William settled on the name Jack. In the early years of the century Jack's Italian grandfather, Peter, had come to Dundee from Belmonte Castello in Italy and eventually settled in the town of Leven, Fife, where he worked down the mines. This is the town once visited by the Duke of Edinburgh, who, in a typical demonstration of diplomacy, called it 'the most hellish place on earth'. The infant Jack was eventually taken from the prosperous environs of St. Andrews to 18 Pirnie Street, one of several near-identical rows of miners' cottages in Methilhill. It was a tough, working-class neighbourhood, scoured by the chill blasts from the North Sea and by the economic hardships of a single-industry town. The Hoggans were by no means the poorest family in the area, but there was certainly little to be found in the way of luxury or comfort. 'Linoleum on the floor, baked beans on the plate', is Vettriano's succinct appraisal.

Yet he looks back on his childhood with affection. Much of it was spent in the company of his older brother, Bill. (By now he had two younger sisters, Karen and Sandra). 'I do remember it as being really great fun. Despite there being no cars, no money and not much entertainment, we did all the things that wee boys do. We made our own weapons and outfits, and I was very keen on collecting birds' eggs. I had quite a decent collection at one point.' He recalls his childhood in seasonal terms: egg collecting from March to May, then a fairground and a circus during the summer, then the football season. He always loved football. The local team was the Methilhill Strollers. 'I used to watch them – as a boy they all seemed huge to me. You'd run along the touchline and if the ball went out of play you'd go and get it for them. It was one of those old leather footballs, so heavy you could hardly lift it.' He and his friends would sneak over the wall at Bayview to watch East Fife, a team in decline during the Fifties. 'They'd go up a division, then come down two. They'd get a good cup draw, say, against Celtic or

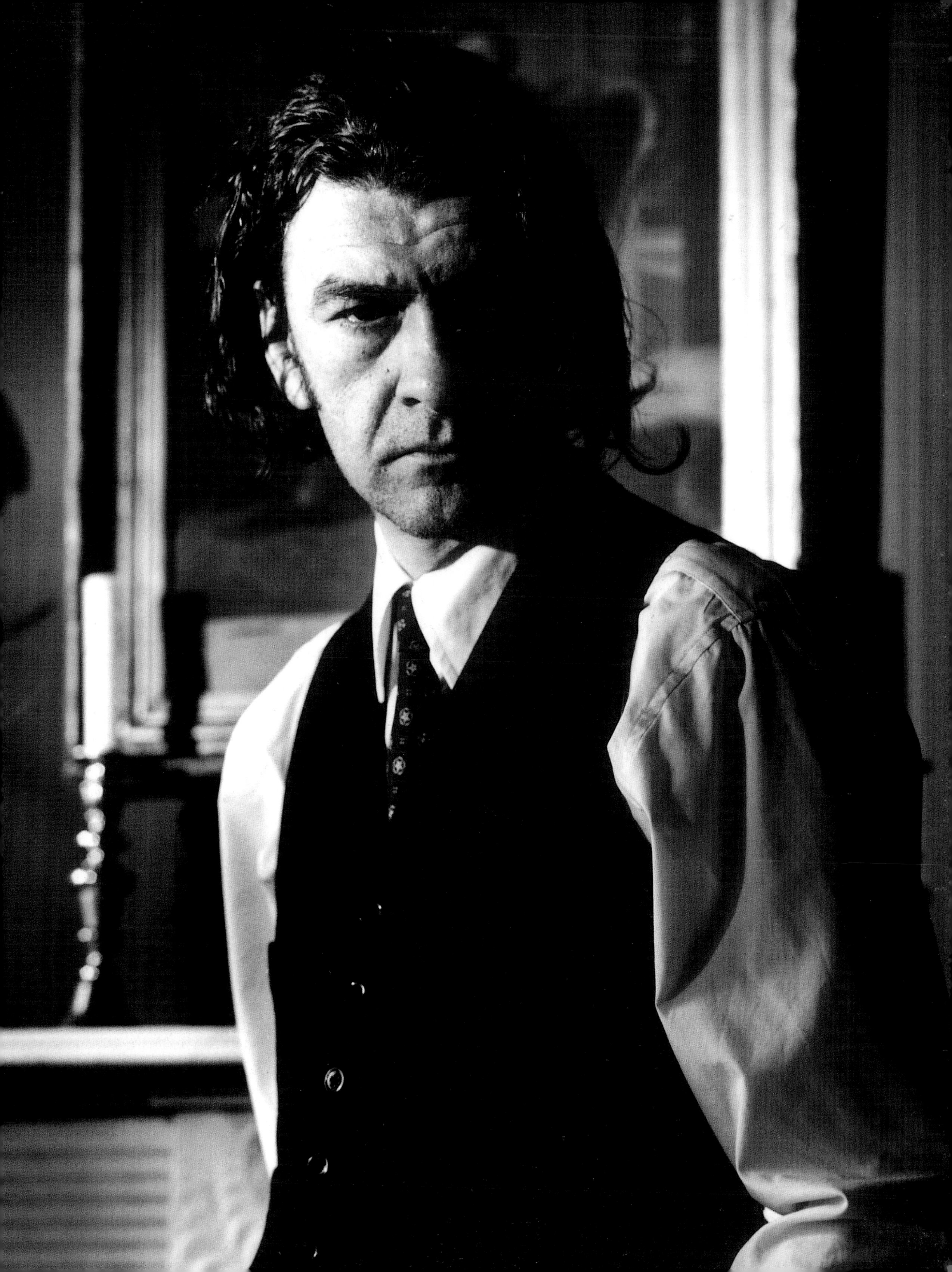

From an early age he liked to draw, and found a ready supply of materials in the six- by four-inch pads of white paper and pencils his grandfather brought home from the betting shop.

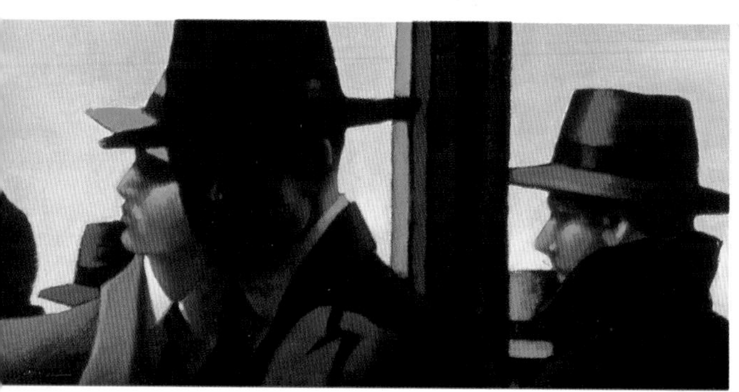

Rangers, where they might sneak a draw – and then they'd get thrashed at Parkhead or Ibrox.'

On his own admission he wasn't at all interested in school, nor was there pressure from his parents to do well. 'You might get a slap round the ear if you fell below "C". It was fairly relaxed at home, I was never encouraged to do homework…I'm quite glad that's the way it was.' From an early age he liked to draw, and found a ready supply of materials in the six-by four-inch pads of white paper and pencils his grandfather brought home from the betting shop. His early efforts included sketches of birds' eggs and 'a lot of goalmouth incidents, quite often starring Denis Law'. Yet the young Vettriano harboured no ambitions to be an artist. The narrow horizons of Methilhill suited him very well, and he aspired not to art school but to the drinking men's clubs and bars that constituted the social life of the area – haunts such as Nairn's shop, for example, where he used to sing as a boy. '"Will you sing for us, Jack?" they'd ask me, so I'd sing them a wee song and they'd give me a packet of Spangles.'

To hear him talk about this nightlife conjures images of rough frontier towns in American Westerns. 'There were always fights, doors opening and people getting thrown out. It was the sort of environment where it paid to be tough. When you're growing up, a year makes all the difference. Whenever my Dad's friends came round to the house there was a lot of shadow-boxing and playful aggression, implying that you had to be pretty tough to make it. I suppose it was from about this time that these hard men became my heroes. I didn't have any inclination to be a scientist or a cricketer or a novelist. I just wanted to be hard man.' In this he was emulating his father, a man who 'didn't take nonsense from anybody'. William Hoggan left school at fourteen, and like his father before him went to work at the Rosie Colliery in East Wemyss. On an eight-hour shift he would lie on his side with a pick and shovel in a coal seam that might be as low as thirty inches. Vettriano remembers proudly going to meet him from work as he wheeled his bicycle up the street. He would lift young Jack on to the crossbar and ferry him home.

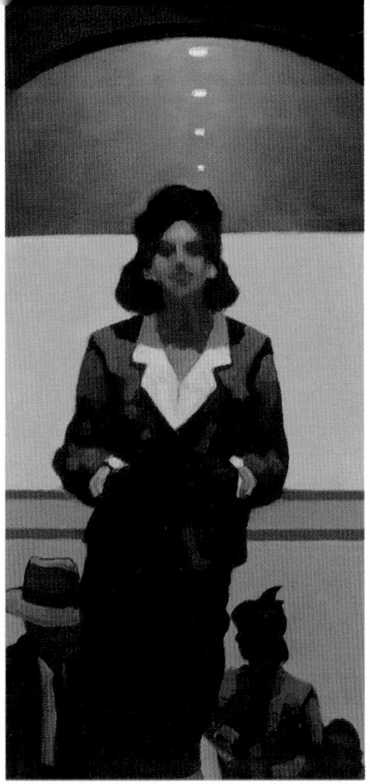

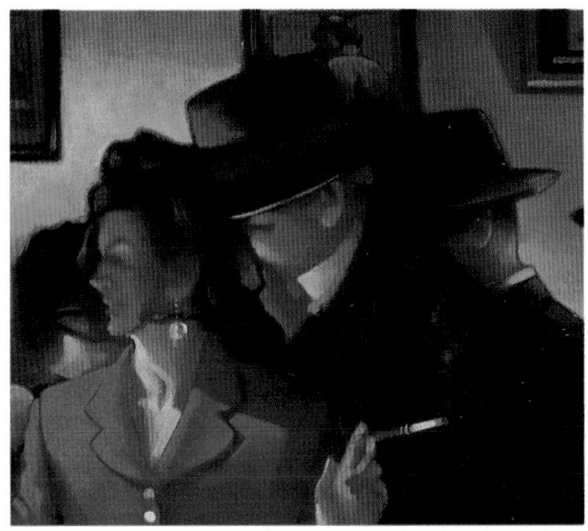

When Vettriano was ten the family moved over the Bawbee Bridge to neighbouring Leven, where they settled in a larger house at Montgomery Drive. The standard of living was improving, and it wasn't long before the family had a car. His father instilled into his children a fierce work ethic. From the age of eleven Vettriano began a long career of odd jobs, from doing a paper round to picking potatoes, from working at the Co-op to calling the numbers at the beach bingo hall. He would also accompany his father on his part-time window-cleaning round. At weekends he would go to a jazz club at the Drill Hall in Leven where he'd collect the empty bottles and return them at threepence each. His father's influence had taken hold. 'It was really drummed into my brother and me', he recalls, 'the idea that if you wanted anything in life you had to work for it.'

Meanwhile he had progressed to secondary school, Kirkland Junior High, where he continued to show little enthusiasm or aptitude for learning. The school on their part responded in kind. 'There were three streams in each year. The top stream were potential O-grades and Highers. The middle stream were the country's future tradesmen – carpenters, electricians, plumbers. The bottom stream was for brickie's labourers and that sort of thing. That was the stream I was in. There was a school bus which would take the top stream to visit art galleries and museums. We went to building sites to learn about construction', he says with a dry laugh. 'I remember one day some guy brought in his granny's sleeping tablets and we all took some while we were meant to be building this wall. We were wallowing around, knee-deep in cement and laughing our heads off. It was bloody hilarious at the time – unbelievably dangerous to look back on.'

As regards his nascent talents as an artist, school was not a source of encouragement. He remembers a 'pretty eccentric' art teacher who got the whole class to paint the Resurrection as a huge mural. 'I did quite a lot of it, as I recall. It was set in a graveyard, with hands rising out of the ground. It was quite spooky for 13-14 year-olds.' Most of the time, however, the only

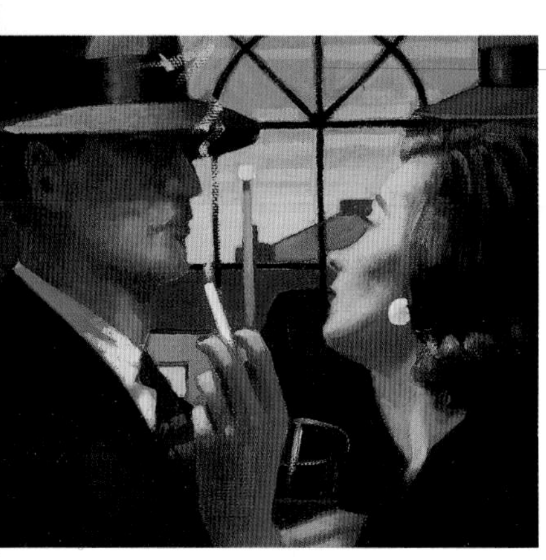

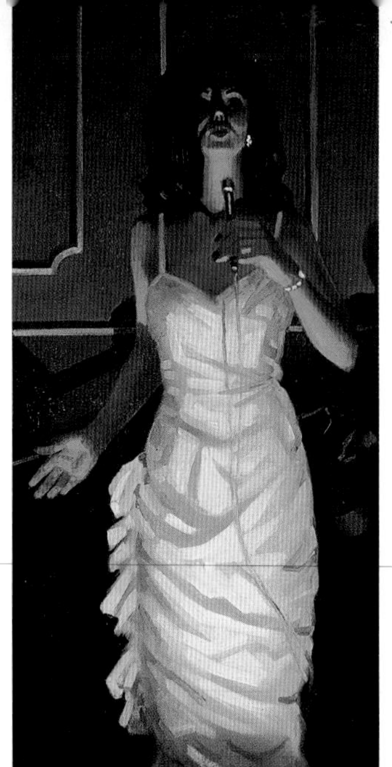

art the school was good for was the art of survival. 'We were treated almost like animals. It was a case of "They're in the system and we've got to get them out in one piece," but there was no question of actually educating us.' He admits now that he did himself a disservice at school, since he was far brighter than he made out. 'There was a hellish mentality among my friends, we regarded boys at the better high school, Buckhaven, as undesirables – they all seemed to have glasses and protruding teeth. It's so limited, that view, but that's how we were.' By the time he was fifteen Vettriano had reached the end of his schooling, and in the summer of 1966 he bid Kirkland High an unfond farewell. He wanted to be a wage earner, not 'the wee boy with a paper round'. A life underground awaited.

In preparation for his training as a mining engineer, Vettriano spent six months at the pithead of the Michael colliery filling sandbags. This was the bottom rung of an apprenticeship that would last four years. Soon enough he was taking home a regular pay packet of around five pounds and giving his mother money for his keep. The work itself was far from rewarding, but he found it hard to resist the extra funds to be had from overtime. 'It was rare to take home just the bare wage', he says. The night shift, from 10pm to 6am, he describes as 'hellish'. 'When I tell people I worked underground they think I was hewing coal. I was actually carrying the tool-bag. By this time it was all mechanized – I was just an apprentice.' Skiving and smoking seem to have occupied long stretches of the training: 'I just wasn't interested. There were maybe a dozen of us, and we treated it as a laugh. I spent more time sleeping underground than I did working. Not many apprentices came to do any actual work.'

What mattered to the young Vettriano was his social life. Strangely, drink didn't play a major part in it, and still doesn't. He has never enjoyed beer, and loathes spirits. When he was twelve or thirteen he got drunk on whisky one New Year and woke up under a hedge in the early hours of the morning, shivering and ill. It was enough to put him off. The passion he did conceive around this time remains unshakeable today: 'Women

What mattered to the young Vettriano was his social life.

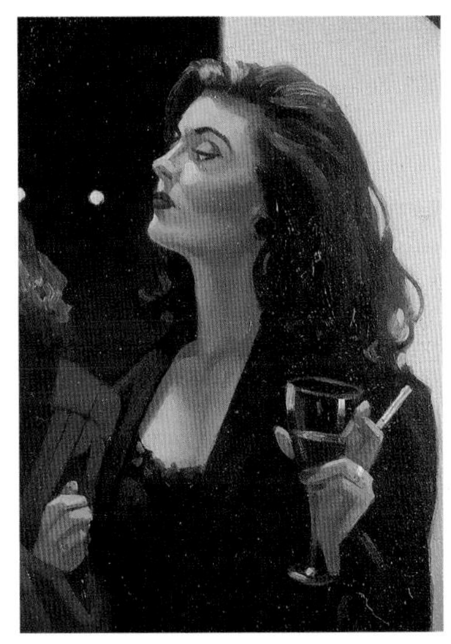

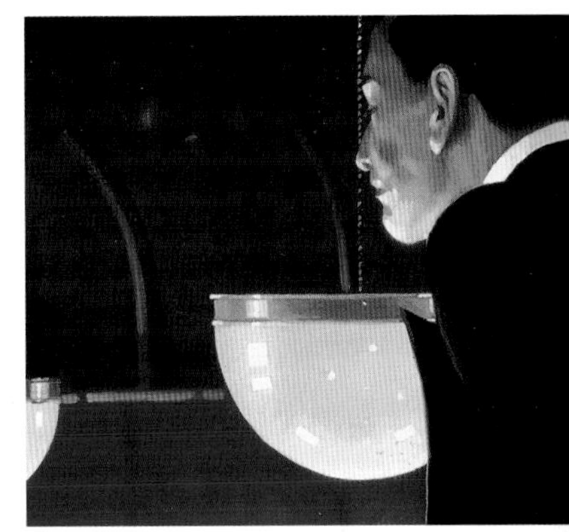

always meant more to me than beer and darts. I always thought the smart thing to do was stay sober and get the woman.' His forbearance has paid dividends. Vettriano seems never to have been shy of female company, as the paintings tend to suggest. 'Those things that awoke me physically are still with me now. The same images – the mascara, the blue eye-shadow, the bright red lipstick, the white stilettos. I remember seeing these women around town on a Saturday afternoon, their hair in rollers with a head scarf around it, getting ready for a night out. It touches me still when I see it in black and white photographs, that ritual of women dressing up.'

Two ballrooms, the Raith and the Burma, formed the centre of nightlife in nearby Kirkcaldy, where Vettriano and his friends would repair to spend their hard-earned cash. Looking sharp was a prerequisite of hitting the town, though in the late sixties it was difficult to realize dreams of sartorial suavity if one lived outside London. Vettriano would get a suit made at Hepworth's, which he would make do for a few seasons. The only off-the-peg suits in provincial Scotland were made for old men. The rest of the time it was a matter of keeping in step with the Beatles, who by this stage were entering the Edwardian moustaches era of *Sergeant Pepper*. 'We were always trying a new look', he says, though the one he remembers with most fondness was the dark suit worn with a plain white shirt and a knitted black tie, *'a la* Fleming's Bond.

The rituals of courtship were played out on the dance floor, where the custom of three fast numbers alternating with three slow ones held sway. He has particularly fond memories of the Andy Ross Orchestra (the same Andy Ross of *Come Dancing* fame) and their signature finale *The Party's Over*; indeed, he named a painting after it. The faded glamour of the ballroom gave way, at the end of the evening, to a rather more mundane walk to the bus stop where he would try to steal 'a few damp kisses'. The youth of Fife swarmed around the bus station in such numbers that it was often difficult to find room for one's romantic goodnight clinch. In the winter months passion was even trickier

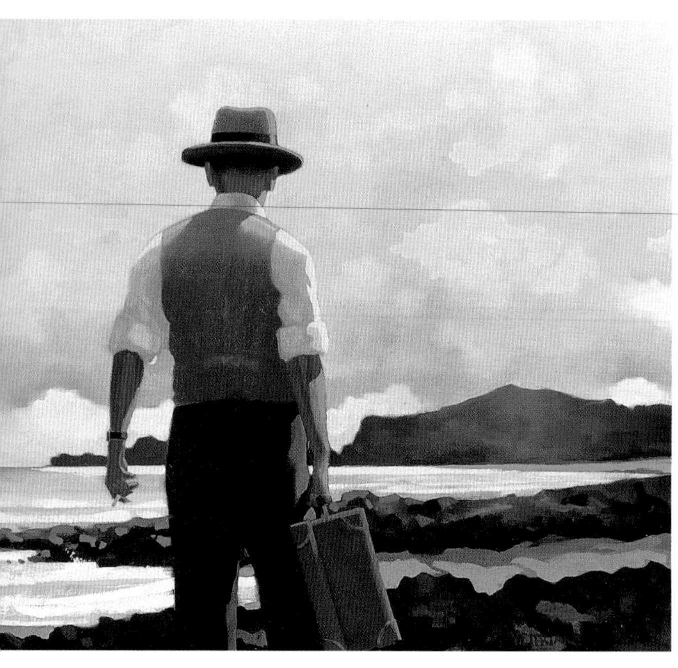

...he was restless and eager for the world beyond the narrow horizons of Kirkcaldy.

to sustain. Vettriano looks back on the time with a mixture of astonishment and horror: 'You'd be standing there snogging while it snowed or rained – just awful.'

AT nineteen his apprenticeship was completed, by which time he was restless and eager for the world beyond the narrow horizons of Kirkcaldy. Thus began a strange and occasionally comical venture into the unknown – England, in other words. He spotted a job advertised in the press as 'interviewer', and applied with innocent alacrity: 'I should have known as soon as they offered me the job on the spot, but I was that naïve. I thought interviewing people meant, you know, being Michael Parkinson – I imagined that in a couple of years' time I'd have my own TV show'. The reality was somewhat different. His brief was to travel to Darlington and 'interview' people, on a door-to-door basis, in order to sell them magazine subscriptions – and usually magazines of a defiantly unglamorous nature. Dreams of his own TV show cruelly dashed, he abandoned the job the very next day and caught a southbound train to King's Cross.

The idea of the provincial boy coming to London to seek his fortune has an enduring romance. Two hundred years earlier, another brash, credulous young Scot arrived in the capital, eager to establish his name and discover his talent. His name was James Boswell. On 19 November 1762 he recorded in his Journal: 'When we came upon Highgate hill and had a view of London, I was all life and joy. I repeated Cato's soliloquy on the immortality of the soul, and my soul bounded forth to a certain prospect of happy futurity.' Whatever hopes of happy futurity Jack Vettriano had nurtured on coming to London, he swiftly came down to earth once the economic realities of survival became apparent. He applied for a job as trainee chef at a restaurant named Auntie's on Cleveland Street, near Broadcasting House.

'Trainee chef' turned out to be as much of a misnomer as his previous 'interviewer'. He was chiefly required to fill the roles of dishwasher and drudge

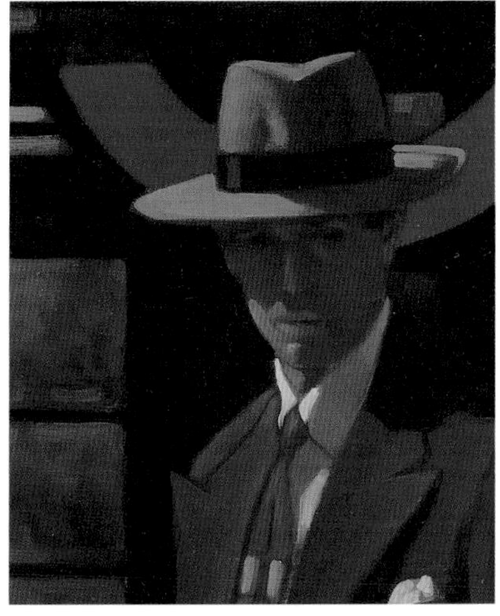

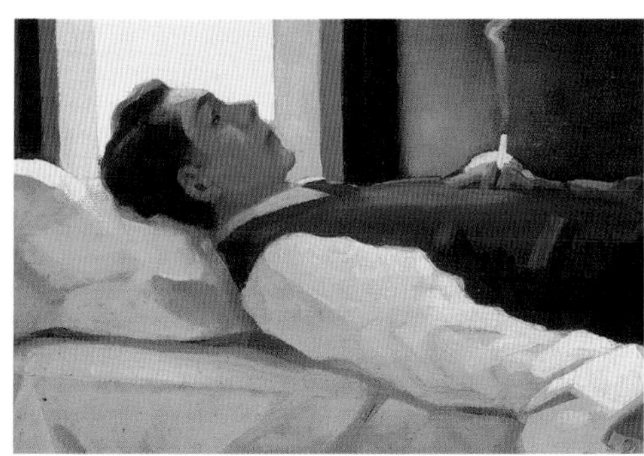

down in the restaurant's basement. Auntie's provided 'Olde English cooking', nursery food for the nearby executives of the BBC, for which it was named. (Among its celebrity clients he remembers Gabrielle Drake, sister of the tragic troubadour, Nick Drake). Most days were spent chopping vegetables and filling pies. He lodged in a bedsit on Camden Road, at that time a miserably run-down area; but for the mice that also occupied the house he was completely alone. He stuck at it for three months and then, not for the first time, he walked out. He admits he would have left earlier but was embarrassed to return home so soon. 'I'd have liked to have been able to come back home and say I'd seen a bit of the world. But I'd just seen a bedsit, and was none the wiser for it. I never made a friend down there'. He wasn't yet ready to make the adjustment from small town to big city.

Back in Scotland he began rifling through the jobs pages. For six months he worked as a trainee shoe-shop manager at Peter Lord in Edinburgh. Sensing a better opportunity to meet women, he took a job as a barman at the Ambassador Hotel in Kirkcaldy, which gave free access to The Garrison nightclub next door. It was here he meet a woman who would have a profound effect on his life. Her name was Ruth McIntosh. 'I'd never been out with anybody who did anything other than a manual job or factory work. Her family lived in a nice house, which was also something I'd never experienced before.' Ruth discerned a potential in Vettriano which he had hitherto denied in himself, and she encouraged him to look beyond the sphere of menial work. They argued a lot, but 'I liked the way she talked and the things she said, it felt new to me. It fitted in with how I felt when I went to London. I knew I wanted to change, but I wasn't capable of working out what to do.' Ruth advised him to seek some qualifications. He enrolled at college to study personnel management, passed the first exam and applied for a job as a work-study officer in Cupar. It was the start of a new career: he had donned the white collar.

'I suppose it was the first time in my life I felt receptive', he says. 'I felt I was getting somewhere.'

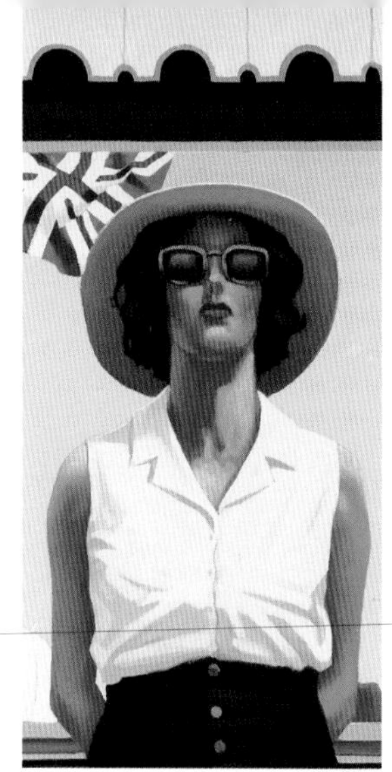

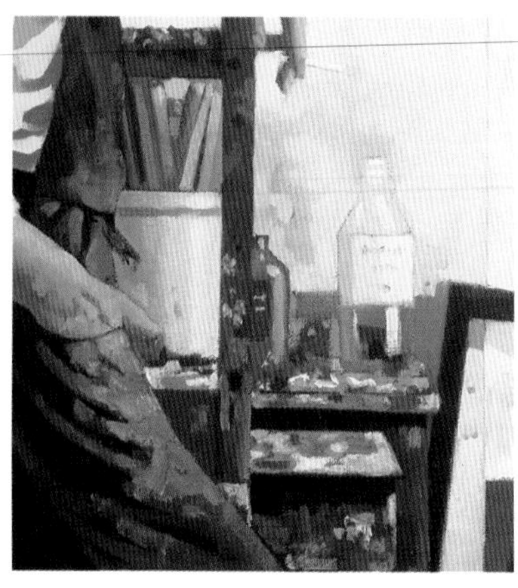

Meanwhile he was sketching, though without much sense of direction or ambition. Prompted by a gift he had made for Ruth – a landscape drawing which he attached to a small calendar – on his twenty-second birthday she gave him a set of poster paints. Encouraged, he began borrowing books from the library to teach himself the rudiments of painting, even though their instructions were largely unrealistic: 'The first chapter would be about materials, which I couldn't afford – the perfect palette and a huge room to work in. Chapter two would be about how to lay your palette before you started work, which was fine if you were in a studio, but in a back bedroom…So I dispensed with all that nonsense and found a way that suited me, squeezed out whatever colours I needed and started from there. I still do what I did then, which other artists would be appalled by, sticking the brush into the tube directly.' He was still a long way from taking it seriously: 'It wasn't important to me at all, it was just a wee hobby that I had. I gave the things away, if they were good enough. I remember doing a self-portrait in a mirror, quite a bold thing to take on. I look at it now with a certain fondness, even though it's not very good – my face in it looks very fixed and uncomfortable.'

Without fully realizing it himself, he began to search for a style, and a subject. His knowledge of art history up to this point was virtually nil, so he started to read around. He discovered the Impressionists, and tried copying them. The first painter who made a real impact on him, however, was Dali. 'I didn't "get" it, I know that now, but I just loved the smoothness and perfection of it'. Graduating from Ruth's poster paints to a set of oils, he took to copying as a pastime. 'It was a twofold thing. One, it was there in front of you. Two, you had to teach yourself how to do it – basic things, like never use pure white. White is always touched by the thing next to it. Nobody taught me that, I had to learn it.' Because he had so little time to spare he learned to work very quickly (and still does to this day). He was impatient for a result within three or four hours, 'something I could take downstairs and say, "Look, Dad".'

'She taught me the importance of visual pleasure, which up until then I'd not really thought about. She also dressed in a way that was terribly stylish – it made me want to listen to her.'

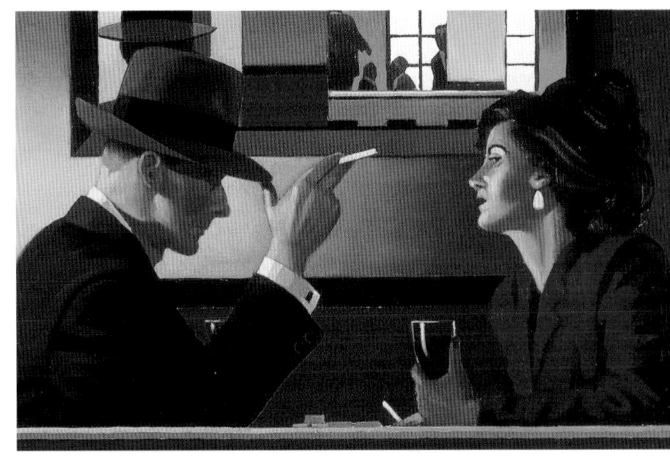

He was by this time earning decent wages, first as an engineer at Cessna in Glenrothes, a Fife new town. He went to night school and took a one-year course of study in time and motion; later he took a job at Scottish & Newcastle breweries based in Edinburgh. He had also met a woman, Marisa Jannetta, who would continue the artistic and cultural education which Ruth had set in train. 'She taught me the importance of visual pleasure, which up until then I'd not really thought about. She also dressed in a way that was terribly stylish – it made me want to listen to her. It triggered something in me.' He describes this period as his own 'Grand Tour'.

He began going to museums and galleries, auctions and junk shops where he and Marisa would buy pieces of old furniture. He had also had a second, and rather more successful foray down to London, this time living in Aldeburgh Street, Ilford, employed as a work-study officer for Redbridge Borough Council. He later moved with two colleagues to Forest Gate, near West Ham. It was around this time he started reading Van Gogh's letters to his brother Theo, which in spite (or perhaps because) of their angst and gloom provided inspiration. He realized for the first time that he could be a painter. 'I was still struggling to know *what* to paint. I'd go and look at Picasso in the Tate and come back home to try a Cubist painting. It was the wrong way to attack it. I couldn't conceive that that movement had passed, that Picasso and Braque were the only ones who would ever get credit for it. It wasn't coming from within me at all'.

Nevertheless, by 1979 he had accumulated enough material to mount his own exhibition – not in Scotland or London but in the unlikely, far-flung climes of Bahrein, in the Middle East. He had gone there after successfully applying for a job in the personnel department of a management consultancy. As a single man surrounded by a largely married workforce, opportunities for socializing were limited. While in Manama, a city of Bahrein, he was invisible amid the super-rich locals, the Rolls-Royce driving classes who had made their fortunes in the oil boom of the early seventies. So he threw his energy into painting, and eventually invited friends and colleagues round to his

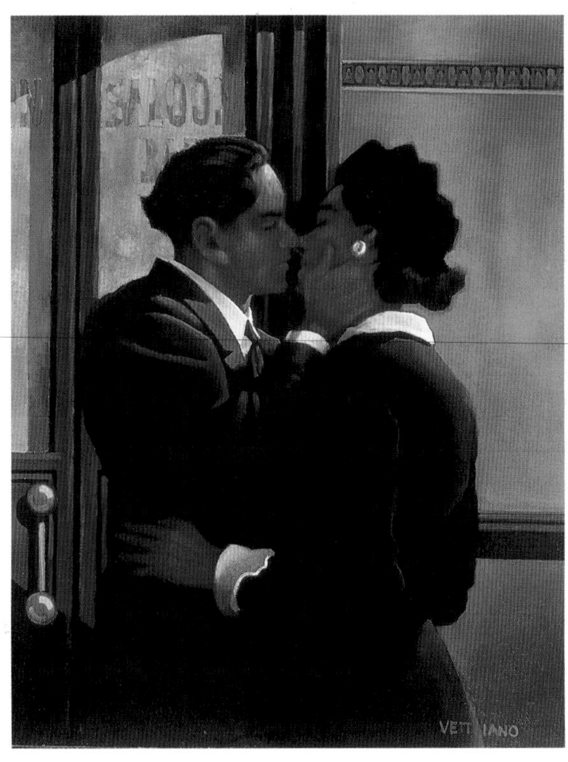

apartment to survey his handiwork, a collection of about twenty paintings. 'They said all the right things, though nobody asked to buy. That didn't disappoint me, because it wasn't about selling. I was just painting for myself.' He gave some away to friends, and even managed to trade one of them for a carpet, which is still in his studio today.

After a year he returned to Scotland, having saved enough money to enable him to buy a flat in Kirkcaldy. He did a one-year postgrad course in personnel management at the Technical College, resuming his old social life around the bars and clubs of Fife. Around this time he met Gail Cormack, a Kirkcaldy lass who was working for her father's newspaper distribution business. They went out together for two years, and in August 1981 they married, in spite of the fact he didn't have a job. They bought a house together in Kirkcaldy which they spent months renovating. The couple moved several times thereafter: Vettriano had found a taste for refurbishing a house and then selling it on at a decent profit. Having worked for Gail's father for some time, he quit full-time employment and worked on converting a garden shed into a studio. In fact, he was in a Catch-22, too old to take a trainee position in personnel but not experienced enough to get a higher position. Eventually he settled once again into Civvy Street, taking a job with the Manpower Services Commission in Glasgow and rising steadily up the corporate ladder.

He began to spend more time painting, copying still – 'wee girls on beaches, mawkishly sentimental stuff' – yet making a little money from it and feeling his way towards a personal style. He became extremely protective of his personal time. 'I was becoming increasingly aware that the talent I had, whilst it was earning me money, wasn't taking me anywhere. I didn't want to spend my life copying other people. I knew I had to start thinking about those things that meant something to me. I became very introspective. I stopped going out as much, my friends were discouraged from coming to the house.' It appears there was a minor crisis going on within him – his

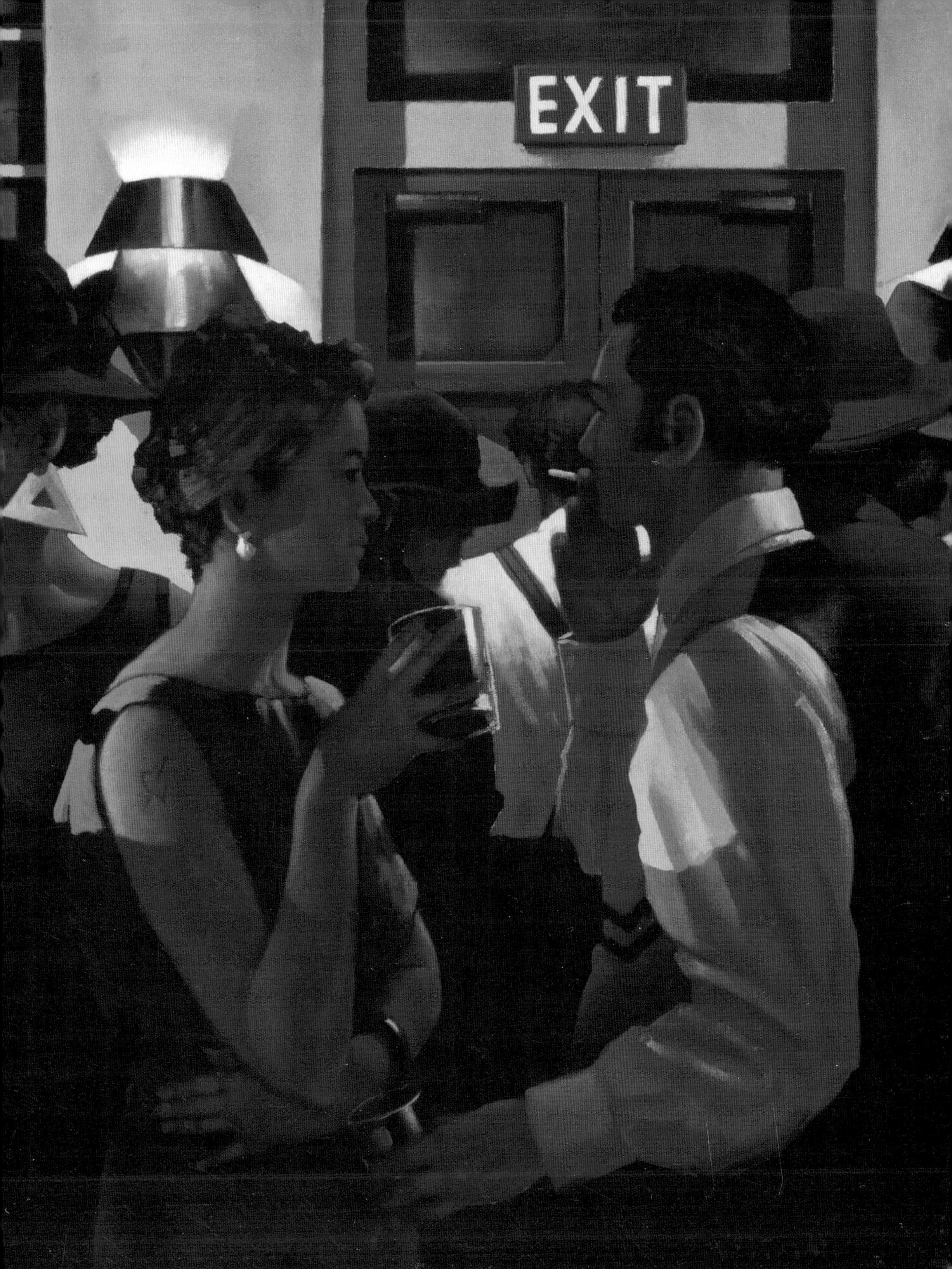
EXIT

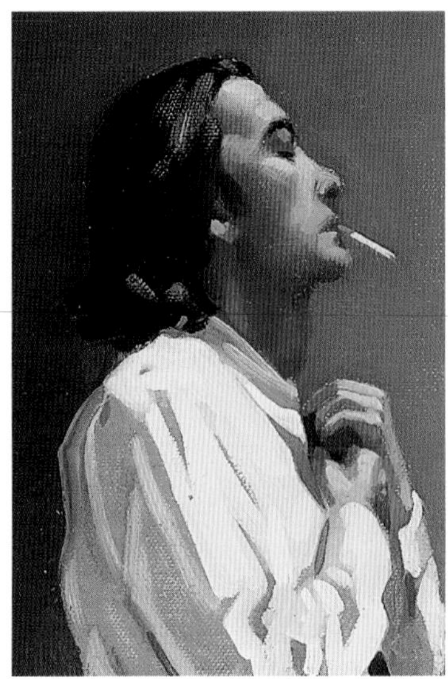

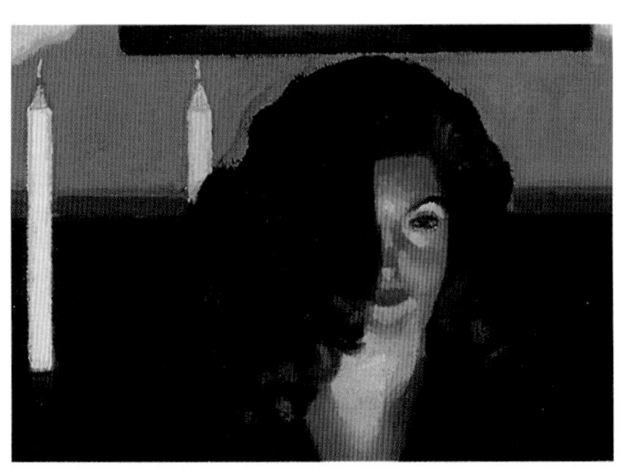

marriage to Gail was on the teeter-totter and he felt trapped in a job he didn't care for. He sensed that things had to change, and so it proved.

BY now technically confident, he realized that his subjects had been always in front of him. The first was his lifelong obsession with women; the second was his romantic-melancholic view of the past – 'No sooner had the Raith ballroom been sold off and turned into a church, and the Burma demolished, than I began to romanticize about them.' He decided to combine these major preoccupations, painting a picture of Gail in a white slip (*Model in a White Slip*) and another of a dancehall couple framed against an Art Deco pillar (*Saturday Night*). He then submitted them to the Royal Scottish Academy's summer exhibition of 1988. 'I remember getting the train from Glasgow, where I'd been working, to Edinburgh and gatecrashing the opening in Princes Street. I saw a red sticker on each of them, and could hardly believe it. It was a shot of pure adrenalin. I'd been judged by the great and the good, and I'd been sold.'

It was a turning point, both in his career and in his life. In November of the same year Gail left, and the marriage was over. He sold up in Kirkcaldy, gave up work and moved to Edinburgh, where his window gave on to a view of the Castle. For the first time in his life he was going to paint all day. He still wasn't certain that he could make the work pay, but something was spurring him on to take a gamble. As extra insurance he let out a room in his flat. The future suddenly looked very interesting: 'I went into overdrive, thinking about situations and looking at my own marriage, at how flawed relationships were.' He decided to mark a break with his past work, which hitherto had been sold under the family name, Hoggan. From this time he would take his mother's maiden name, Vettriano, a decision which he worried over: he didn't want people to think he was beginning to get above himself. 'Because there were so many paintings I'd done that were copies – which I was no longer proud of – and

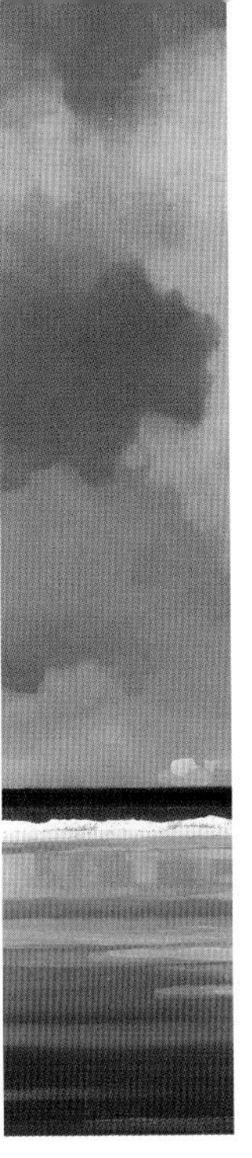

‘Most people would have been saying “Take me”, but I tried to keep a distance from them.’

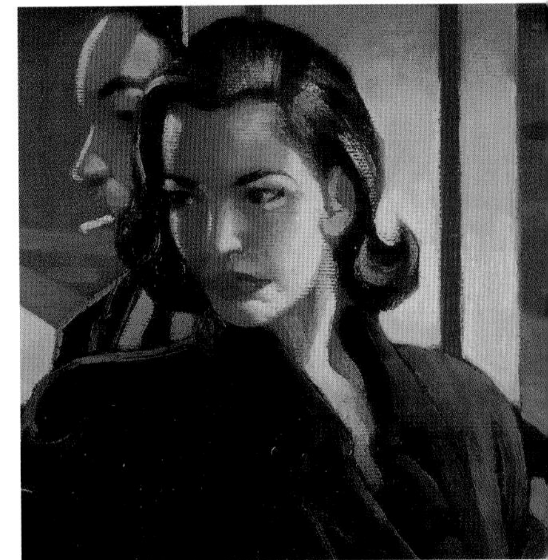

because I was subconsciously planning a new future, I thought I'd change my name. It felt like I was leaving a world behind.'

He was not misled by his instincts. As a result of his success at the RSA exhibition he was courted by three different galleries, in Dunkeld, Edinburgh and Newcastle, all of them highly eager to include him in a group show. He wrote back to each gallery, thanking them for their interest and inquiring about their terms. 'I don't know where I got that gall', he muses today. 'Most people would have been saying "Take me", but I tried to keep a distance from them. They were constantly after me for work, and most of what I gave them they sold.' It was to become a familiar pattern. Around this time he was also thrilled by his first celebrity purchase: Valerie Singleton, BBC TV's *Blue Peter* presenter and icon of the baby-boomer generation, bought one of his paintings at the Dunkeld Gallery. To be sought out by a woman whose presence had infused his childhood was a strange but very gratifying experience.

He was still hounded by insecurities – about his lack of formal training, about his adoption of his mother's name, about his place in the world. This sense of inferiority was at odds with the fact that his work was selling as quickly as he could paint it. The Vettriano style had struck a chord, and demand was on a sudden upward curve. 'I was scratching my head and thinking, "Why is this happening?" I loved it, but I was quite alarmed by the way it had developed its own momentum.' Once installed in Edinburgh he abandoned most of his social life in favour of painting. His regime became almost monkish in its solitude and austerity. 'I'd get up at five or six in the morning and start painting. It wasn't uncommon for me to work twelve hours or more a day. I've always hated walking away from a painting when it's not finished.'

By now the Solstice Gallery in Edinburgh was trying to persuade him to launch a one-man show. To a painter who had only recently found his style it was a daunting prospect. He was, in a word, 'petrified'. 'In group shows you can hide behind people if things go

If he had ever harboured doubts about public interest in his work, they were conclusively laid to rest.

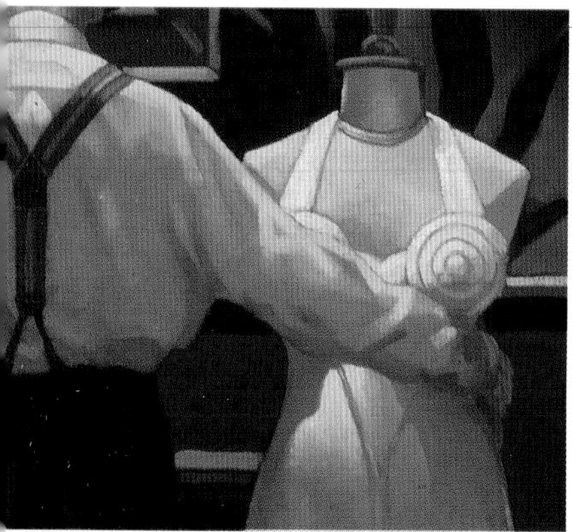

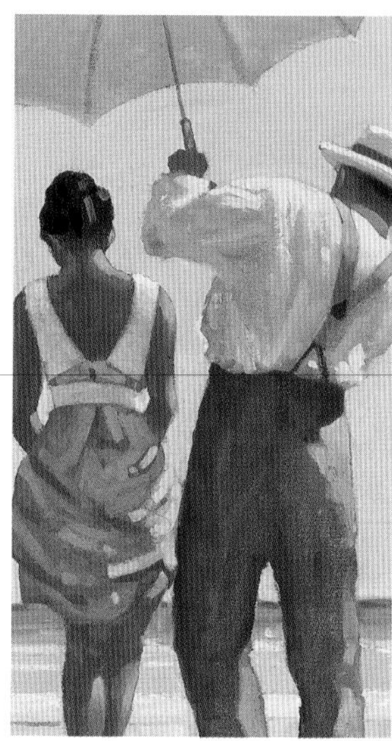

wrong, but to stand alone is frightening.' He backed off, still feeling he wasn't ready to go it alone, but agreed instead to take part in a two-person show during the 1991 Edinburgh Festival. It was entitled *A Contrast of Styles*, and paired him with Joan Renton, an Edinburgh School painter who had already found a following. It was around this time that Vettriano found his earliest champion. W. Gordon Smith, the art critic of *Scotland on Sunday*, was introduced to Vettriano's work, and became a loyal, though by no means uncritical, admirer. A profile of Vettriano he wrote in July 1991 created an immediate buzz around the painter, which a Scottish TV arts programme, *NB*, quickly picked up on: their five-minute programme during the Festival sharpened critical interest.

The show, which provided Edinburgh with its first proper look at Jack Vettriano, was an overwhelming occasion. If he had ever harboured doubts about public interest in his work, they were conclusively laid to rest. 'I don't think I've ever experienced anything like the opening of that exhibition. A couple of paintings had been sold beforehand, but on the night it was a frenzy.' He felt thoroughly vindicated, though his joy that night was not completely unalloyed. His fellow exhibitor, whose sales didn't stand up to comparison, had invited the gallery owner to her after-show party but omitted to include Vettriano. He felt the snub keenly. 'I suppose it was my first brush with establishment pique', he reflects mildly. 'She was well entrenched in the Edinburgh scene, I was the green newcomer. I remember feeling quite hurt by that, though I can sympathize with her, too.'

Heartened by his success, he agreed to Jim Heggie's proposal of a solo show at the Edinburgh Gallery in Dundas Street. *Tales of Love and Other Stories* opened on 15 May, 1992, and W. Gordon Smith wrote an enthusiastic introduction to the catalogue, calling Vettriano 'a phenomenon' and invoking the shades of Hopper, Sickert, Boudin, even Goya. 'Slowly but surely', he wrote, 'he becomes the Vettriano he wants to be. If it is a wonder that he has managed to teach himself drawing, perspective, the manipulation of paint

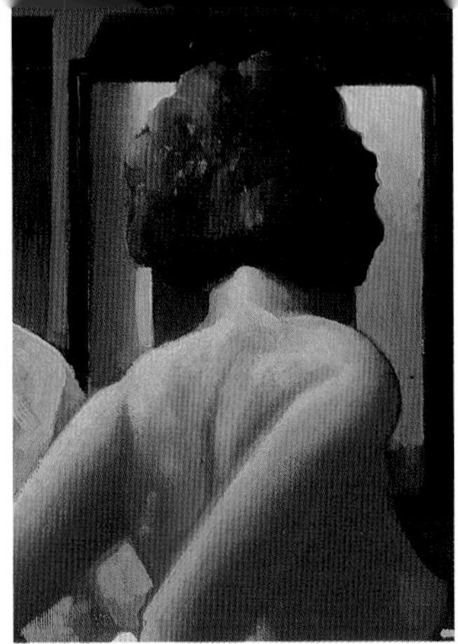

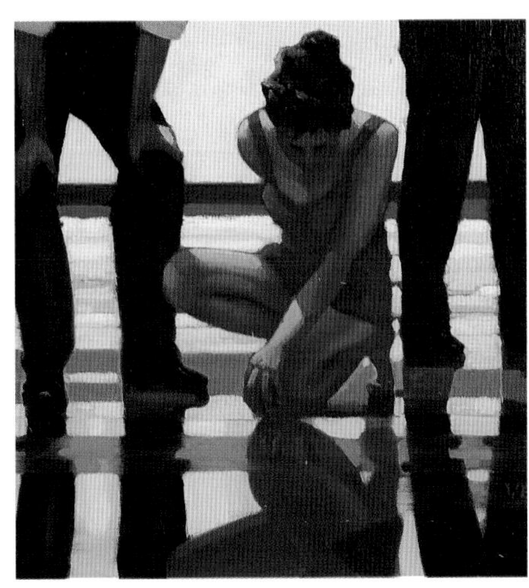

in veiled glazes and meaningful shadows, the music of colour and the dramatic focus of compositions, it is even more remarkable that he has evolved such an identifiable personal style.' Vettriano continues to acknowledge the importance of Gordon Smith's support, which came at a very timely moment in his career. Smith was the first person to whom he talked seriously about his lack of formal training. 'He told me that it wasn't a handicap, and that those who *had* been trained were the ones at a disadvantage. I thought it was such an encouraging thing to hear from this man, a respected art critic. He made me feel OK for being an outsider – I can't underestimate his contribution.'

Not all of Smith's wise words were heeded. He had noted Vettriano's increasingly louche ways, and suggested to him that living the seamy life wasn't essential to painting it. Inspiration could come from within as well as from without. 'I think he saw that I wasn't a man of the world at all – I was a wee boy who'd come to the city from Fife in search of wild times. He could see that I'd easily get into tricky situations, but I couldn't.' The following years would be marked by a succession of 'tricky situations', many of them short but intense involvements with married women; the furtiveness required to conduct such relationships seems vital both to his romantic nature and to a side of his paintings. He has a need for the illicit and complicated. Carolyn Osborne, a close friend for twenty years, has remarked on his inclination to secrecy: 'When I first met him in Kirkcaldy I had no idea, for instance, that he had a girlfriend. He wasn't prepared to tell me. It came as a complete surprise when I found out he was getting married.' She also regards Vettriano's romanticism as a complex form of nostalgia: 'It goes back almost to childhood, and the idea you can't remember a summer that wasn't sunny. That's where the beach paintings come from, I think.'

Jim Heggie meanwhile suggested that Vettriano prepare a one-man show in London. Buoyed by his successes, he felt eager to test himself outside Scotland, and by October 1992 he had thirty-seven paintings to exhibit under the title *God's Children*.

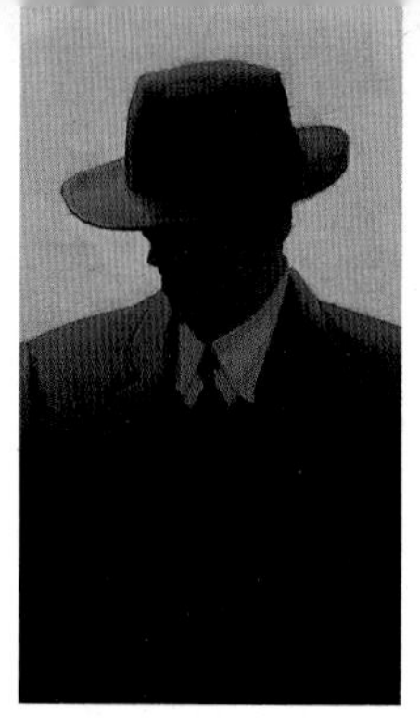

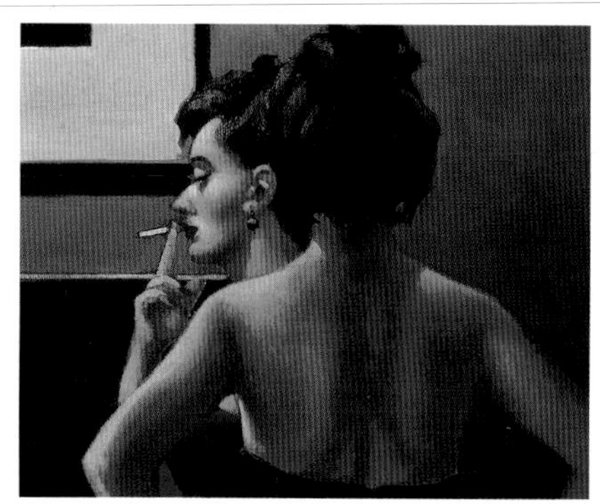

...these canvases betokened a mature and idiosyncratic style, earned from those years he had spent fine-tuning his craftsmanship.

They included *Mad Dogs...* and *The Singing Butler*, which would become his signature pictures, endlessly reproduced on posters and greetings cards. Yet it's the darker, lesser known paintings here that fire the imagination – the strangers on a train station in *Angel*, the contemplative solitude of *Heartbreak Hotel*, the sinister elegance of *Evening Racing*. It was idle to talk any longer of the painter's 'promise': these canvases betokened a mature and idiosyncratic style, earned from those years he had spent fine-tuning his craftsmanship. Audiences assumed from the retro atmosphere of the paintings that Vettriano was a connoisseur of old movies and pulp fiction, yet this was not the case: 'It's a perfect world I would like to have lived in but didn't. It goes back to a time when there was a clear distinction between men and women – nowadays it's all androgynous.'

Heggie chose the Mall Galleries as a venue, which proved to be a mistake. On opening night the place was heaving, but it transpired that most of the guests were clients of Dickson Minto, the corporate law firm which sponsored the show. When Vettriano returned the next day he found it practically deserted. In retrospect he reckons the problem was partly to do with location and partly with the lack of a thrusting gallery owner who would get people interested in the work. The paintings were sold, but it didn't lift the painter's gloom. 'The gallery was geographically in London, but it could have been on the moon for all that people knew about it. There was no coverage in the press. The fact is, I showed in London and nobody knew.'

BACK in London, meanwhile, Tom Hewlett of the Portland Gallery, which specialized in contemporary Scottish art, had just received a tip from a broker friend in the City. This wasn't a tip about stocks or shares: the broker, Adam Walford, suggested that Hewlett take a look at the work of a rising Scottish painter, name of Vettriano. In early 1993 Hewlett travelled up to Edinburgh and visited the painter in his studio at Castle Terrace. He recalls: 'I was impressed,

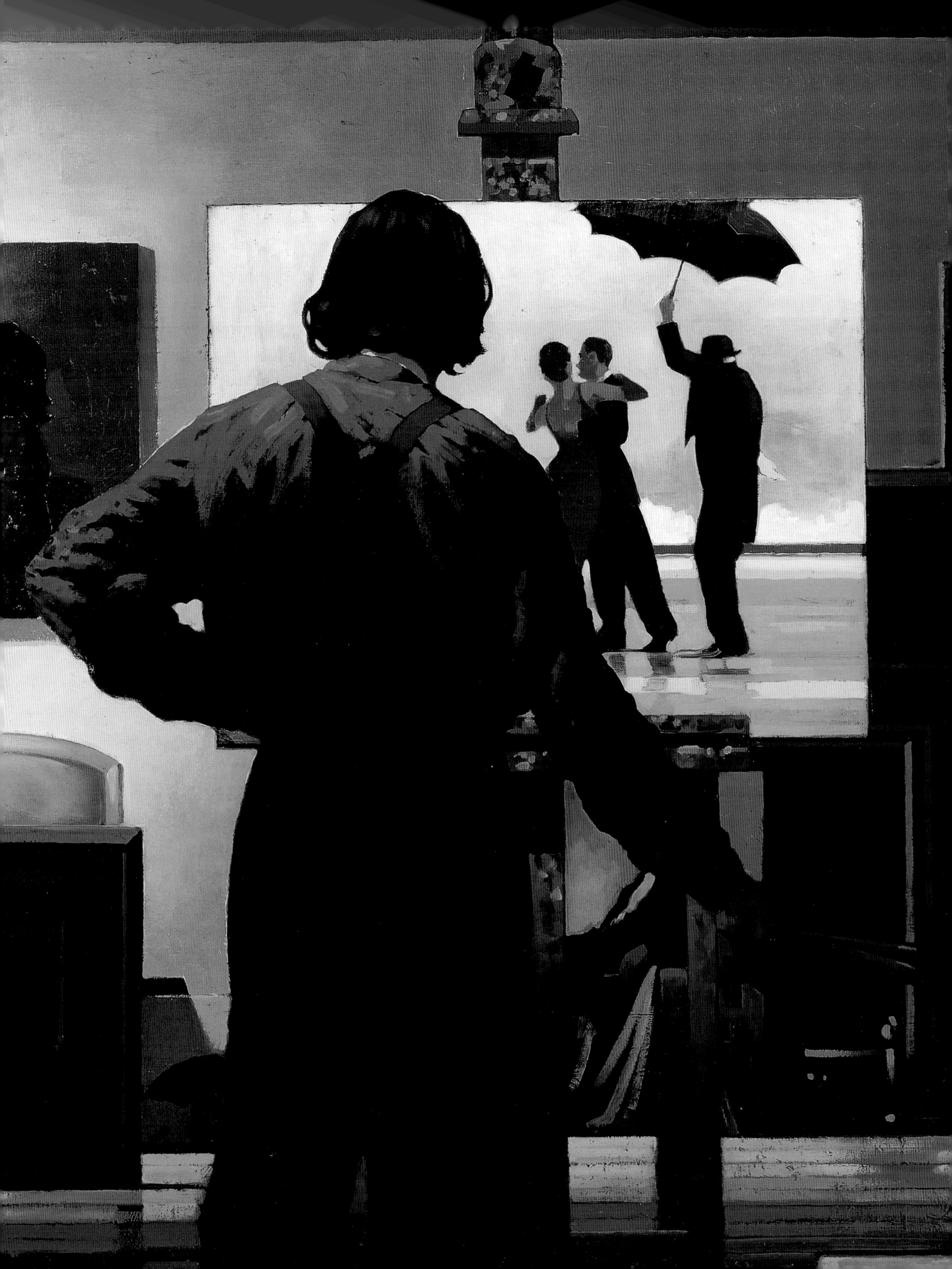

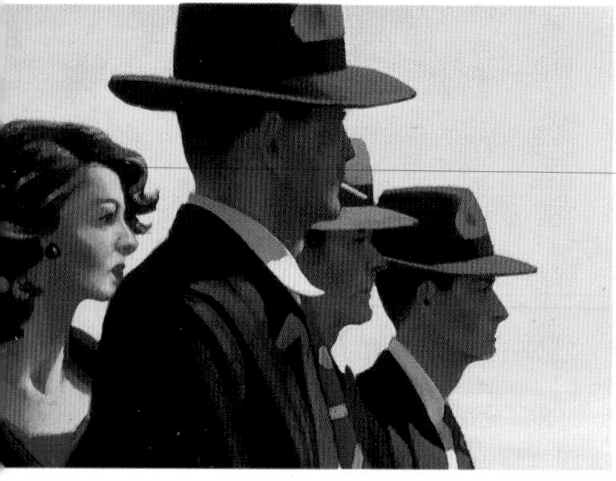

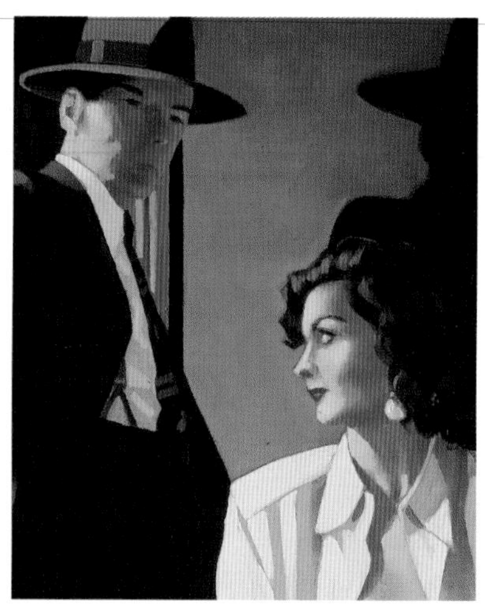

then as now, by Jack's ability to create atmosphere, and more importantly, to engage the viewer in the picture. There's a tremendous narrative quality which draws people in.' Hanging on one wall was a large painting Vettriano had recently completed and was interested in selling; he asked Hewlett how much he thought it was worth. 'I told him a figure', says Hewlett, 'and he said, 'Well, if you can get that for it, then do'. So I did, and that was the start of it.'

Vettriano's relationship with the Edinburgh Gallery had deteriorated to the point where he was seeking other representation. The Catto Gallery in Hampstead had made overtures to him, and it was time to part company with Heggie: 'He couldn't accept that I wanted to grow. He could have let me go gracefully, under conditions that would have allowed the friendship to continue. In fact he'd still be getting my work now if we'd parted on good terms.' By the end of 1993 he had exhibited at the Catto Gallery (*Fallen Angels*) and, in November, at the Corrymella Scott Gallery (*Summers Remembered*) in Newcastle.

He decided to join Tom Hewlett at the Portland Gallery. Vettriano agreed terms with Hewlett, and a partnership was up and running. They celebrated with a dinner at Raymond Blanc's Manoir aux Quat' Saisons. Blanc was so impressed with the painter that he hung a whole suite at the Manoir with Vettriano originals and named it after him. Vettriano's first Portland Gallery show, a collection of forty-eight paintings under the title *Chimes at Midnight*, opened on 12 October 1994. It sold out. Yet neither painter nor dealer would have dared to predict the level of success they were about to enjoy. 'When you first start representing somebody', says Hewlett, 'you're full of enthusiasm – it would be disingenuous to take on an artist if you *weren't* enthusiastic – and you think, "Well, I've been wrong before, but I don't think I am this time." With Jack the paintings all sold, and the people who came along seemed just as enthusiastic as we were'.

The show was combined with a book launch. Alert to the ground swell of public interest, Pavilion Books had

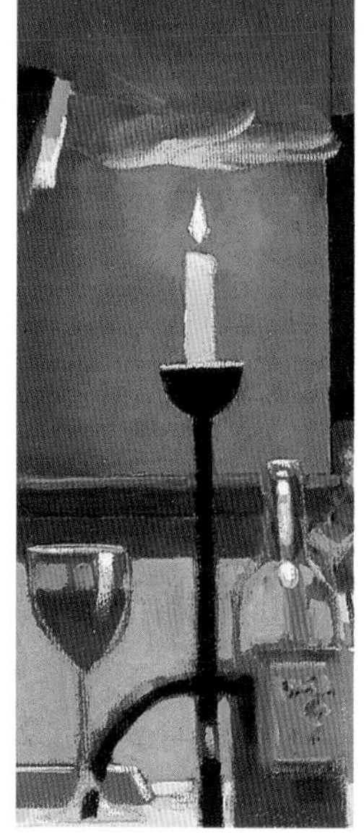

All the years he had spent cultivating his taste were now brought to bear upon his new home

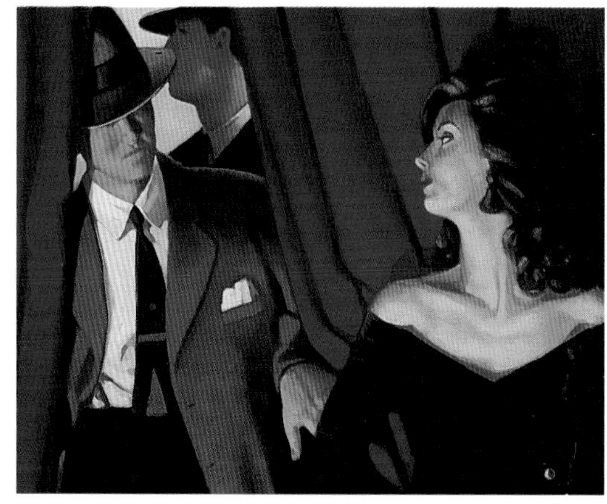

commissioned Gordon Smith to put together *Fallen Angels*, in which over forty Vettriano images were reproduced, accompanied by a selection of Scottish writing. Poets, playwrights, novelists and actors were asked to respond imaginatively to the paintings, or else a poem – by Burns or Robert Louis Stevenson – was selected to complement an image. Smith himself provided an excerpt from his play about Van Gogh to accompany *A Test of True Love*, a dramatic picture of a man confronting a woman in a restaurant by calmly placing his hand over the flame of a candle.

After four years in Castle Terrace, he moved to a house in Lynedoch Place, a fine old Georgian terrace in the west end of Edinburgh. The idea of turning the drawing room into a studio immediately appealed to him. Three large sash windows overlooked the street, and would provide him with a generous source of light. All the years he had spent cultivating his taste were now brought to bear upon his new home, which he slowly transformed from a neglected suburban villa into a house closely resembling its original incarnation. This was not just a step up to gracious living: it would be the stage set for his paintings. With the exception of the studio, he had the other rooms painted a theatrical shade of burgundy. Candles and candelabra lined every surface. A cupola at the top of the stairwell offered abundant natural light for his preparatory photographs. An original Georgian handrail provided a focus not only for interior paintings but for many beach scenes, which he could simulate quite conveniently indoors. Paintings such as *The Purple Cat* were conceived around the house's hallway, where he hung drapes in the manner of tableaux from Peter Greenaway's *The Cook, The Thief, His Wife and Her Lover*. The fireplace became a favourite framing device, and the bathroom too figured prominently – even the back garden served as a backdrop in two of the Bluebird paintings.

He would rise as early as four in the morning to begin painting – within minutes of getting out of bed he would be standing before a canvas, coffee and cigarette in hand. His dedication was unwavering,

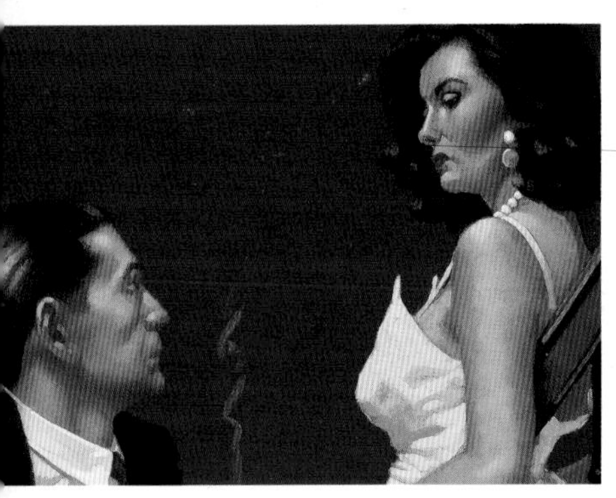

…she looked like a woman to whom a pledge of eternal love might provoke her to stab you with a stiletto.

which may explain why he lives so determinedly alone to this day. There was never any question that Lynedoch Place was a house for more than one person. His life became that of a career bachelor. His dining habits confirmed him as a creature of habit: he would go to no more than three different restaurants in town – a local Italian, Pizza Express and a swish eaterie named Atrium, where a Vettriano beach painting adorns the entrance. His love of the comfortable and familiar made him impervious to exotic holidays. When he flew to Hong Kong for his one-man show he stayed at the Mandarin Hotel as a guest of David Tang. Yet despite the red-carpet treatment, he couldn't suppress a desire to be back home in his familiar surroundings.

Around this time a model, Genevieve Solecki, took a central role in Vettriano's paintings. He had met her some years before when she was working in a perfumery, and her dark, voluptuous look was like a moth to a flame. At his 1996 Portland show, *The Passion and The Pain*, she dominated the canvases, while the picture titles – *Shades of Scarlett*, *Edith and the Kingpin*, *A Woman Must Have Everything* – indicated that Vettriano had been listening quite intently to Joni Mitchell's 1975 classic *The Hissing of Summer Lawns*. Genevieve, with her gimlet eyes, haughty demeanour and vampish nightwear, exuded an abrasive sexual energy – she looked like a woman to whom a pledge of eternal love might provoke her to stab you with a stiletto. For Vettriano the appeal was consuming. He had always liked women who dressed in a glamorous way, who 'didn't worry that other people regarded high heels as only for tarts'.

His passion for glamorous-looking women has sometimes led him astray. Some liaisons have been more dangerous than others: 'I have, under the pretext of research, visited a few odd places in my time, but it's not a habit. I enjoy women being overt in their sexuality, and that goes way back to the first time I saw prostitutes around the dock area – I was about eleven.' So it might come as a surprise that he has used in his career only thirteen or fourteen women as models. Given that this is a man who could use the line 'Come

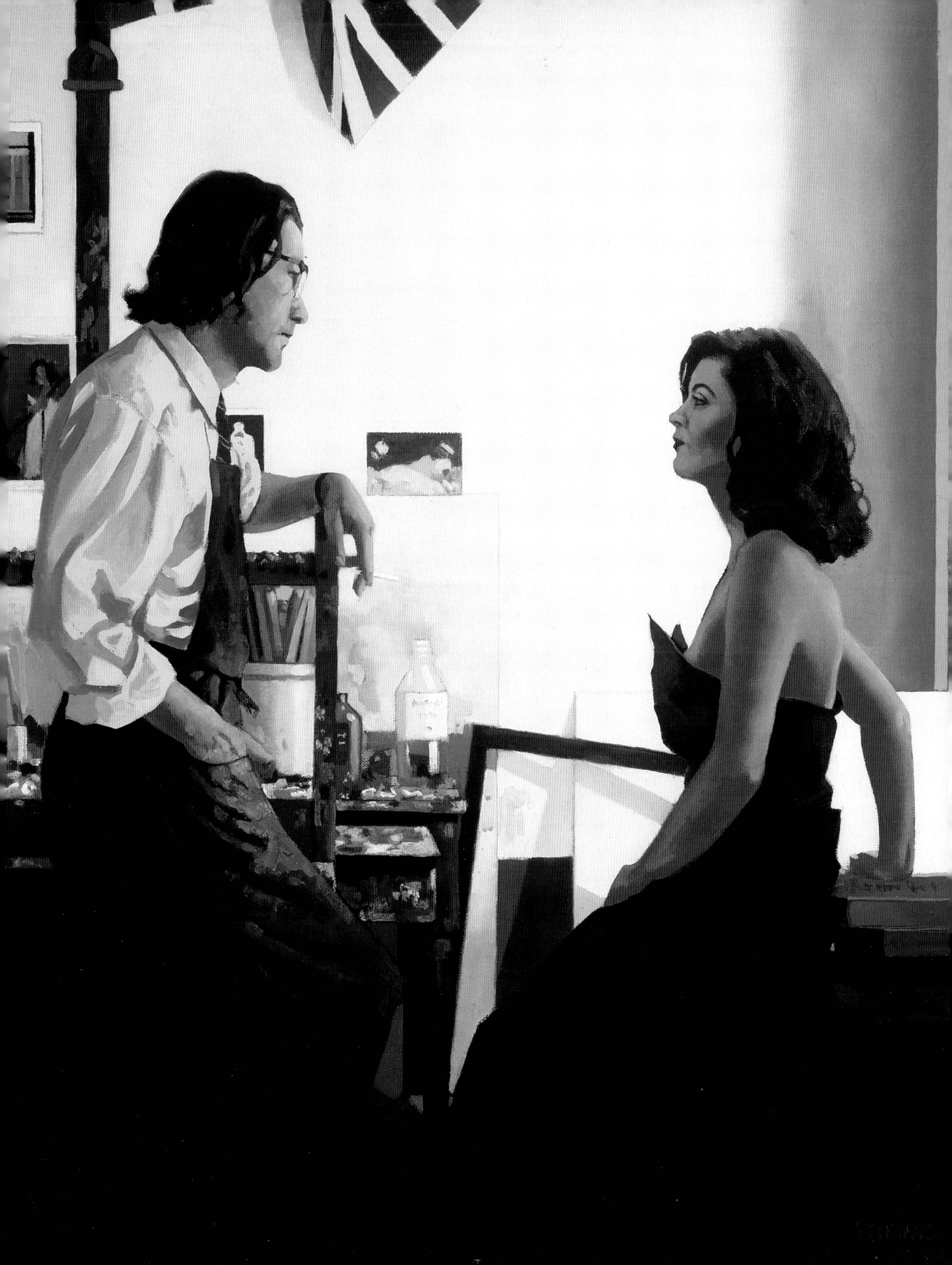

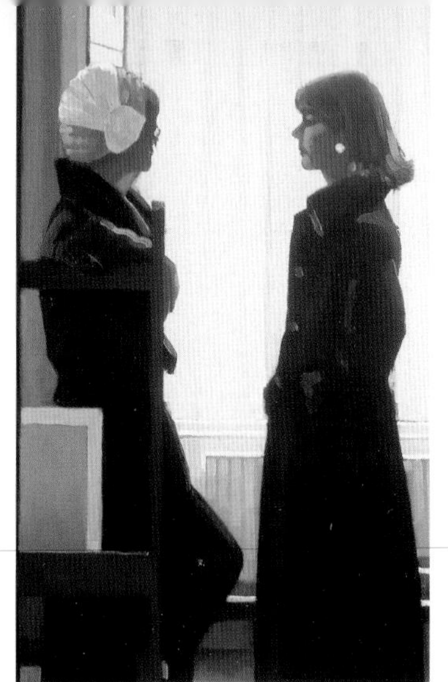

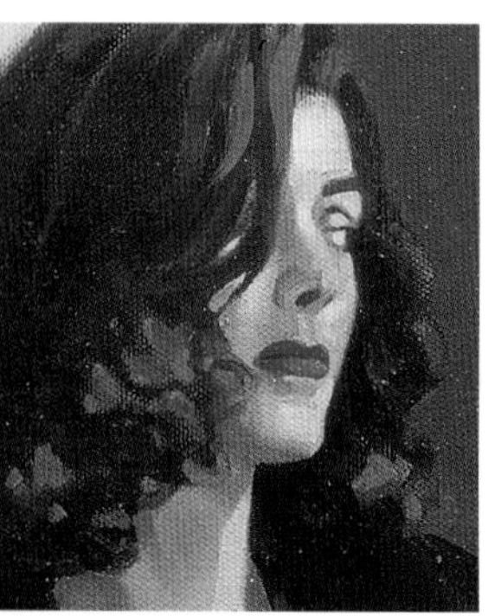

His methods are briskly professional. He will ring his model the week before a session and discuss one or two ideas of how he sees the painting

up and see my etchings' and actually mean it, his restraint seems almost chaste.

Aside from his own eyes, he relies upon friends to recommend suitable models. 'Once people are on the case it's amazing how many come along for interview.' His demands tend to be so specific, however, that no more than one in five is ever taken on. Some years ago a photographer he knew suggested to him that he might like to paint his girlfriend, assuring him that she had 'the Vettriano look'. He invited Vettriano round to his flat, where the girlfriend was waiting, already kitted out in underwear so revealing and cartoon-saucy that she might have stepped out of the window of Anne Summers. As introductions go, it wasn't the subtlest. The prospective portraitist admits that he 'didn't know where to look', and after a mortifying fifteen minutes of chat, fled.

His methods are briskly professional. He will ring his model the week before a session and discuss one or two ideas of how he sees the painting, then ask them to bring whatever props – dresses, stilettos, hair clips – he feels necessary. Once he has set up in the studio, he takes photographs of her, from which he works straight on to a small canvas. Carolyn Osborne, who began modelling for him in the mid-nineties, describes the process as 'very straightforward': 'Jack is an absolute gentleman, so there's no feeling of discomfort. We also share a similar sense of humour, which helps a lot. Perhaps other women who didn't know him so well would feel a bit more intimidated.' Vettriano himself takes pains to put his subjects at ease. As far as he's concerned, modelling is simply another form of acting: 'It's a job, and they shouldn't worry about being perceived as vamps. Nonetheless, it's not always easy asking a girl to take her clothes off. I'd never ask a girl to undress in front of me – they're always given a room to change in.'

It has been asked why he paints women naked but not men. His answer is simple: 'Men aren't very attractive naked, all that tackle they have to cart around with them. Speaking for myself, if I can perform the act and keep my clothes on I always feel much

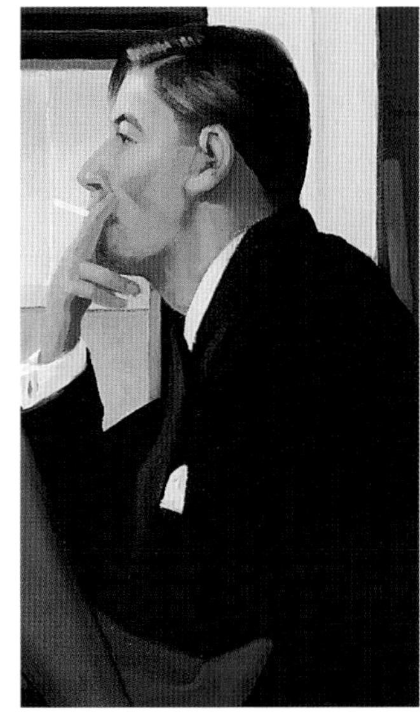

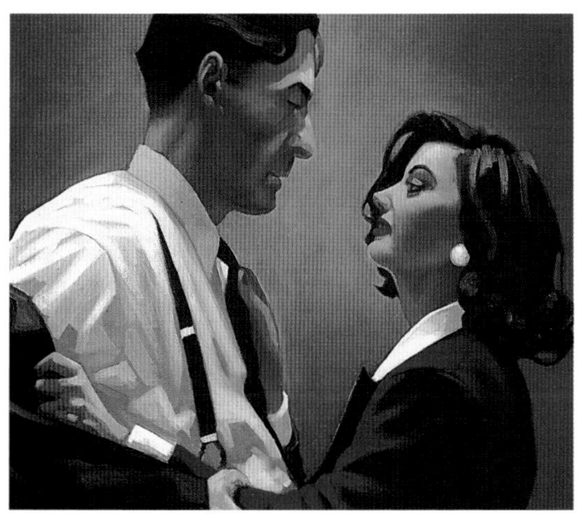

better about it. It's also to do with the fact that I'm ageing. It's like that Leonard Cohen song, *Tower of Song* – 'My friends are gone, my hair is grey/I ache in the places where I used to play.' As you get older you inevitably find the machinery starts to break down, you lose the bravado of youth'. As a young man he was attracted to older women, though he has happily not succumbed to the embarrassing tradition of the older man who chases after younger women. His view of relationships remains pessimistic – 'a battlefield', in his words: 'It's not just about sex, it's about how we're driven to go out to a bar, pick up a woman and know full well that twelve hours later we'll be disgusted with ourselves. But we do it all the same.'

Aside from Gail, he has never had a long-term relationship with a woman, nor has he any strong yearning to have children. (When he married Gail, however, he legally adopted her daughter, Victoria). 'I've never had a great sense of passing on my genes', he says. 'I'm not sure I'd want anyone to have these genes…Recently, I suppose in the last five years, I've thought that if I met somebody and we had a reasonable chance of success, I'm sure I'd feel differently about it. And because I've got no dependents, it would also solve the problem of what to do with what I leave.' But, as Carolyn Osborne suggests, the woman he is looking for probably doesn't exist. His unsentimental analysis of his romantic future suggests a man who has reconciled himself to being alone. Socially he seems to be retreating further into the shadows. He recently moved to a place outside Edinburgh, with a startling view over the Firth of Forth and two gleaming vintage Mercedes parked in the garage. In London he keeps a studio in the expensive anonymity of Mayfair.

His decision to leave Edinburgh has not caused him much regret. As popular as his paintings are, he is not represented in the Scottish National Gallery of Modern Art, while the art establishment, he feels, misses no opportunity to undermine him. He stopped showing at the RSA five years ago. 'Because the paintings are

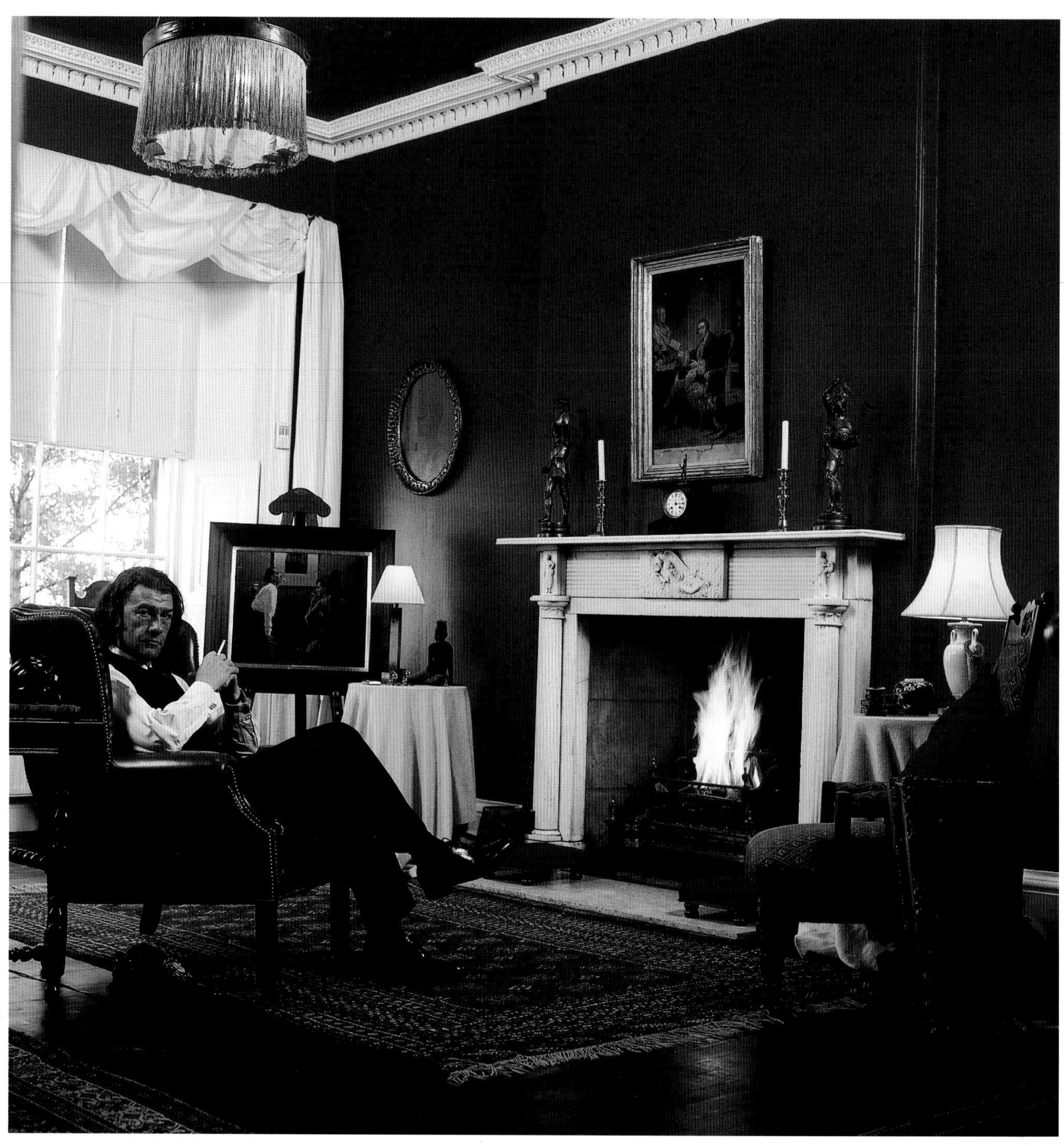

judged by a jury of your peers, I always felt it was a thrill to show there. I suppose my feelings just changed. They have a gala evening when the academicians all go round in their gowns talking to the public – I was invited to it one year, and foolishly believed it represented some kind of acceptance of me. But then someone explained that the only reason I'd been invited was because I'd bought something the year before. I was totally ignored, not one academician came and said hello. And it's not as if they're showing the cream of Scottish art – the Conroys, the Campbells, Alison Watts, Jenny Savile, they weren't touching the place either. So it wasn't a heartbreaking decision for me not to show'.

Photograph of Jack Vettriano by Robin Matthews.

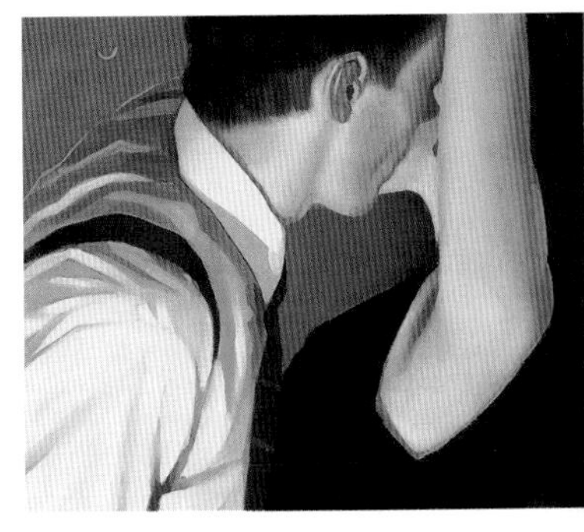

He is especially offended by those who disdain his work as pornography.

In February 1999 *Scotland on Sunday*, no longer a bulwark for him after Gordon Smith's death, ran an article investigating 'Scotland's love-hate relationship with Jack Vettriano'. The writer, Iain Gale, tried to gussy up the piece by insisting that Vettriano had 'disappeared', indeed had 'ceased to exist', but stuck for evidence he fell back on a precis of the career so far: 'Vettriano is that breed of artist who singlehandedly embodies the hoary old chestnut of the argument between high art and popular culture. Perhaps without intending to do so, he has successfully split Scotland in two. Mention his name anywhere, from a Stockbridge dinner party to a Glasgow bar and you will not find any shortage of opinions. He is, by turns, "gallus" and "crap". Even in the national press, opinion has been divided.' Vettriano takes a deeply cynical view of the debate: 'The art world has nothing to do with art – it's only to do with people and power and money. If I thought my critics were just concerned with art I might worry. I wish they'd say something I might learn from.'

He is especially offended by those who disdain his work as pornography. 'The word is not used in a remotely accurate or interesting way, it's used about my work the way a thug uses a club. The person who called it that knows it's a lie.' The person in question is Duncan Macmillan, Professor of Scottish Art History at Edinburgh. 'He wrote recently that my work was "instantly forgettable". Well – to whom? Try telling that to the thousands of people who've bought it in the last ten years. Anyone who says it's pornography just hasn't *seen* pornography. I choose to paint the moments before or after sex, not the act itself.' Hewlett wonders whether Macmillan has seen any meaningful body of Vettriano's work at first hand. If Vettriano has a genuine grievance with the likes of Macmillan, there might be just a bit of him that needs to feel embattled and misunderstood. Carolyn Osborne thinks that it suits the painter to believe that he's got at: 'If you look at it, there's Duncan Macmillan and maybe one or two others who lambast him, but Jack has had a lot of publicity and I think he has to expect some negative side to that. He's naïve if he doesn't.'

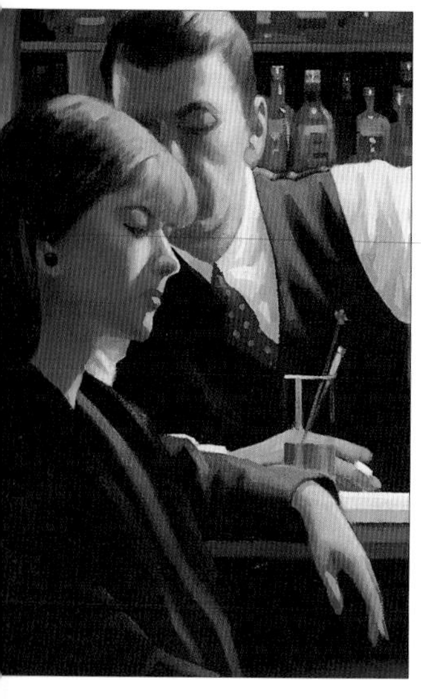

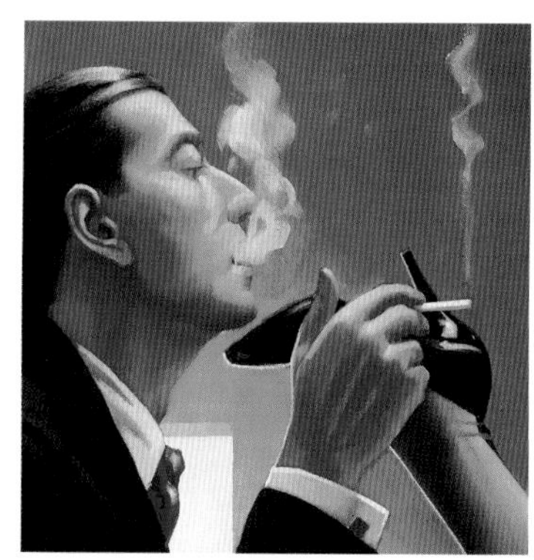

After six years of sell-out shows in London, Edinburgh, Johannesburg and Hong Kong, Vettriano can brave the brickbats. The paintings featured in his June 1998 show, *Between Darkness and Dawn*, revealed not only a greater technical accomplishment but a wider tonal range. The play of light in *Models in the Studio II* rates as one of the most beautiful effects he has ever set down in oils. As well as the signature nocturnes – *The Purple Cat*, *Girls' Night*, *Weaving The Web* – there were lovely wistful mood pieces such as *Portrait in Silver and Black* and *The Very Thought of You*. And nostalgia for the Raith and Burma ballrooms resurfaces in the dancing partners of *Defending Champions* and *Couple No.8*. In 1997 a series of paintings was specially commissioned by Sir Terence Conran for exclusive display in his new Bluebird Club on the King's Road.

Carolyn Osborne decided that it was high time a public place exhibited his work, and two years ago donated one of her own Vettrianos – a study of *One Moment in Time* – to Kirkcaldy Art Gallery. Such was the interest that the Gallery contacted the painter and asked him to come and be interviewed before an audience. The response from the public was overwhelming, so much so that Vettriano was asked to do a second night. Kirkcaldy then contacted Hewlett and a transfer of *Between Darkness and Dawn* was arranged from the Portland. It was an enormous success, breaking all visiting records at Kirkcaldy, and for Vettriano it afforded a very personal satisfaction: 'For the first time ever my parents were at an opening on their home patch. What really touched me was that, if I had any fears that my own people would reject me, the absolute opposite turned out to be true. People were just so generous.' Quite a homecoming.

What continues to please him, and baffle his critics, is the diversity of his fan base. His work appeals across the board, from city brokers to bus drivers, and mail from all over the world lands on his doormat every week. The sales figures on posters and cards alone are staggering, yet there is no shortage of buyers 'at the top end'. His name has now reached the other side of the Atlantic. In November 1999 his paintings were shown

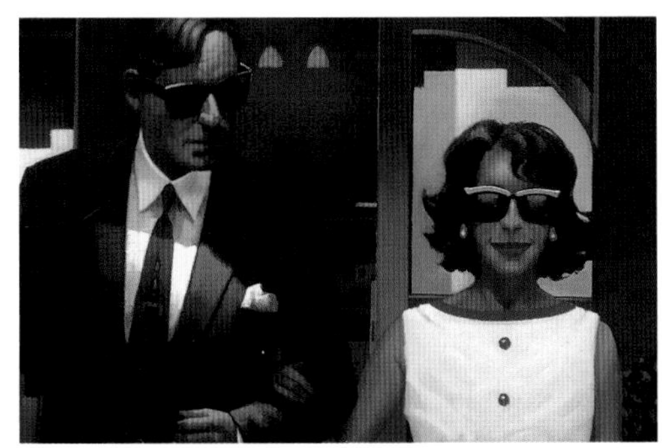

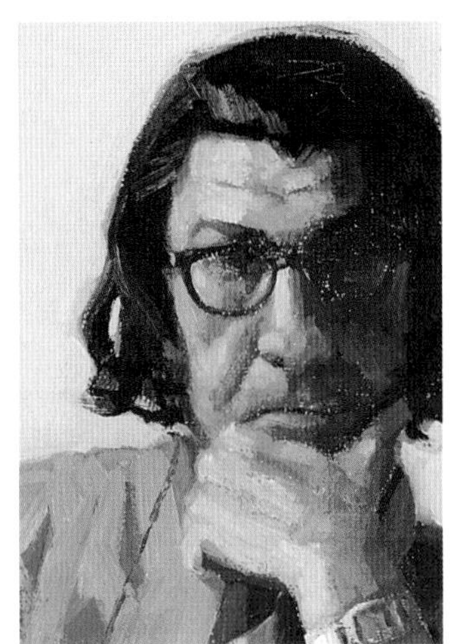

He reads a little, smokes a lot, devising new situations, angles, intrigues, to set down on canvas.

publicly for the first time in New York, at the Twentieth-Century Arts Fair in Park Avenue. Such was the fervour that many Vettriano fans in the UK, anticipating a rare opportunity, flew over simply to buy a painting. The twenty pictures on exhibition were sold within fifteen minutes of the opening. At the Portland Gallery inquiries about his work, whether by e-mail, phone or personal visit, now run to about thirty per day. As Tom Hewlett says, 'I don't know of any other gallery that enjoys such interest in a single artist'. Will his stock slump? Vettriano has considered the prospect, and seems philosophical on the matter: it might have a bearing on his output, but it certainly wouldn't change his passion for the work. 'One generation might rubbish me, and because they do the next generation is bound to praise me. You come and go, so there's no telling.'

Like any true romantic, he is most himself when alone, working in one or other of his studios. While he paints he listens to music that will kickstart his memory, or else set him dreaming – Joni Mitchell, Leonard Cohen, Elvis, golden oldies from the sixties. He still likes to haunt auction houses and junk shops, searching for props (dresses, shoes) to put in the paintings. He collects a little art – Jenny Savile, Alberto Morrocco, Robin Philipson, Stephen Conroy – but nothing too flash or pricey. Around London he keeps a low profile; back home in Kirkcaldy people are more inclined to say hello. At Giovanni's restaurant in Dunnikier Road there's always a welcome from the staff. He reads a little, smokes a lot, devising new situations, angles, intrigues, to set down on canvas.

What to make of him? So obsessive is his privacy that few will get the opportunity to find out. Carolyn Osborne, who knows him as well as anybody seems to, describes him as somebody who 'shuts out the things that disagree with him' – and one of those things is surely intimacy. On the other hand, there might be a very good reason for saying that Vettriano is open about himself, for what are his paintings if not an artfully dislocated expression of his fantasy life? And within their small dramas of duplicity and desire, do we not see an expression of our own?

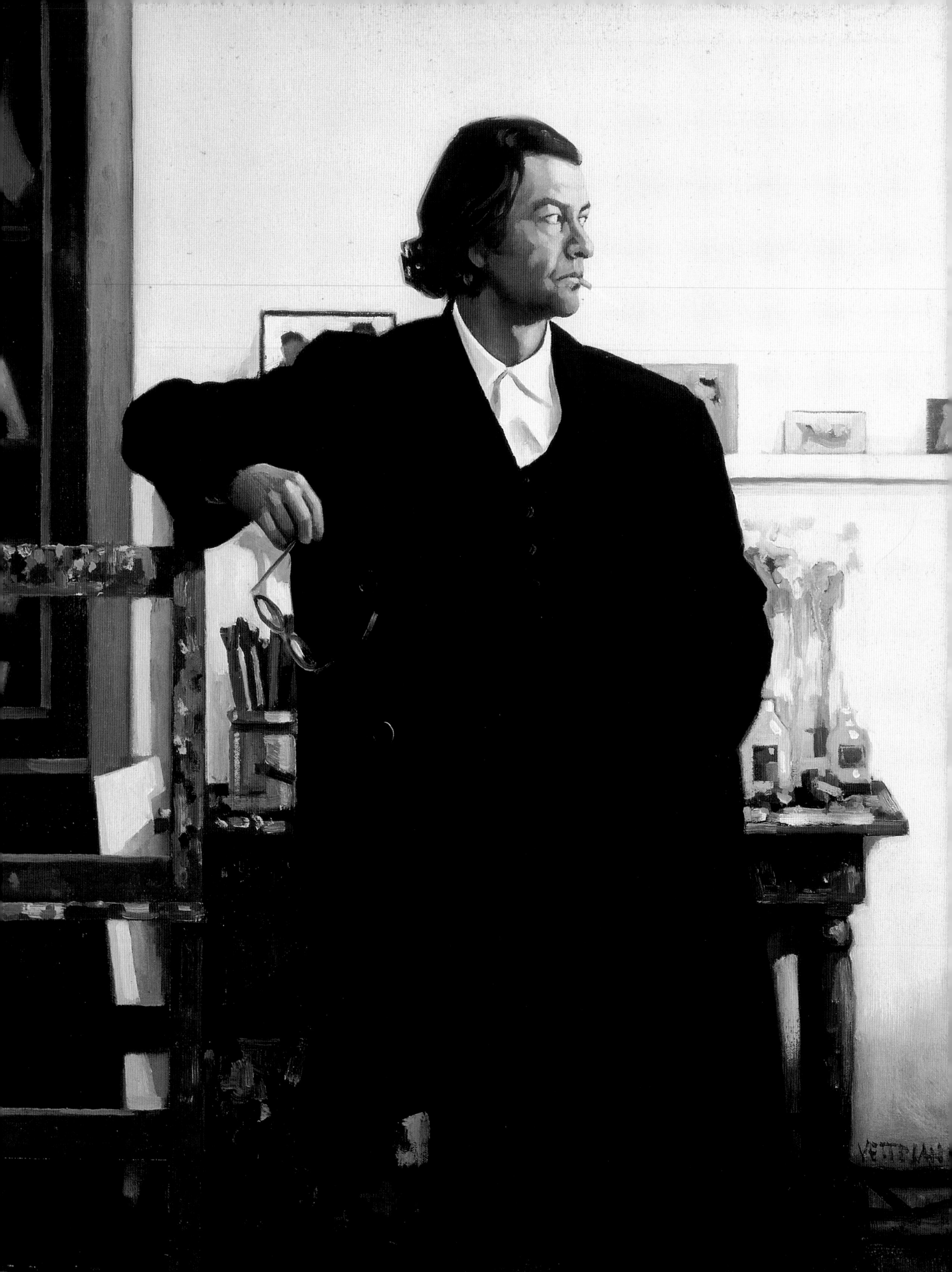

GALLERY

Angel

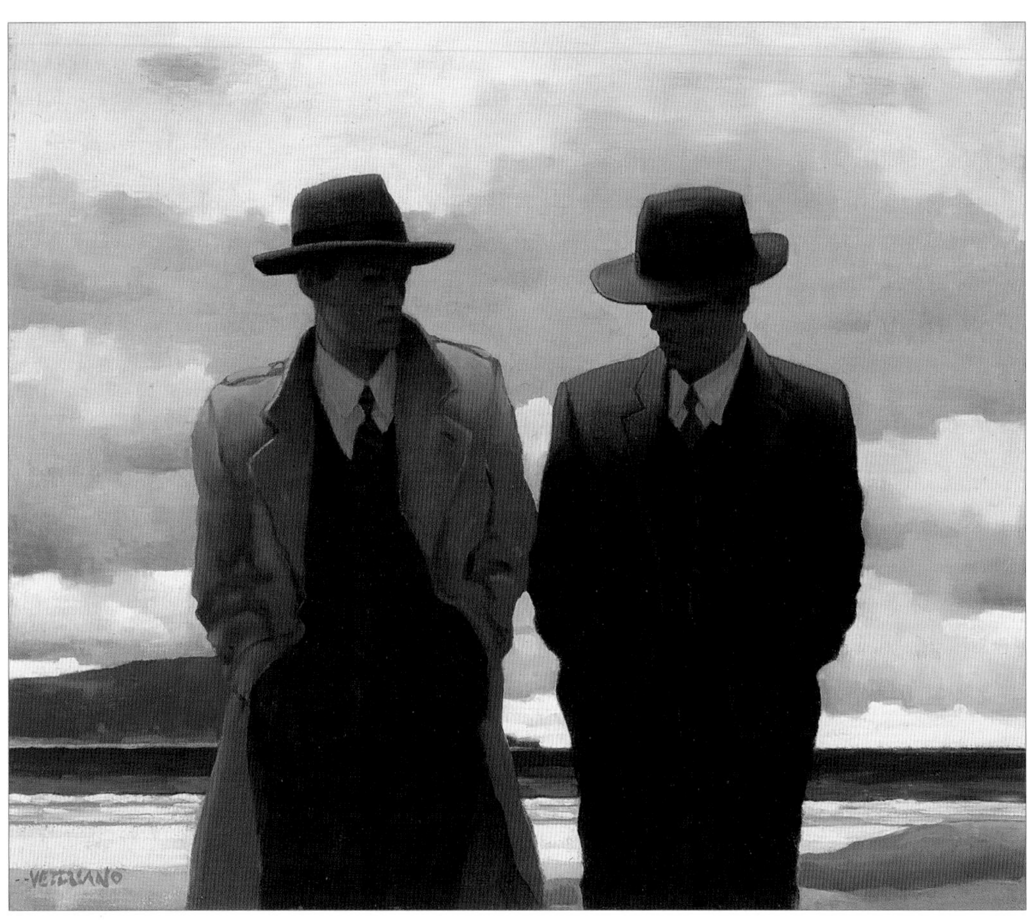

Amateur Philosophers

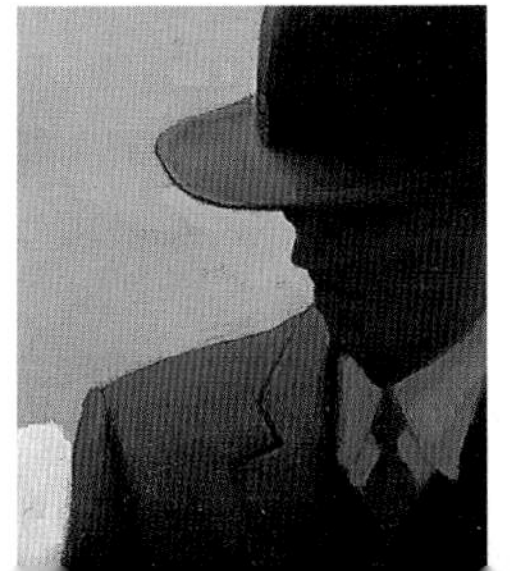

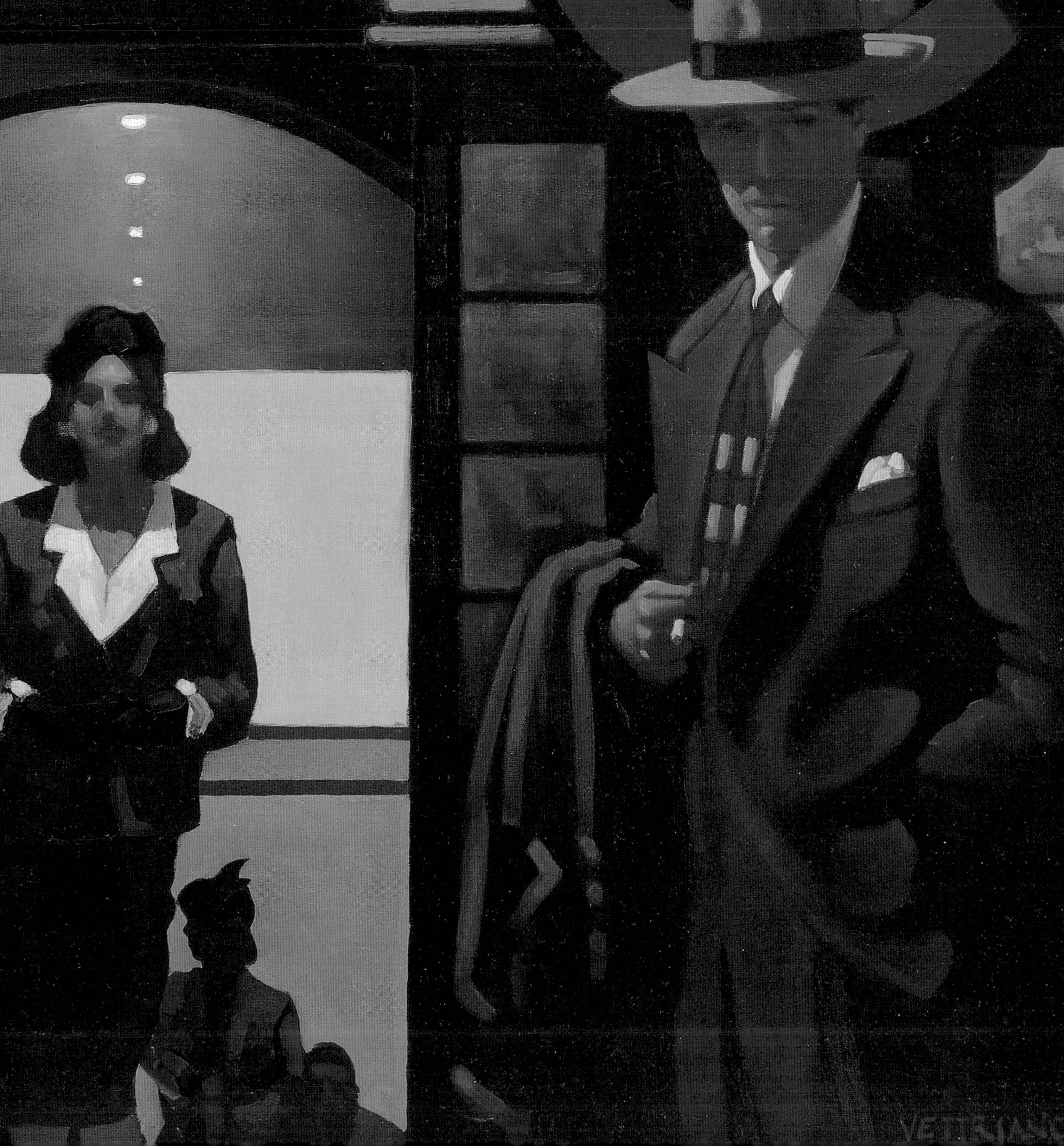
ANGE

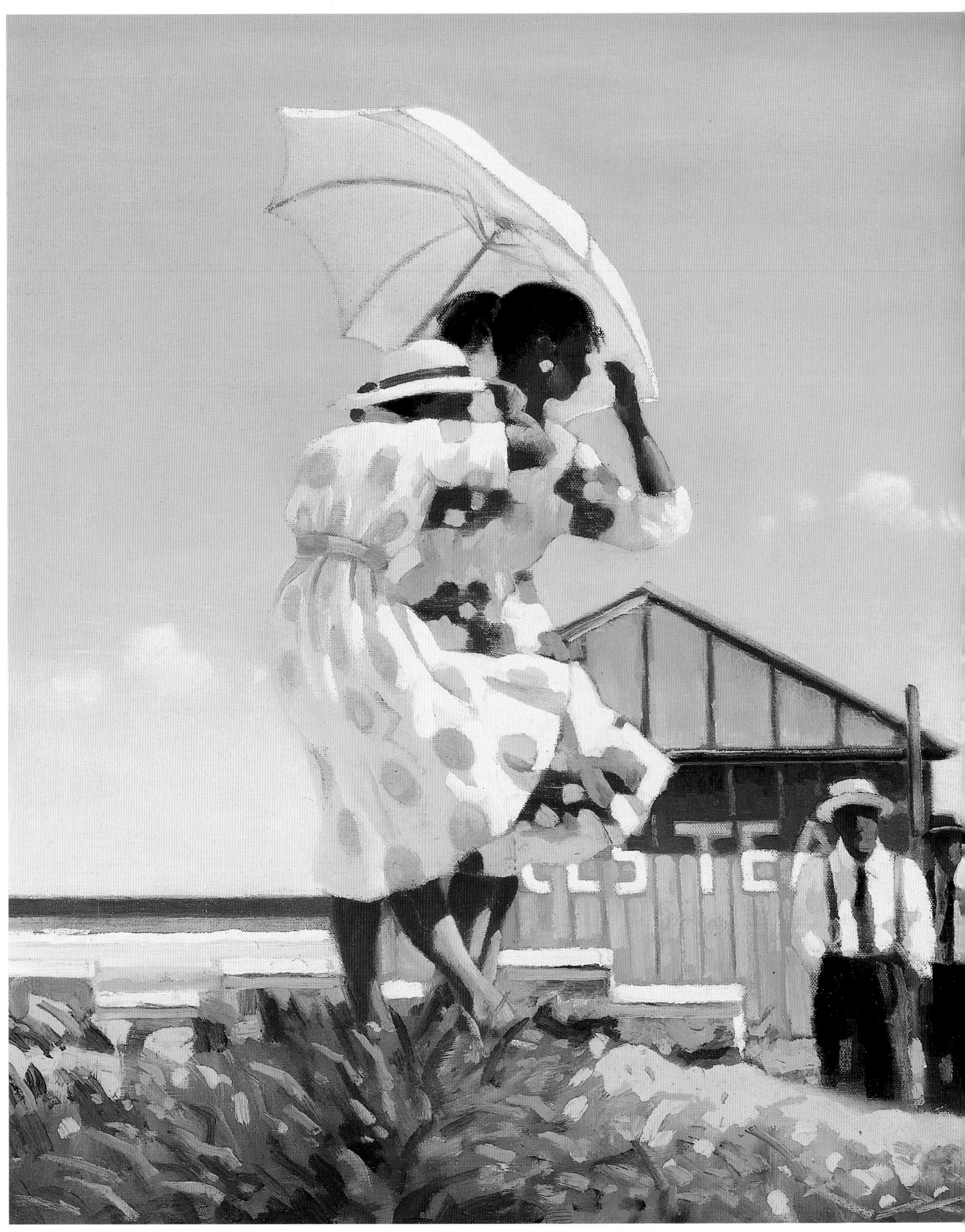

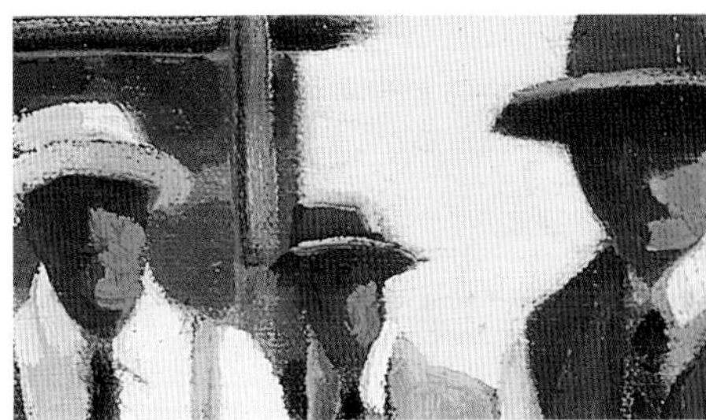

A Very Dangerous Beach

Evening Racing

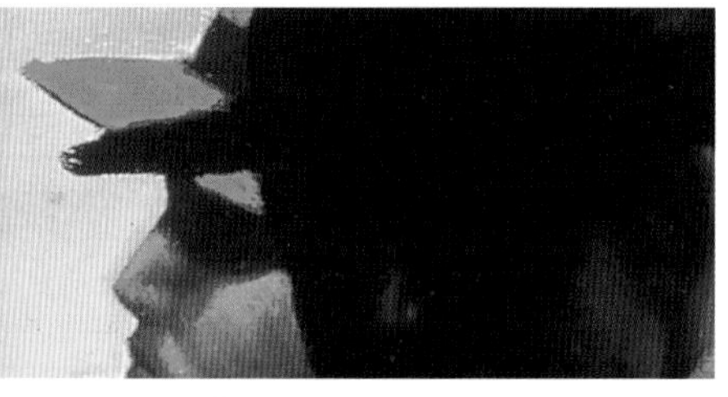

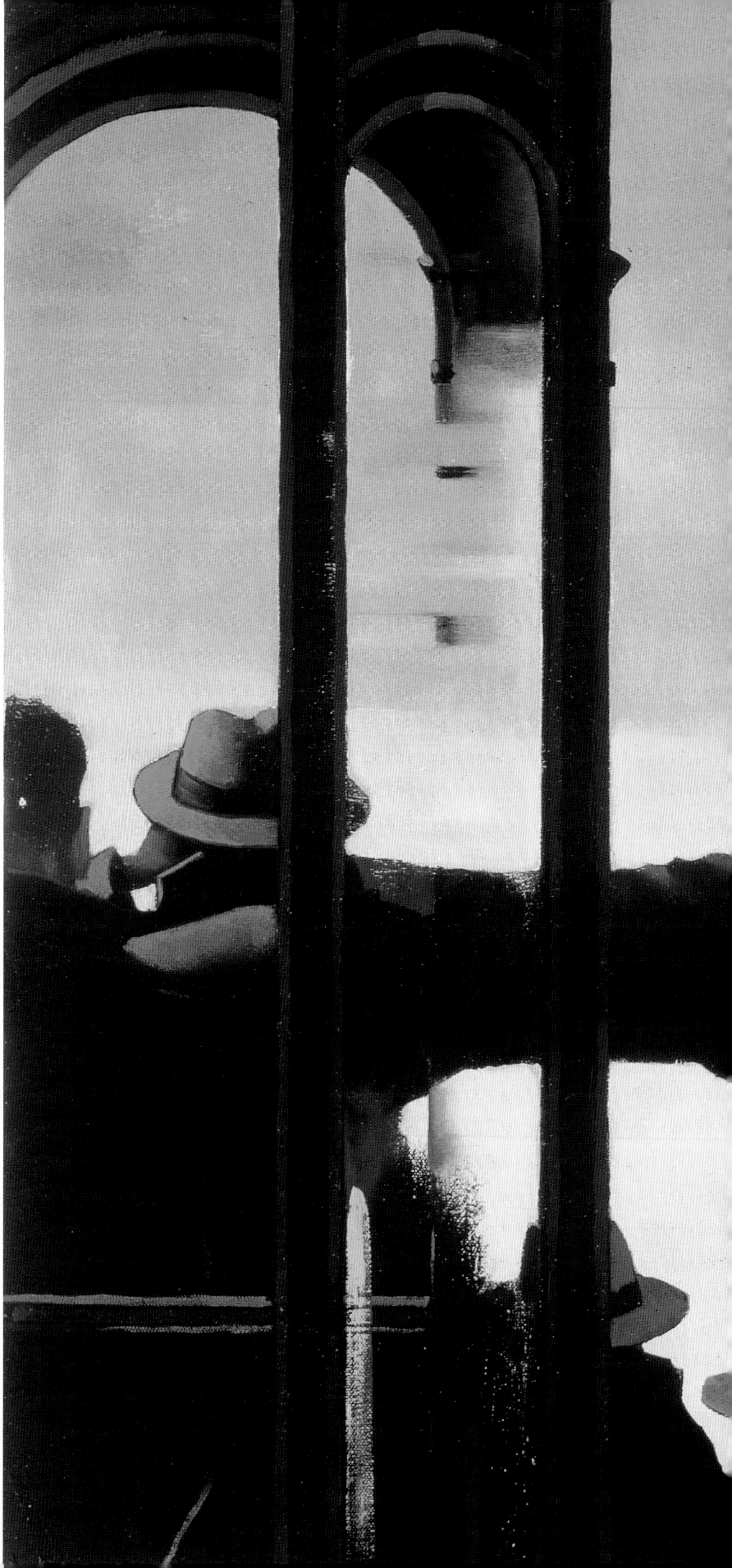

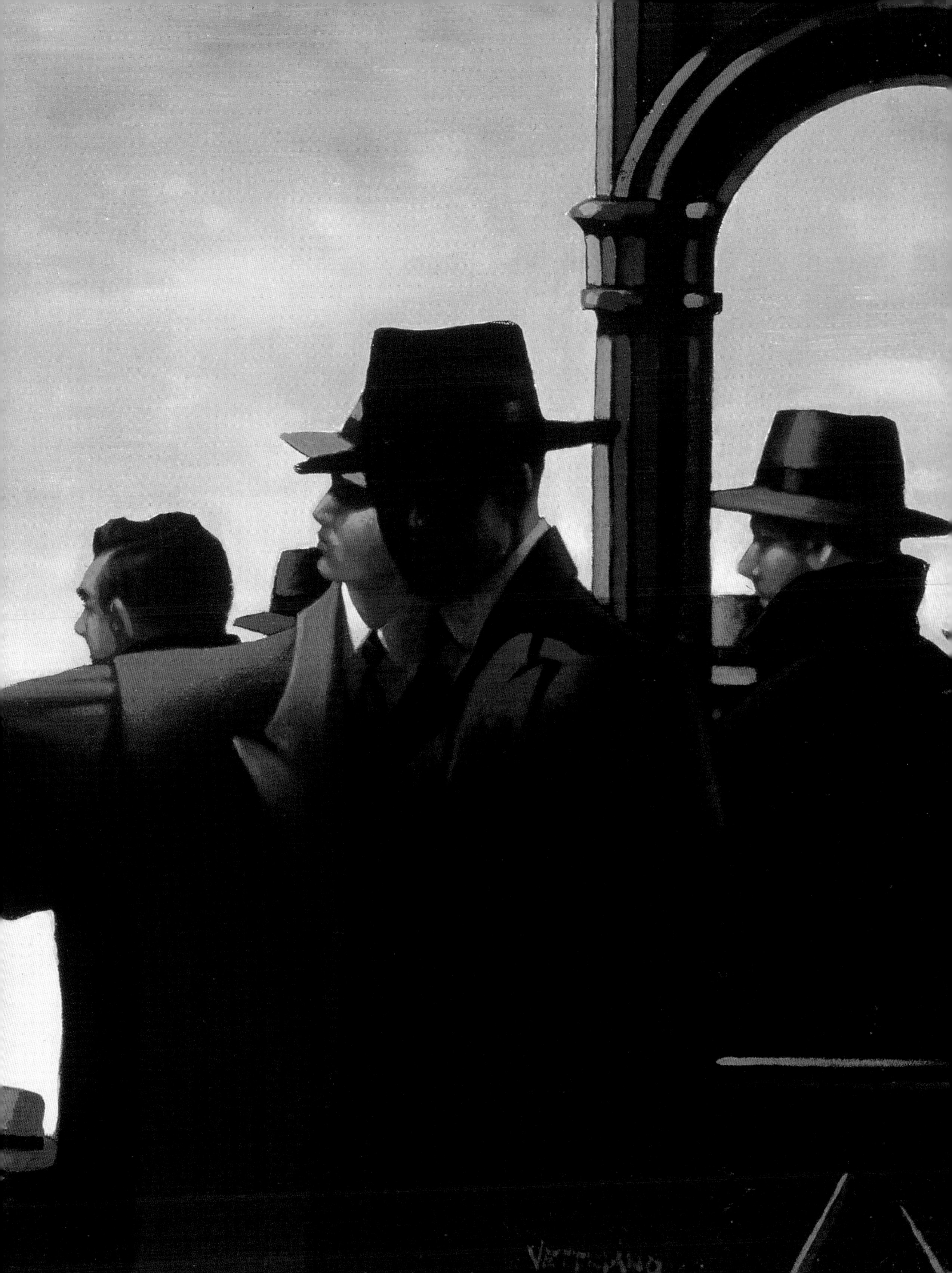

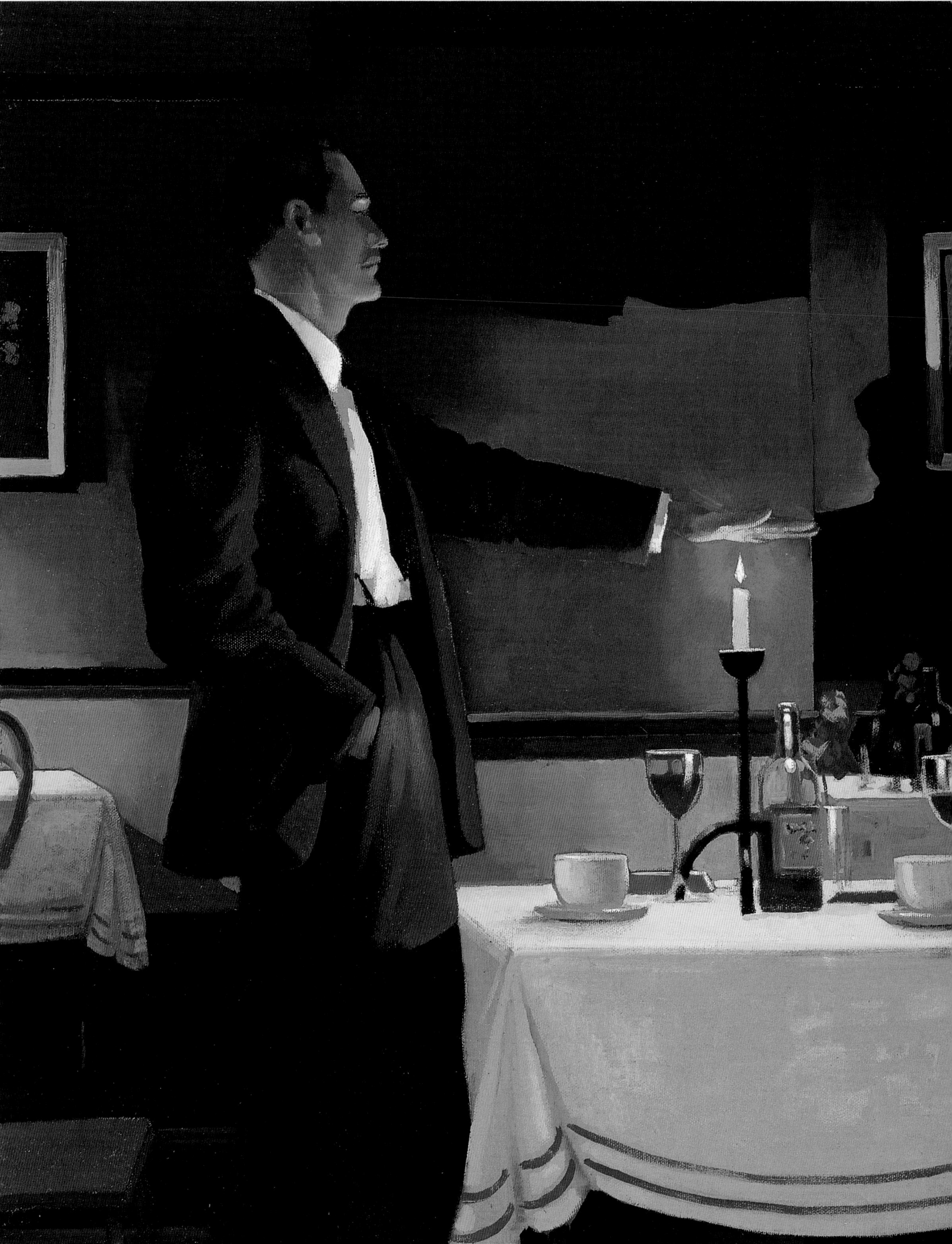

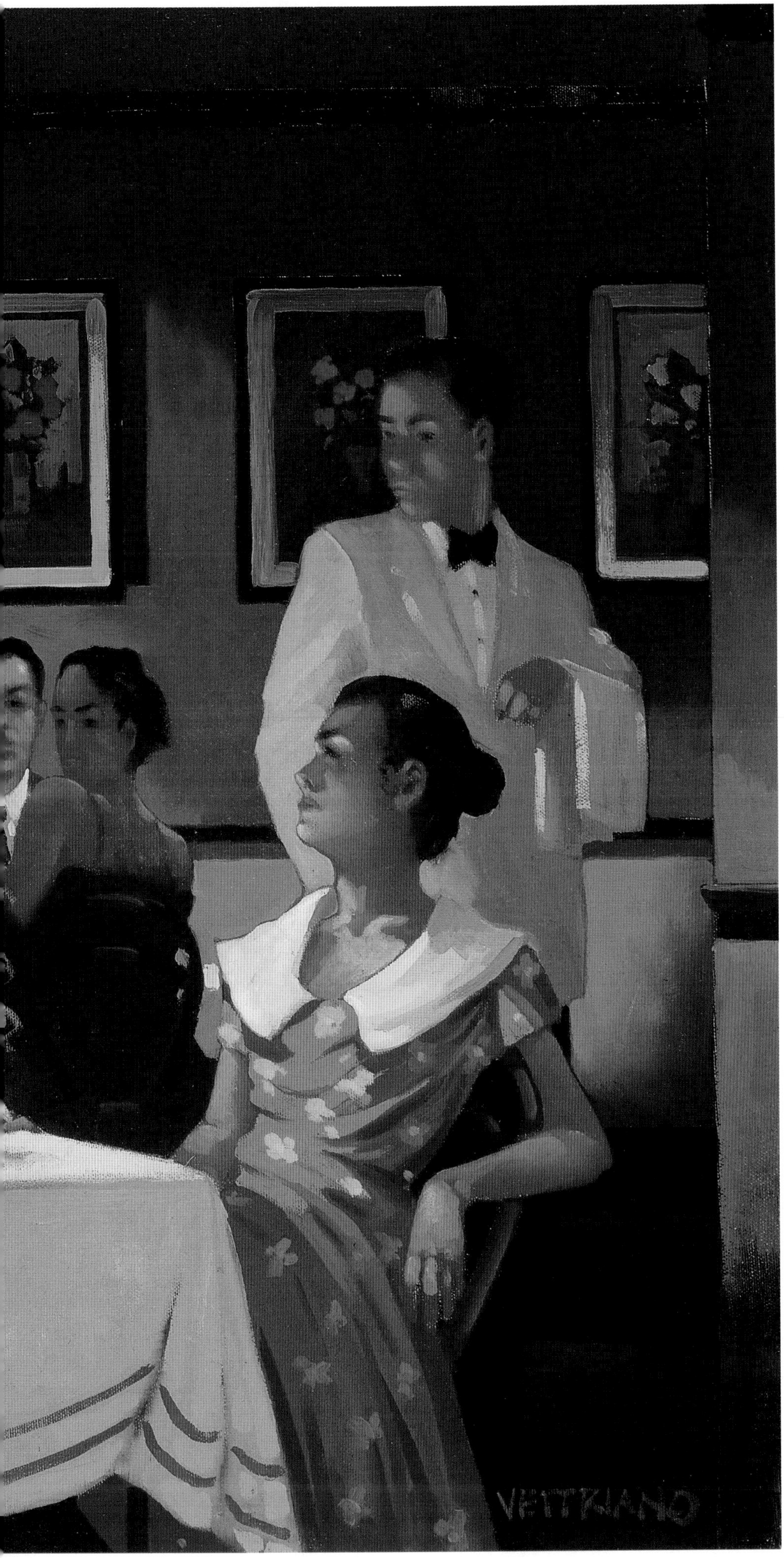

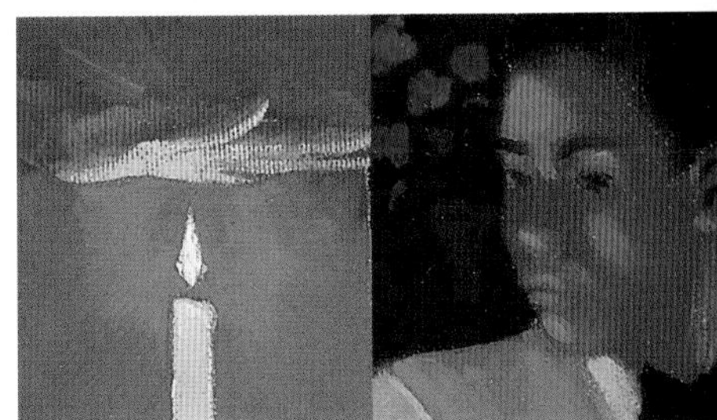

A Test of True Love

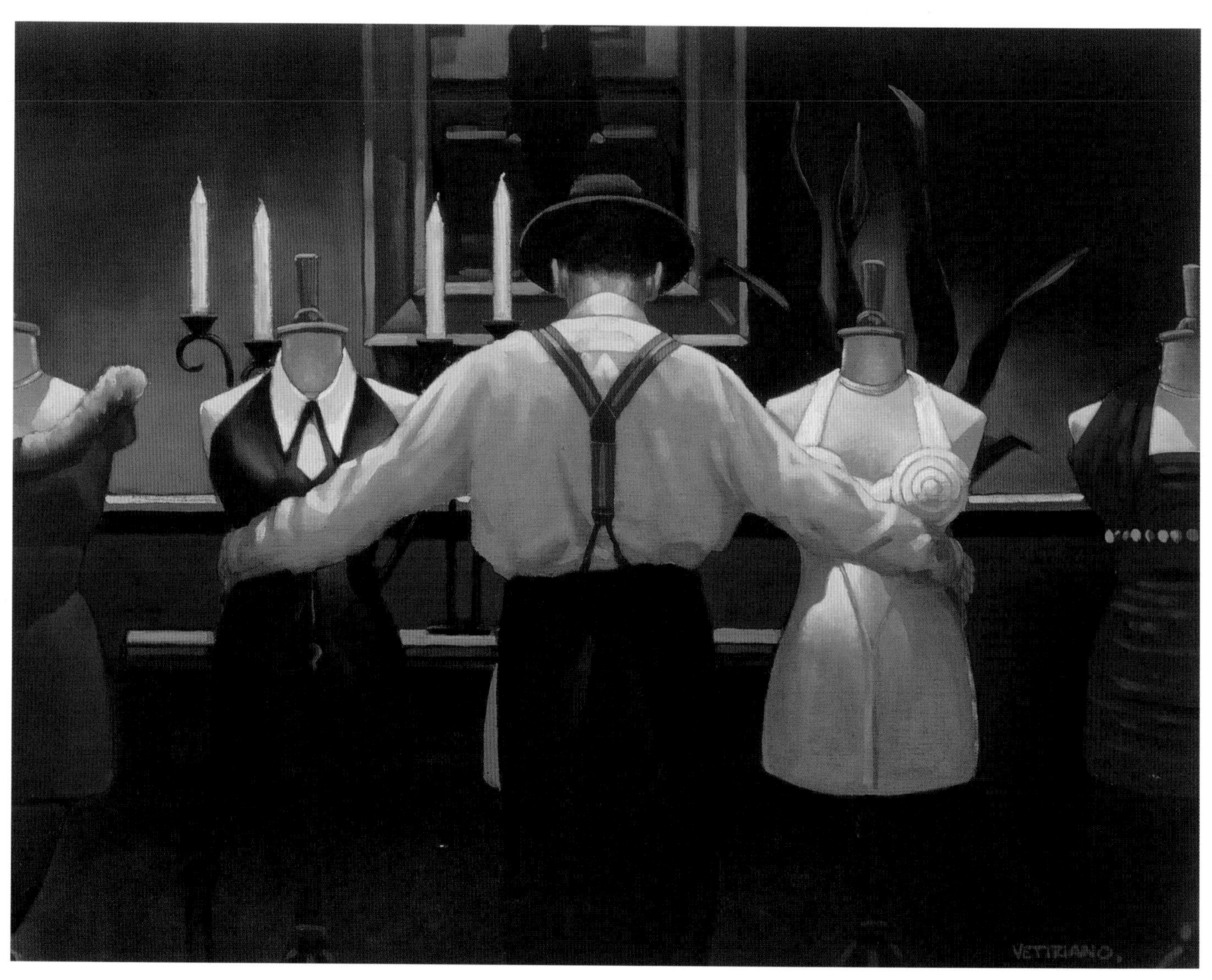

A Kind of Loving

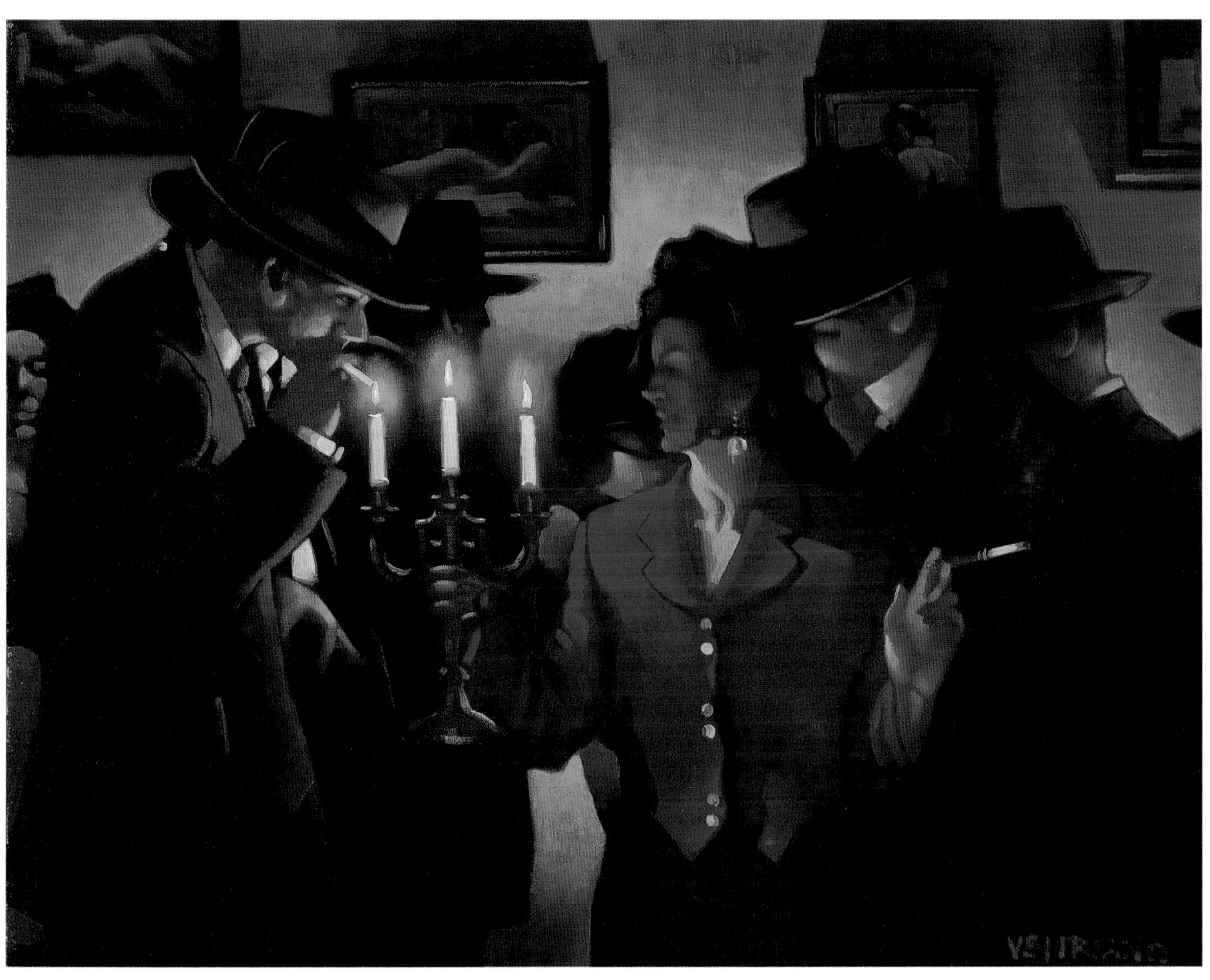

Queen of The Fan-Dan

Strangers in the Night

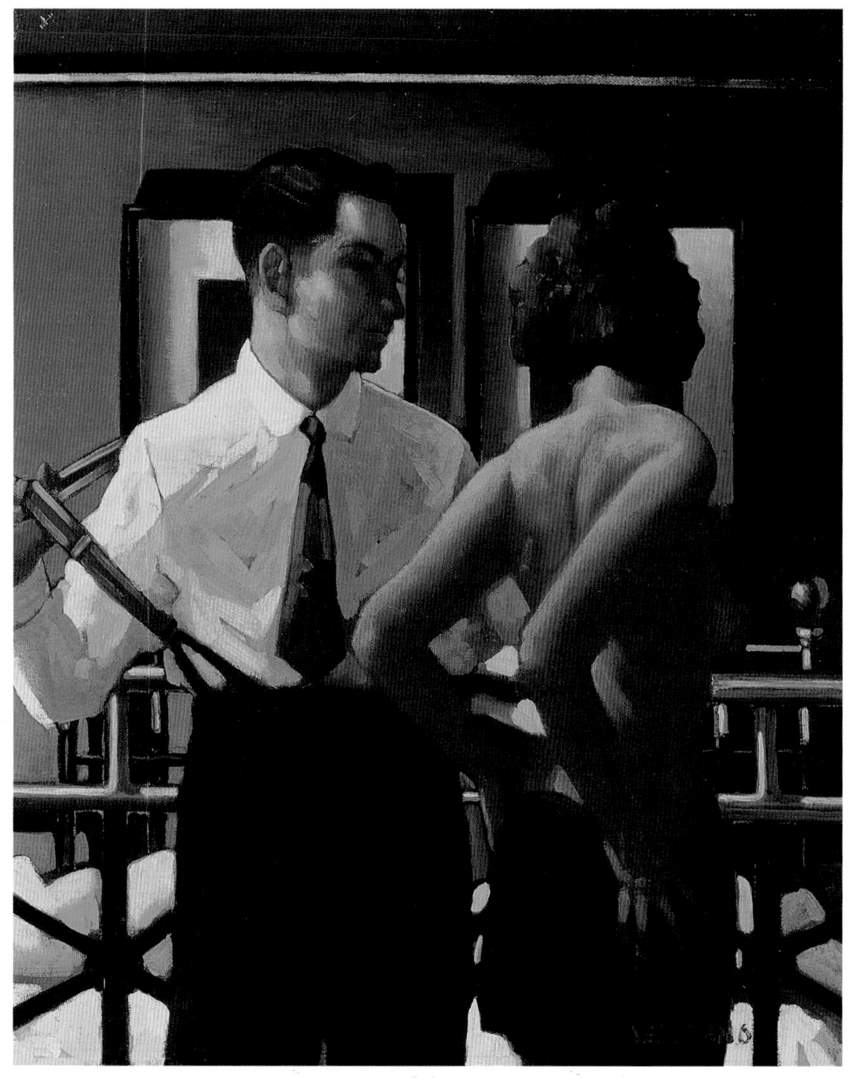

The Same Old Game

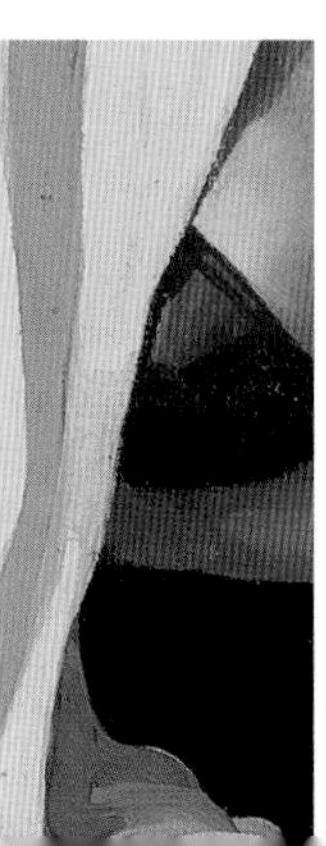

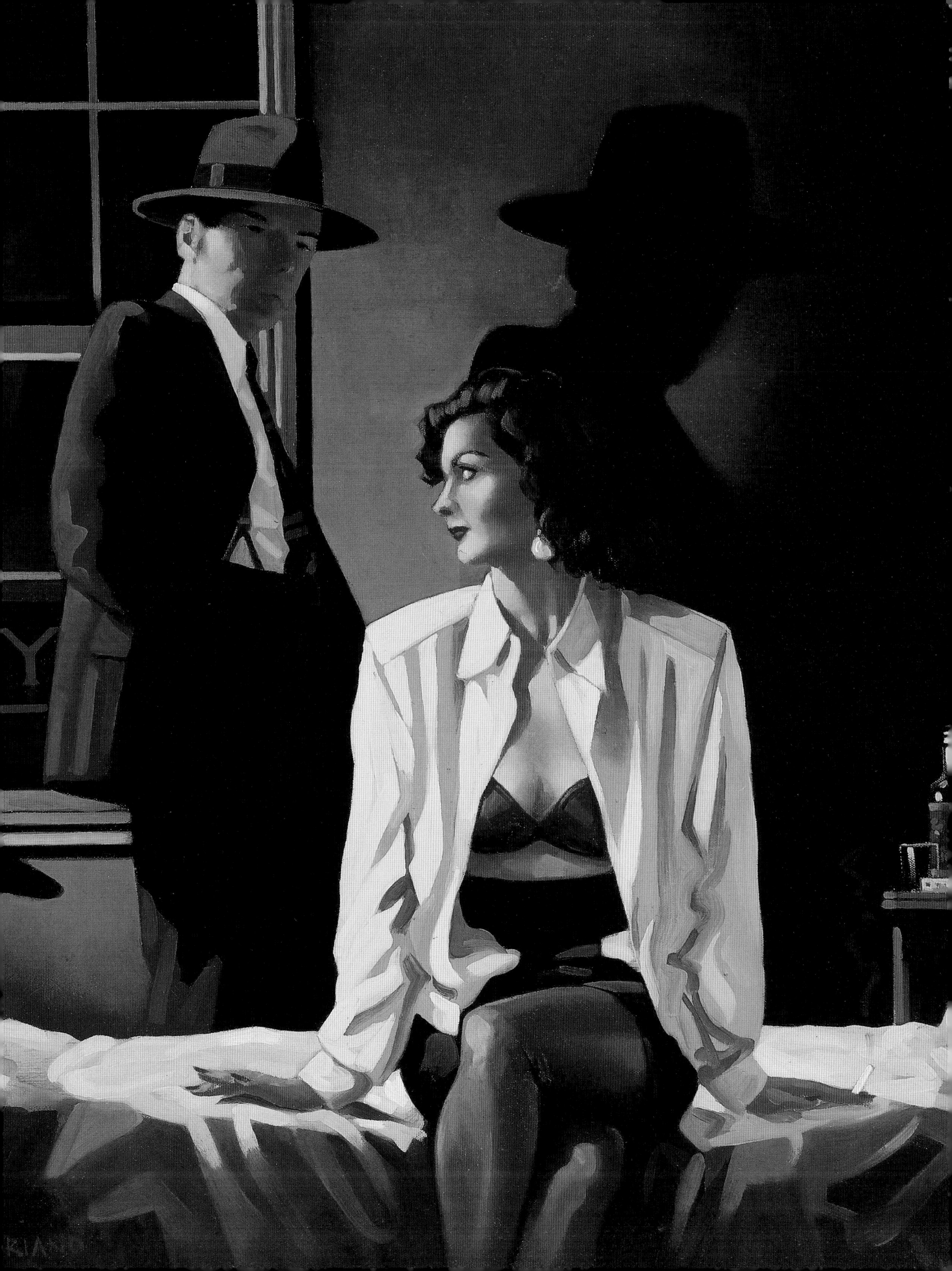

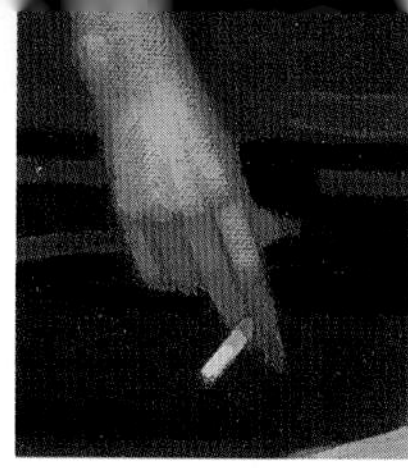

After the Thrill is Gone

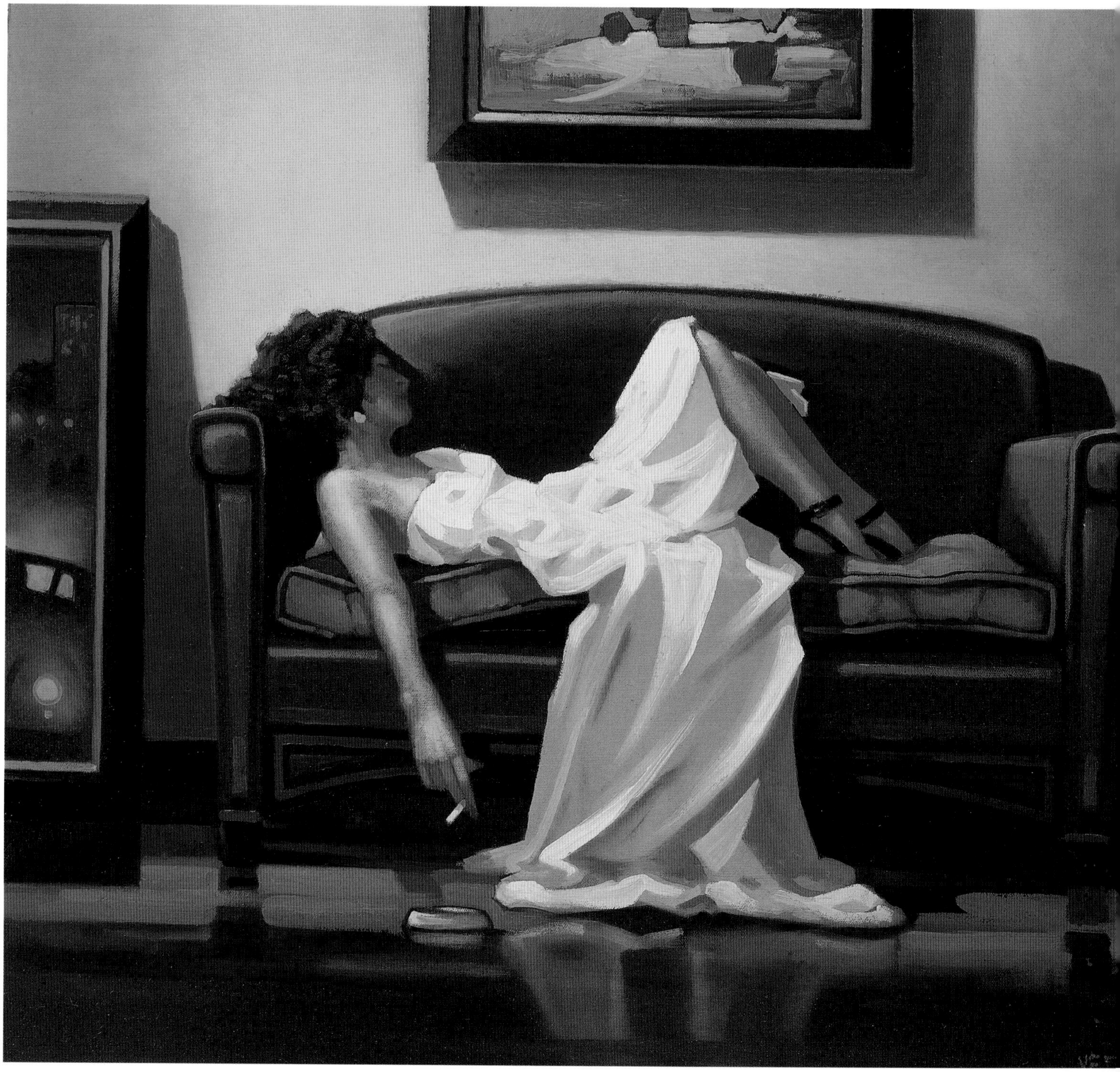

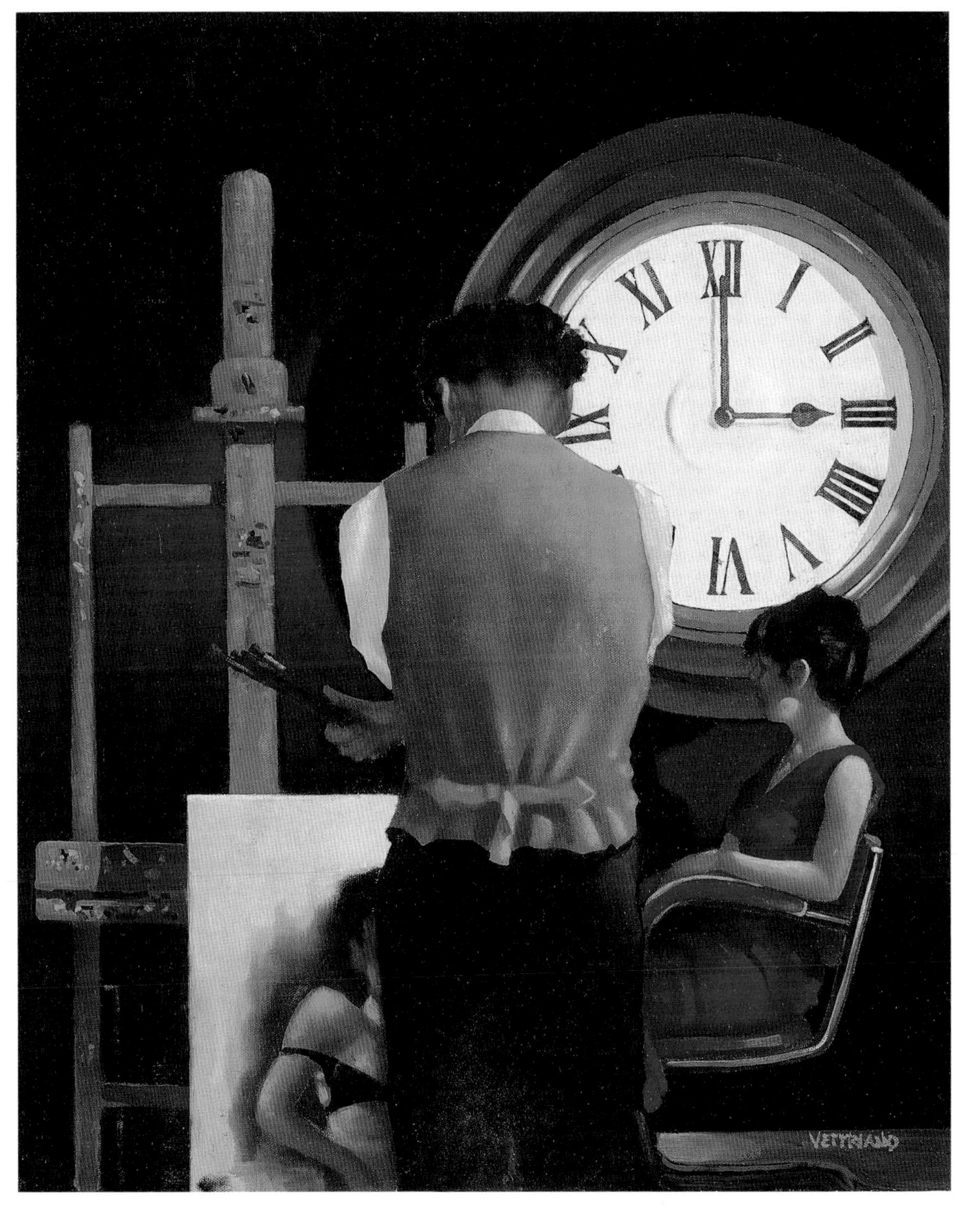

The Critical Hour of 3am

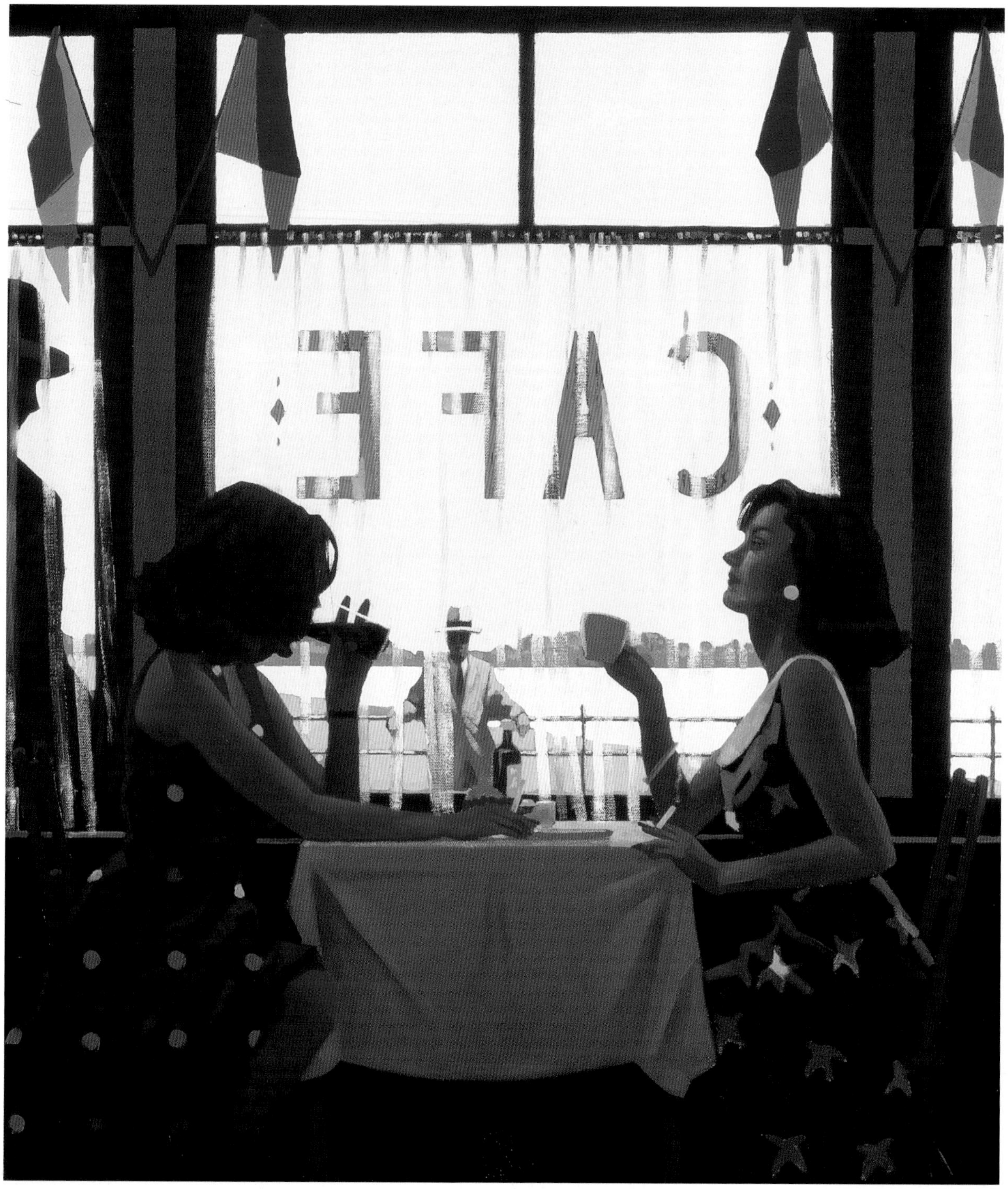

Café Days

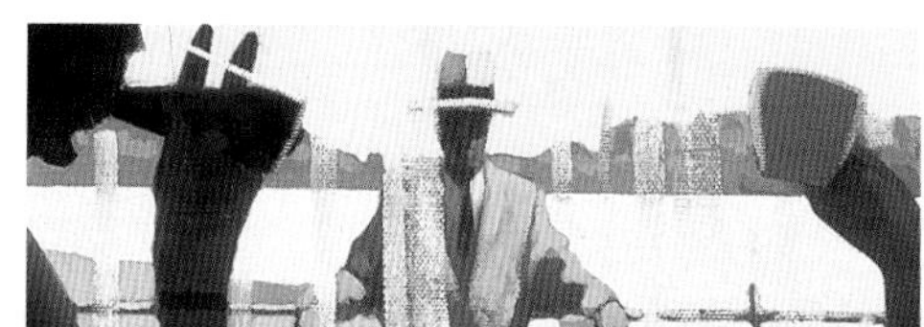

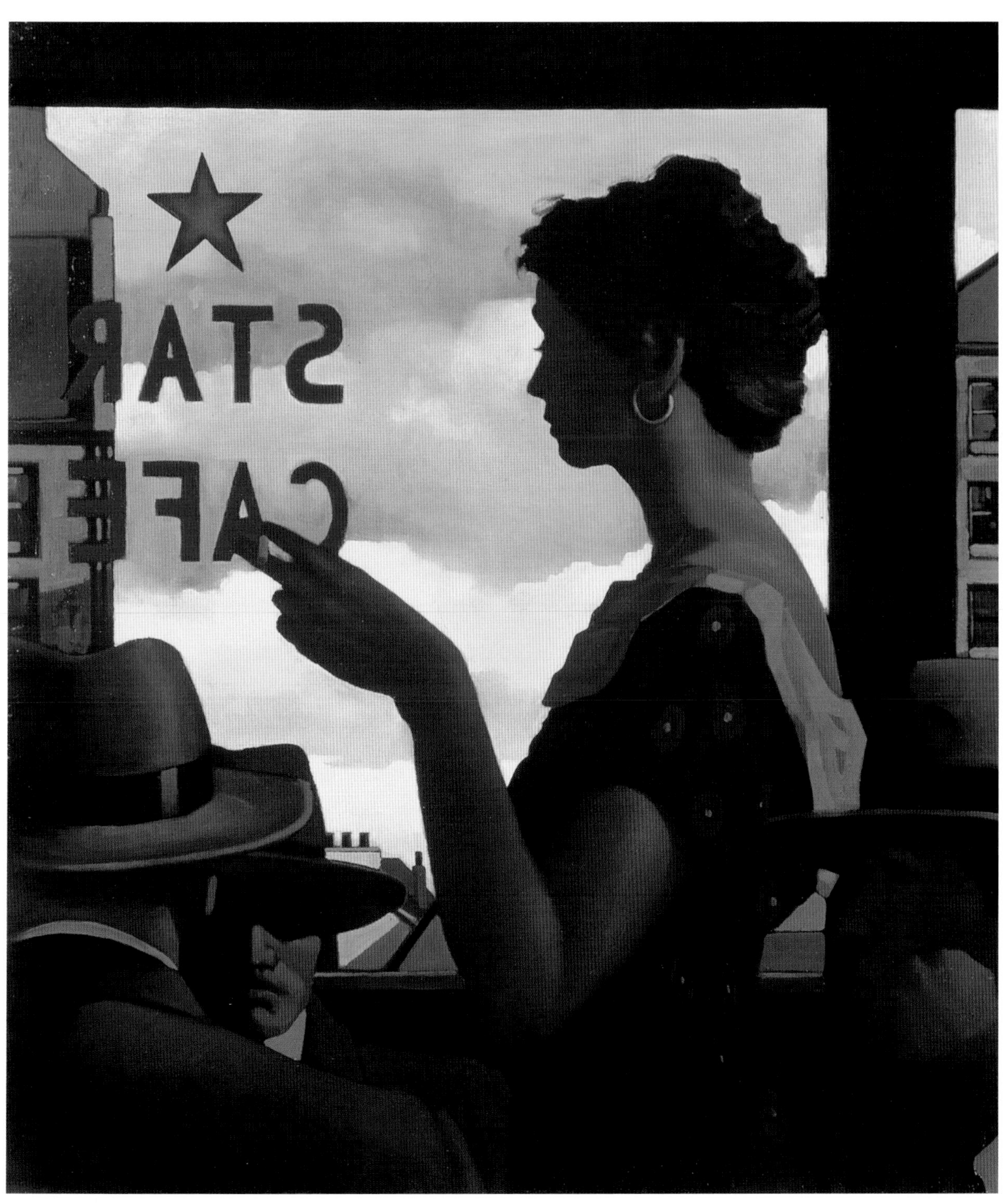

The Star Café

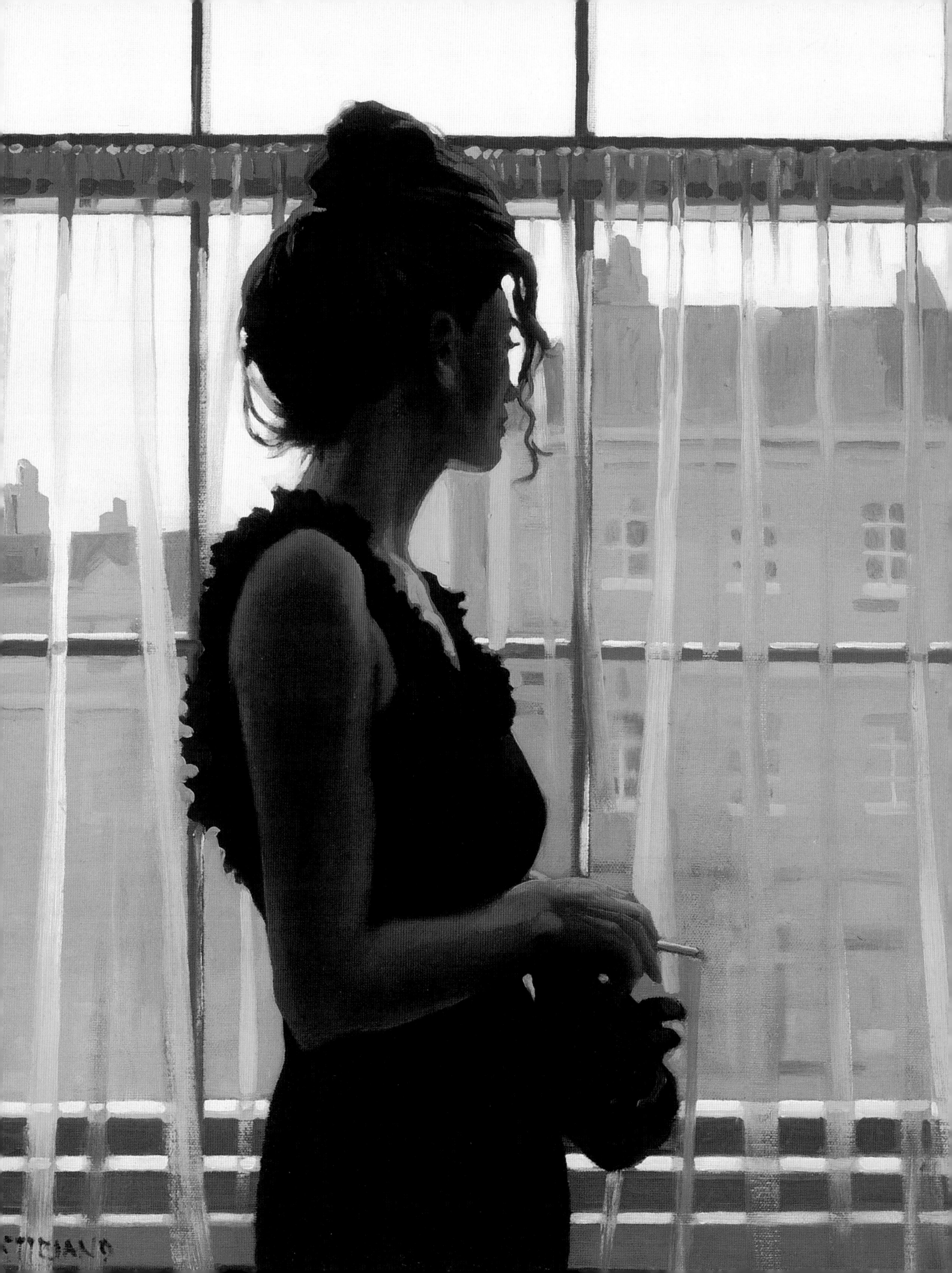

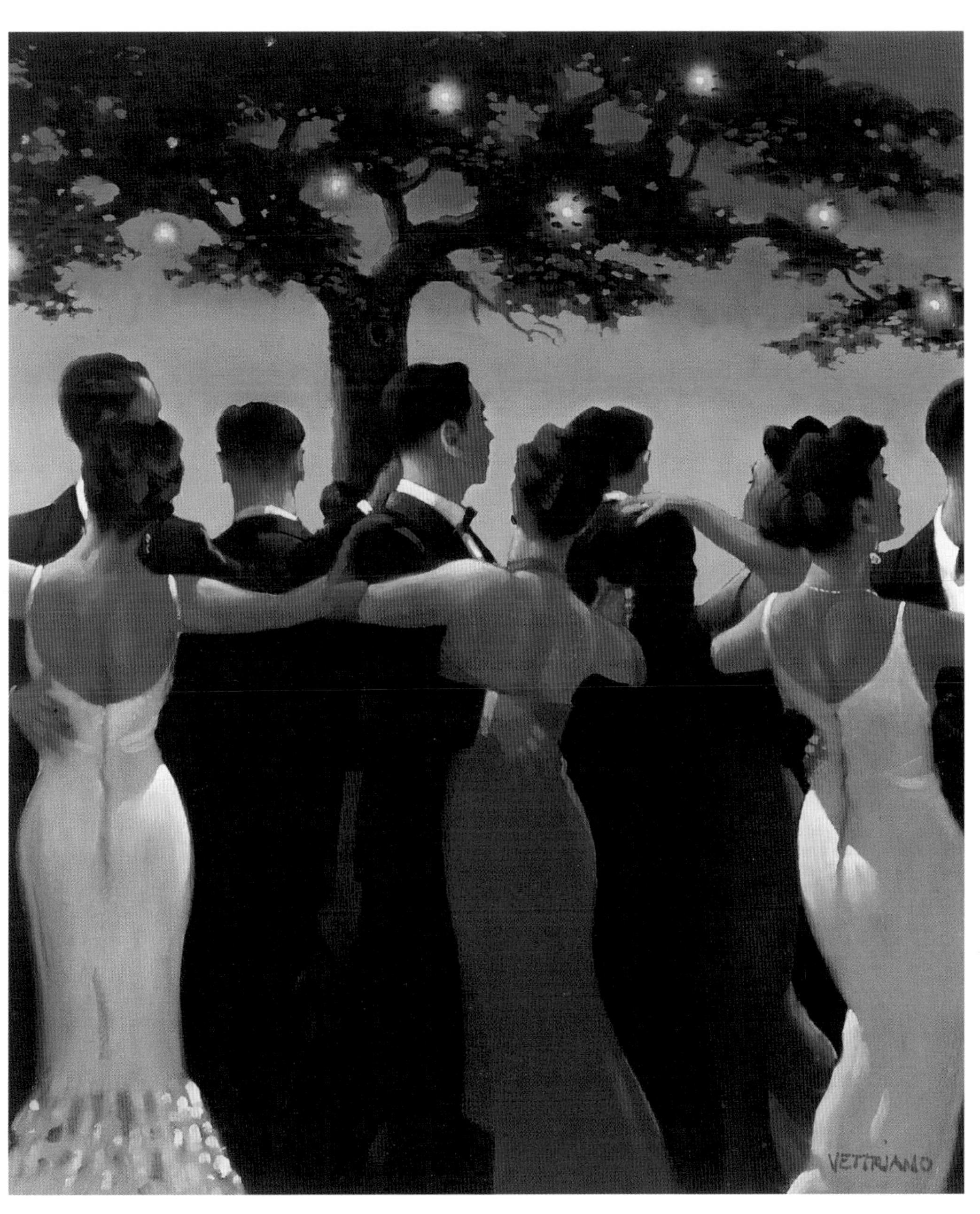

Waltzers

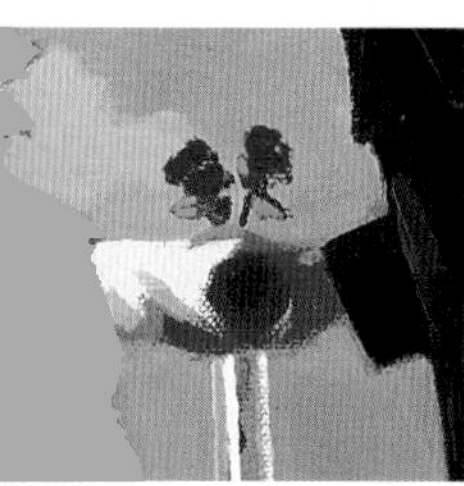

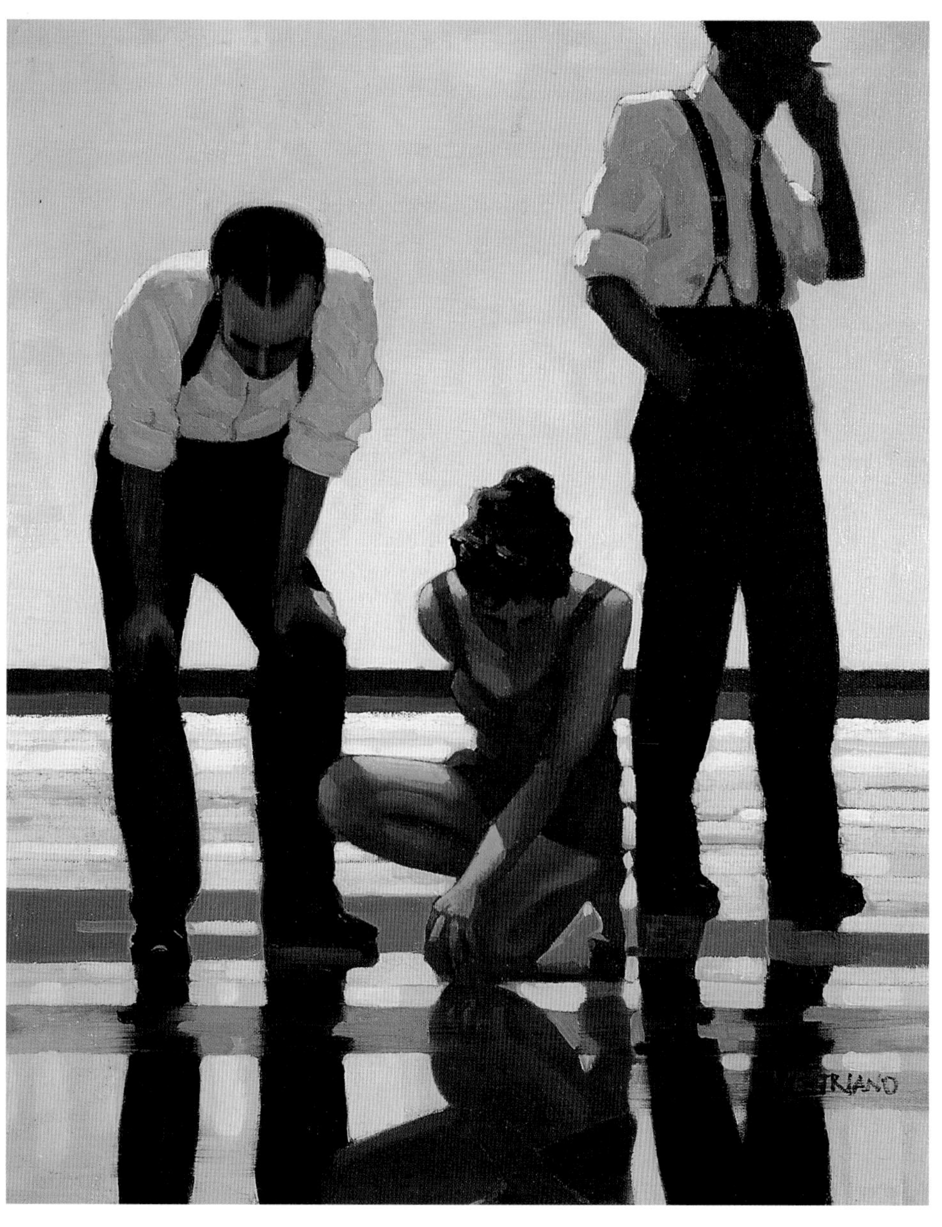

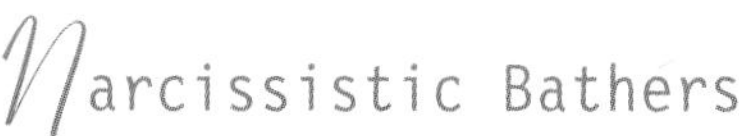

Narcissistic Bathers

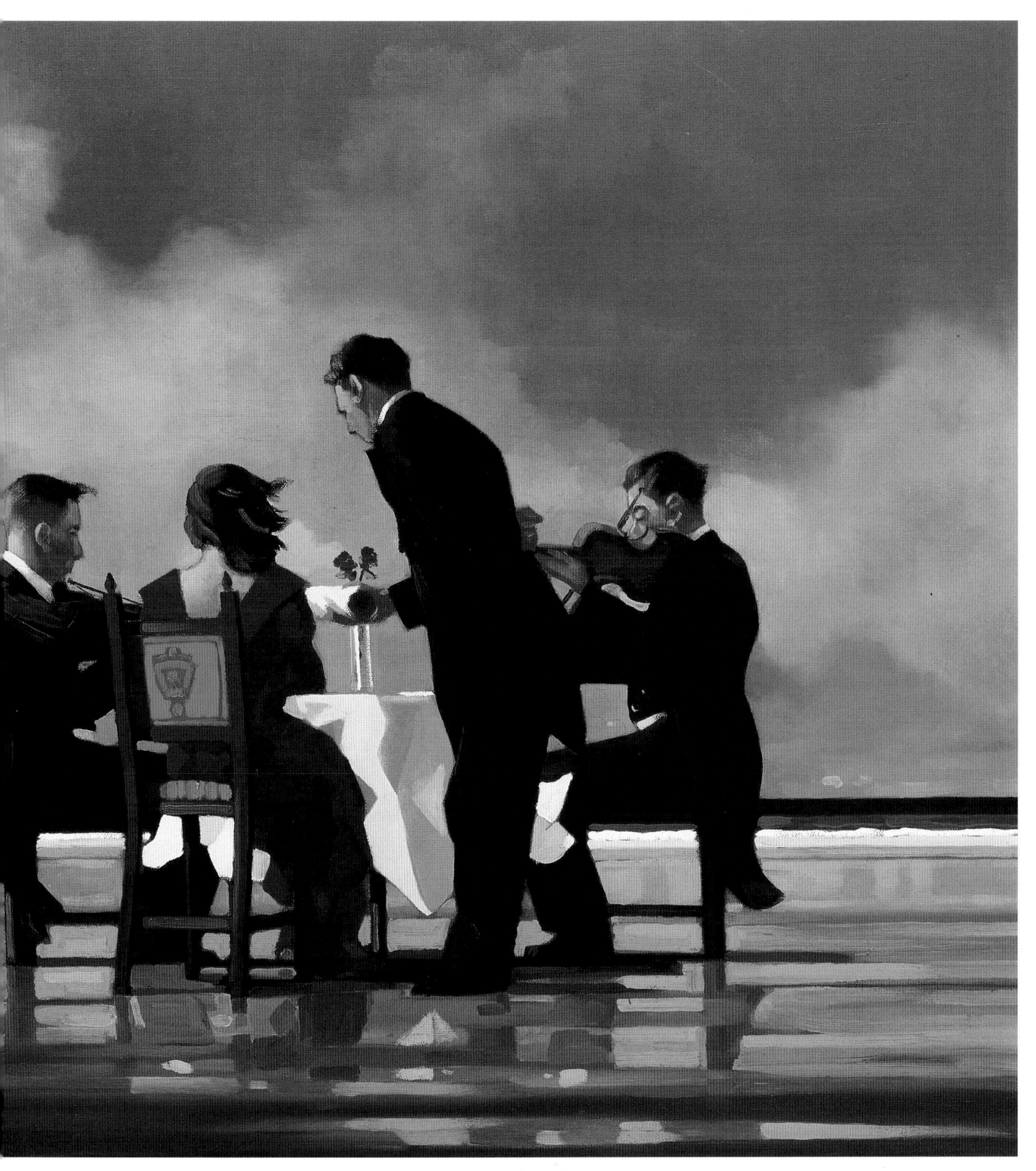

Elegy for the Dead Admiral

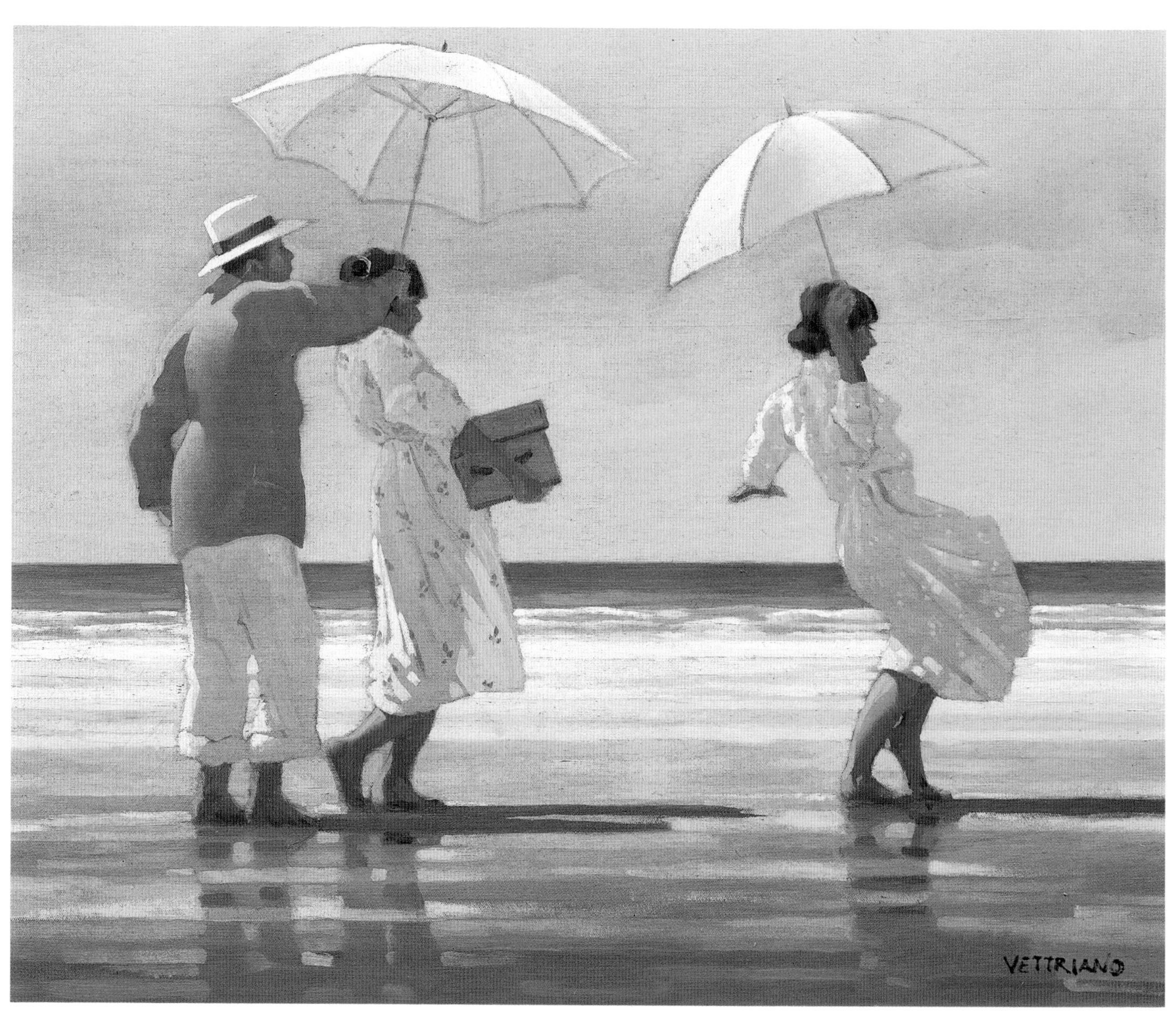

The Picnic Party

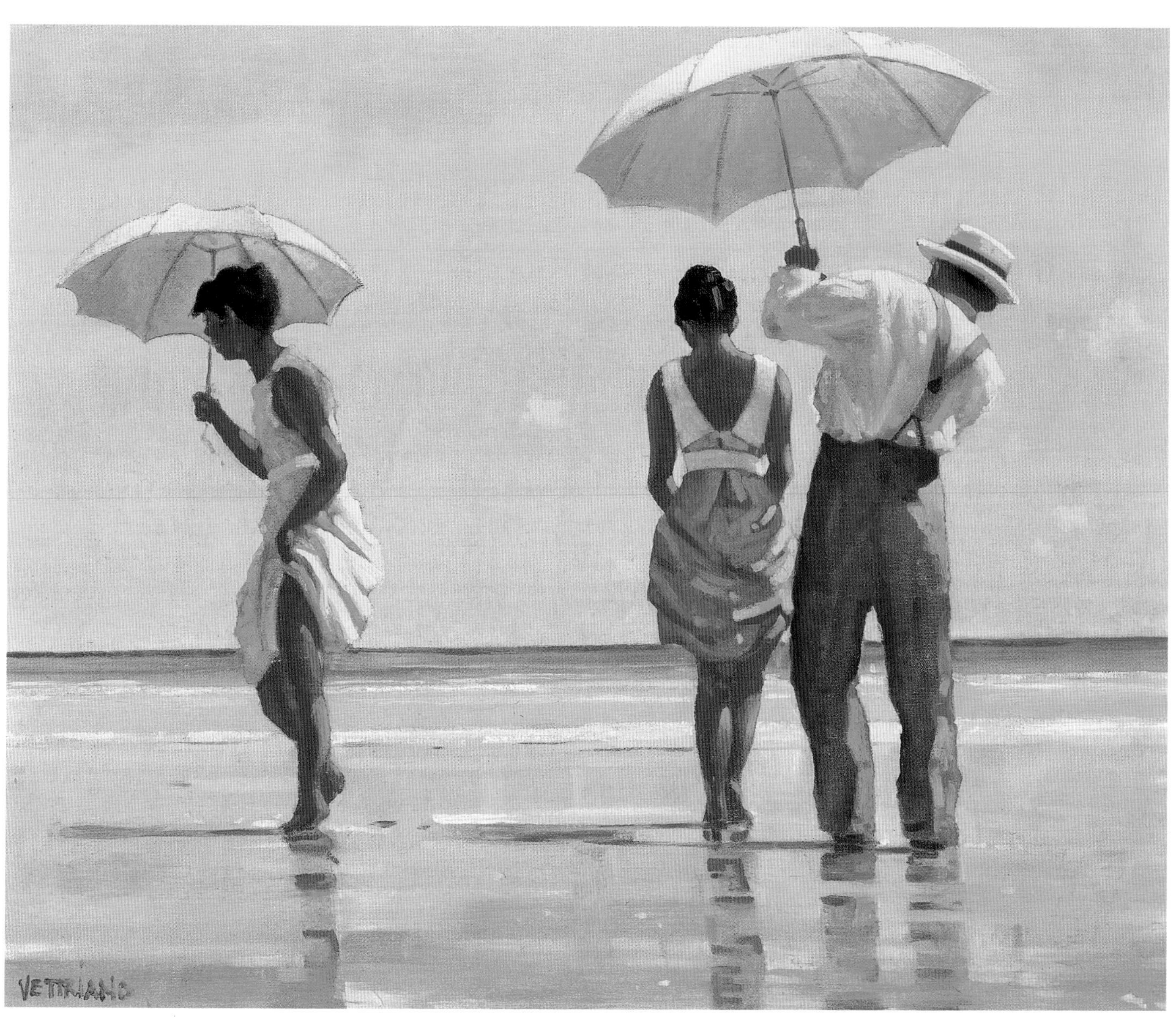

Mad Dogs...

The Singing Butler

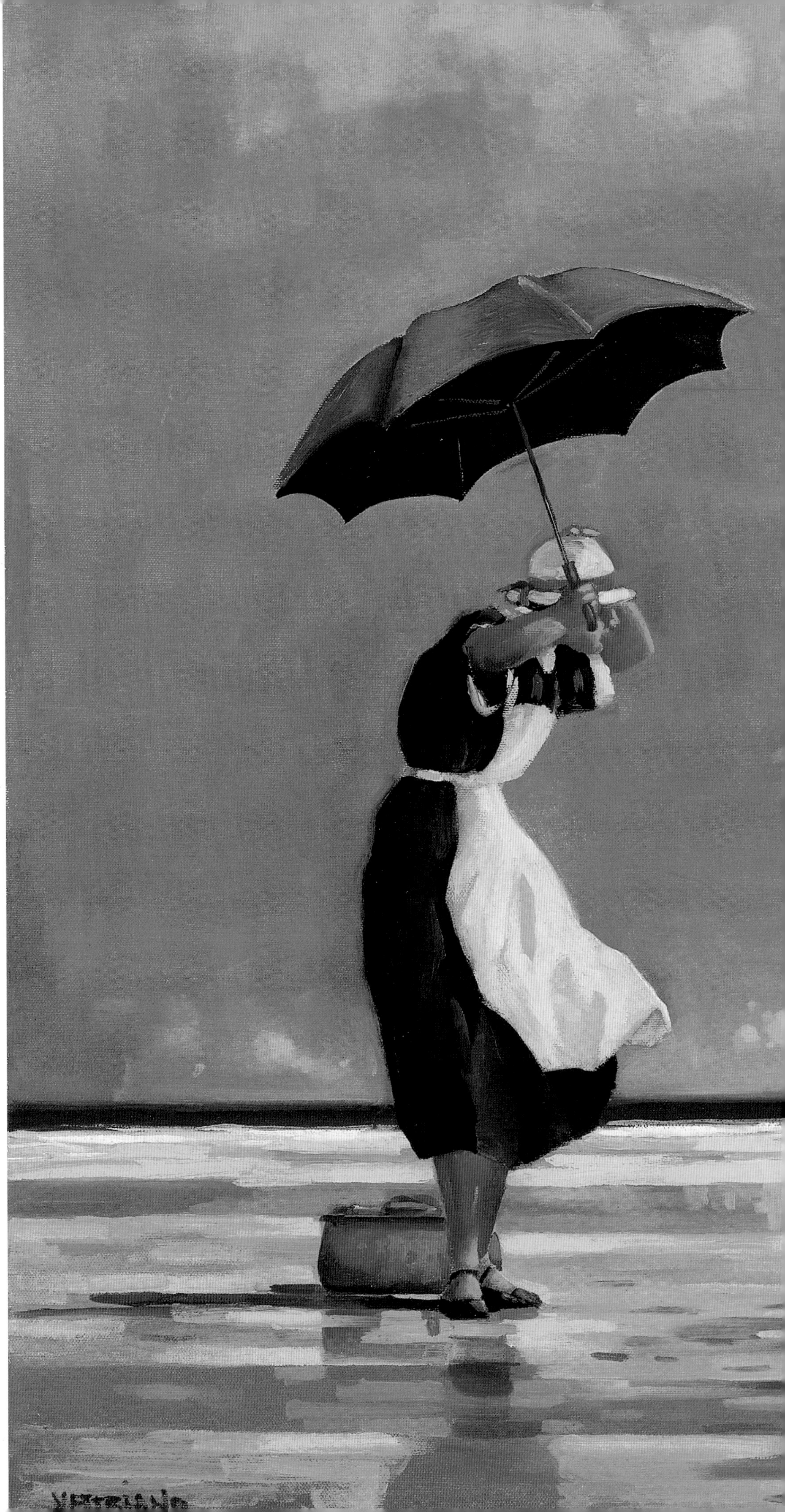

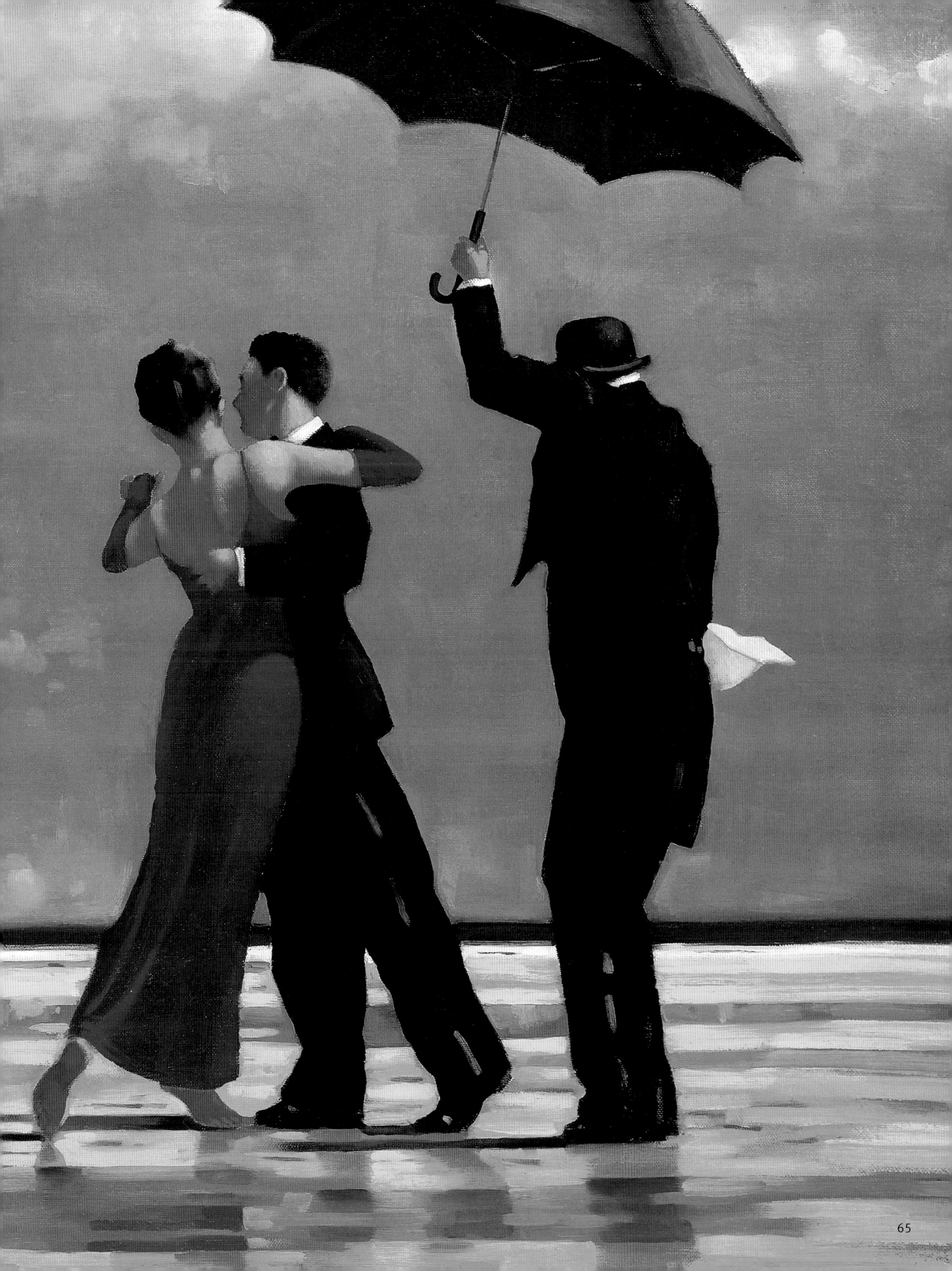

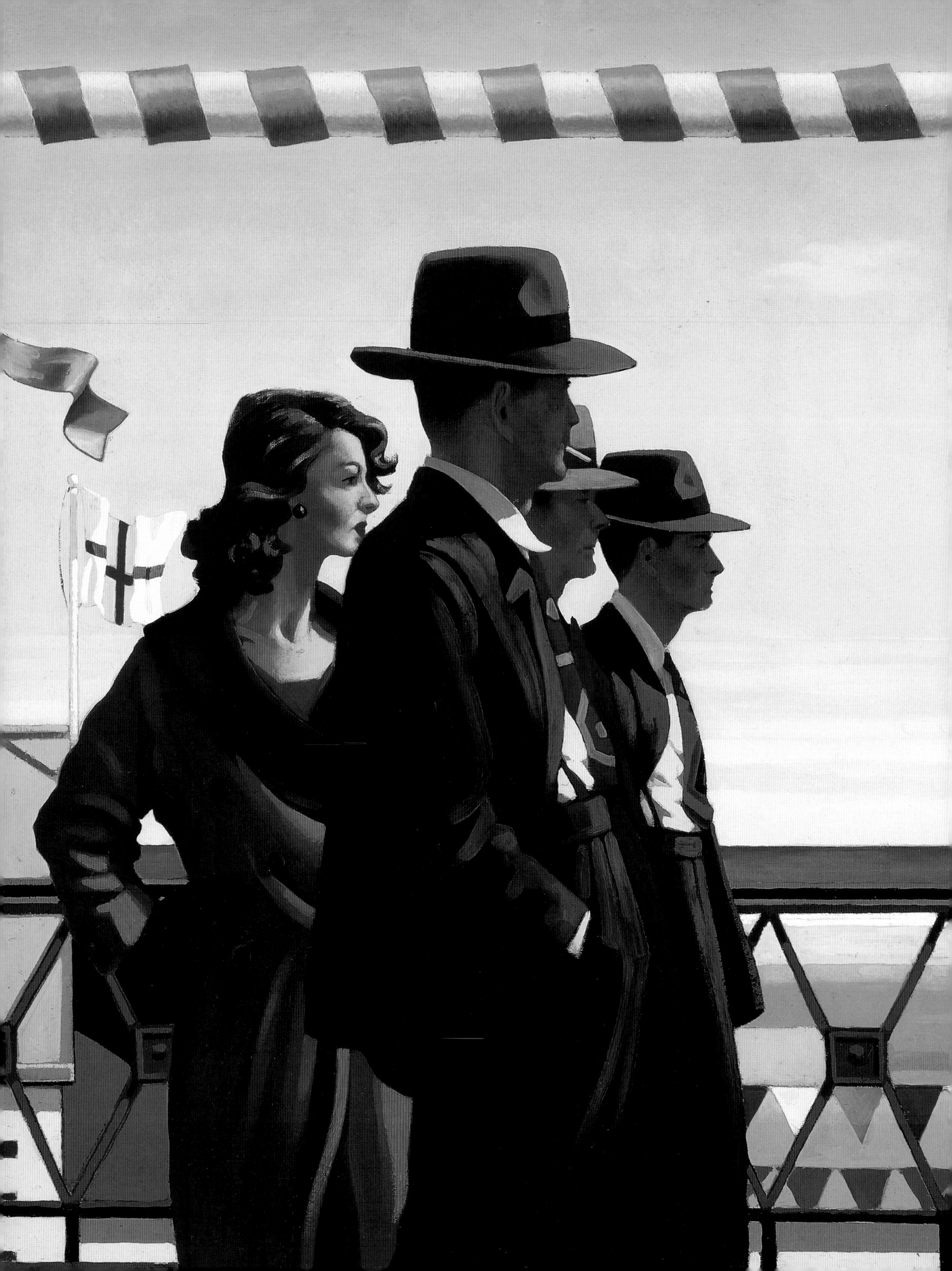

The Defenders of Virtue

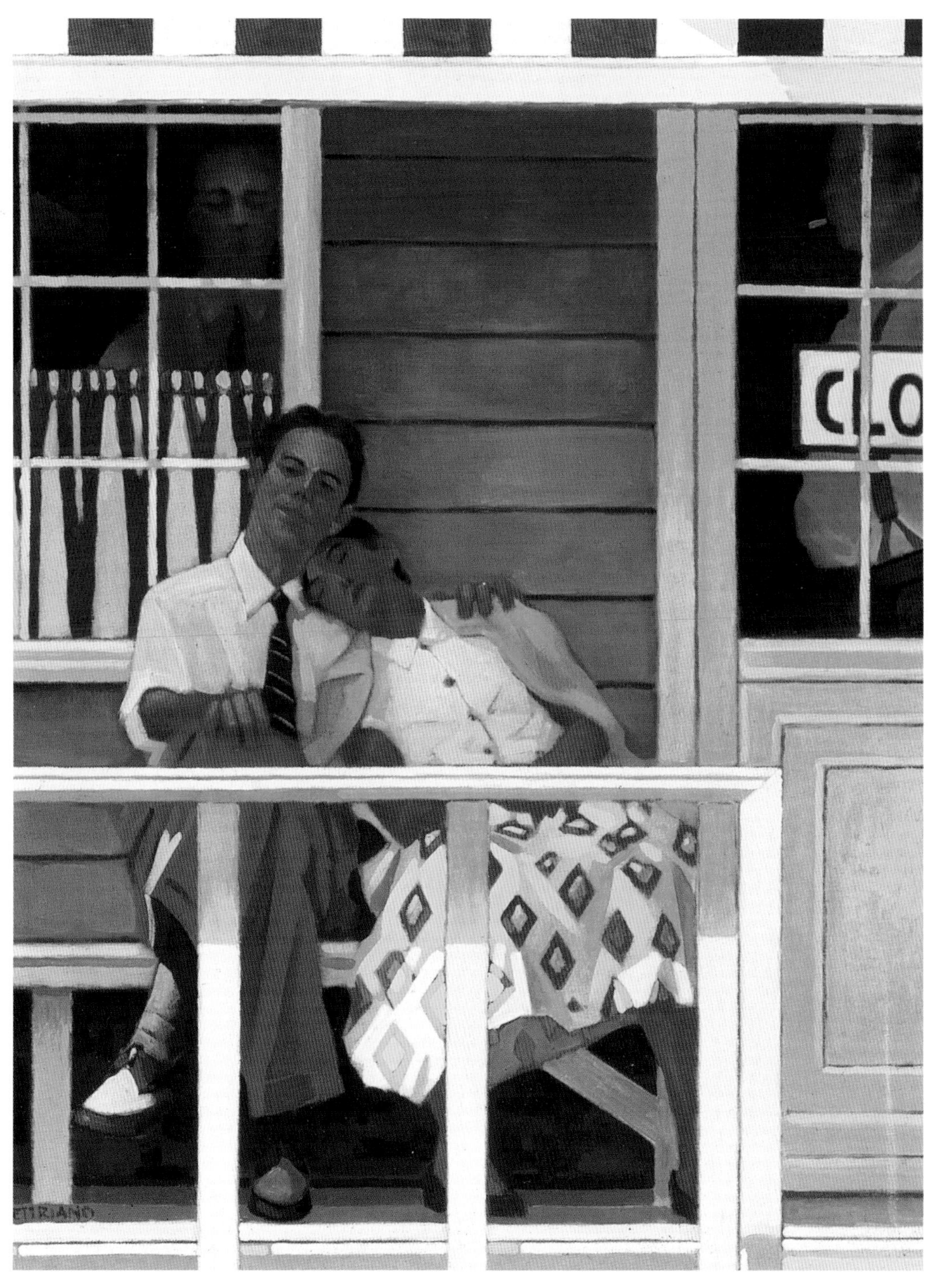

The Innocents

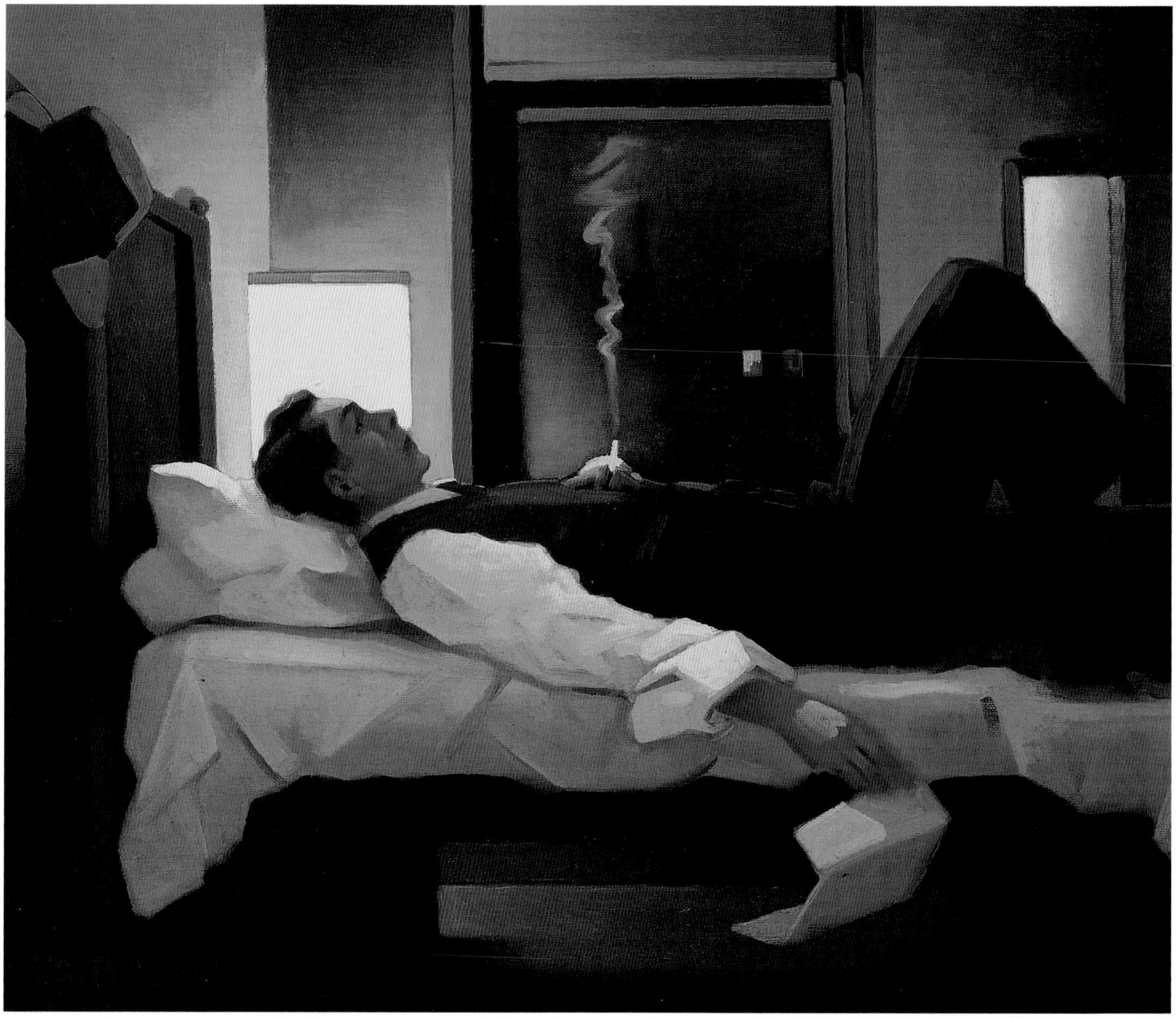

Heartbreak Hotel II

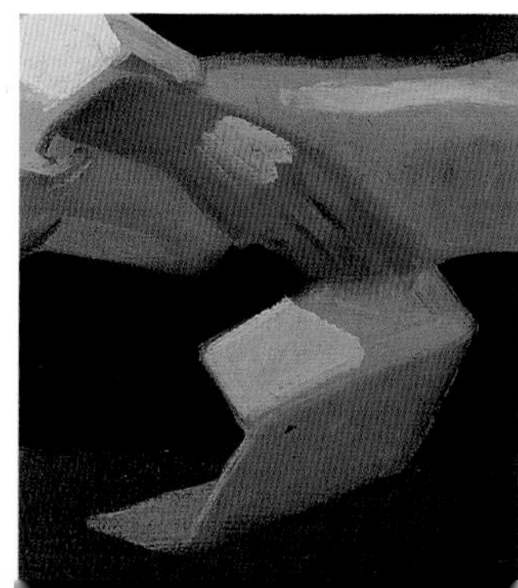

Model in Black

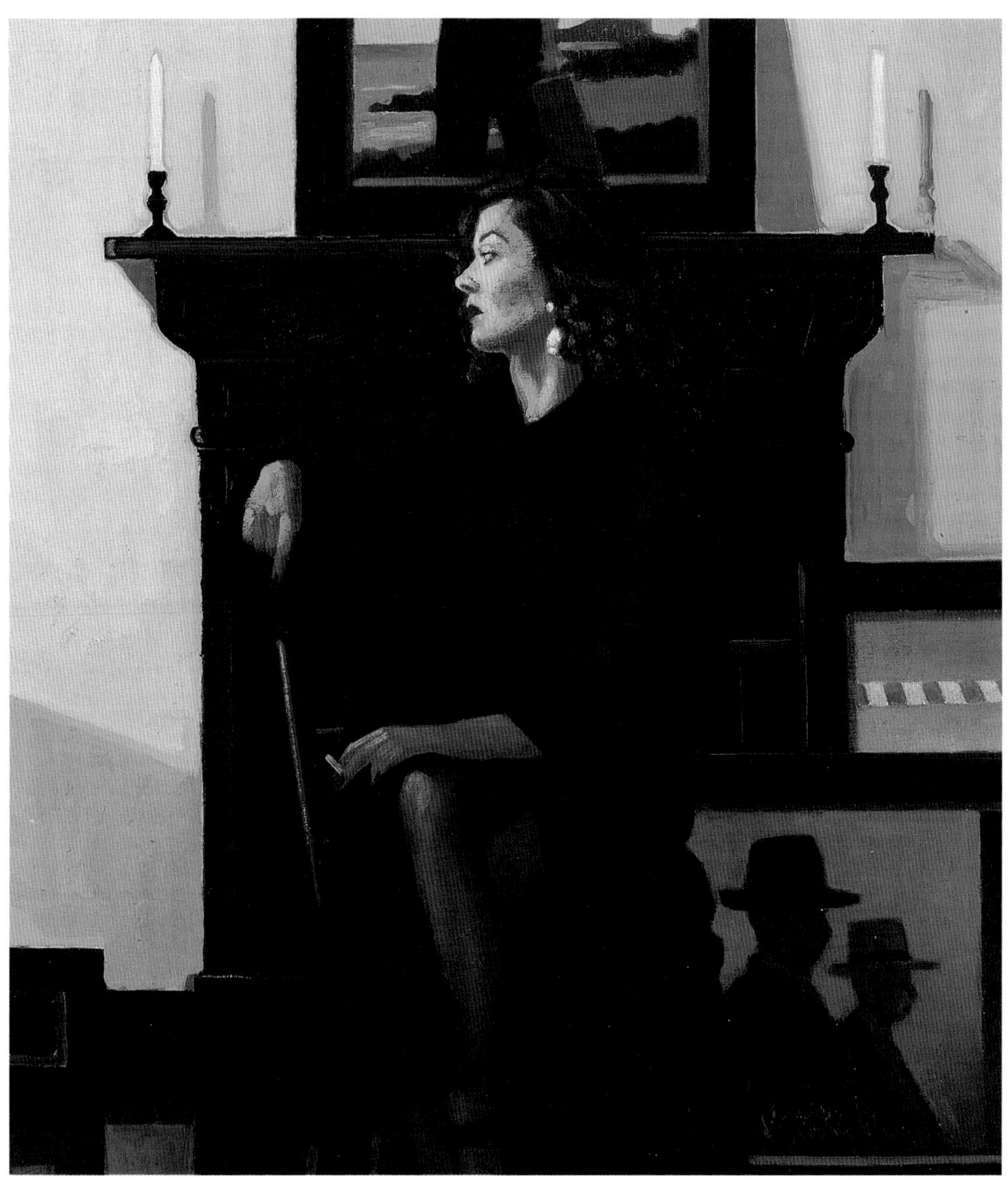

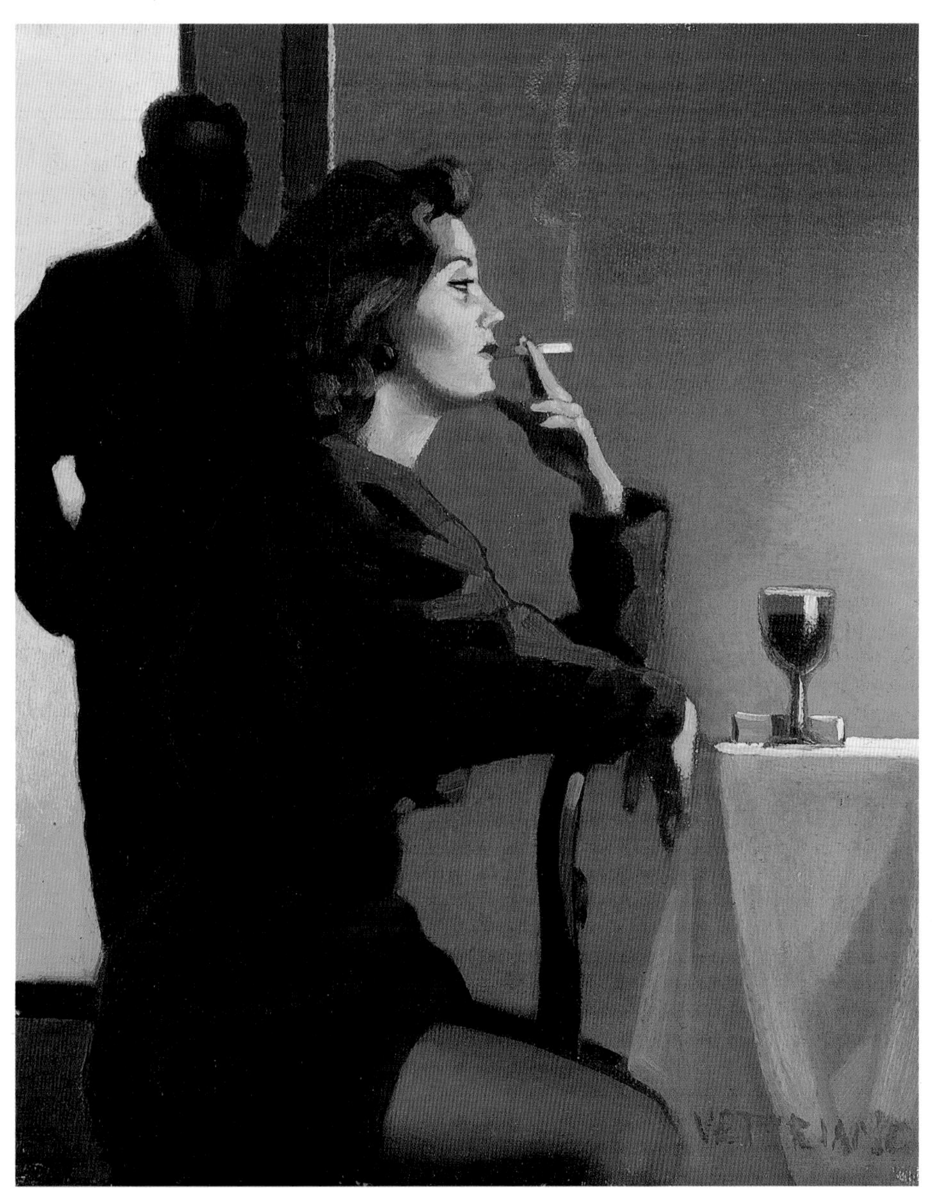

Someone to Watch over Me

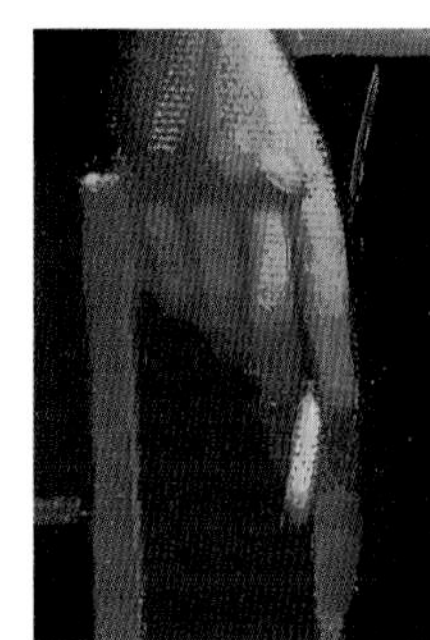

The Main Attraction

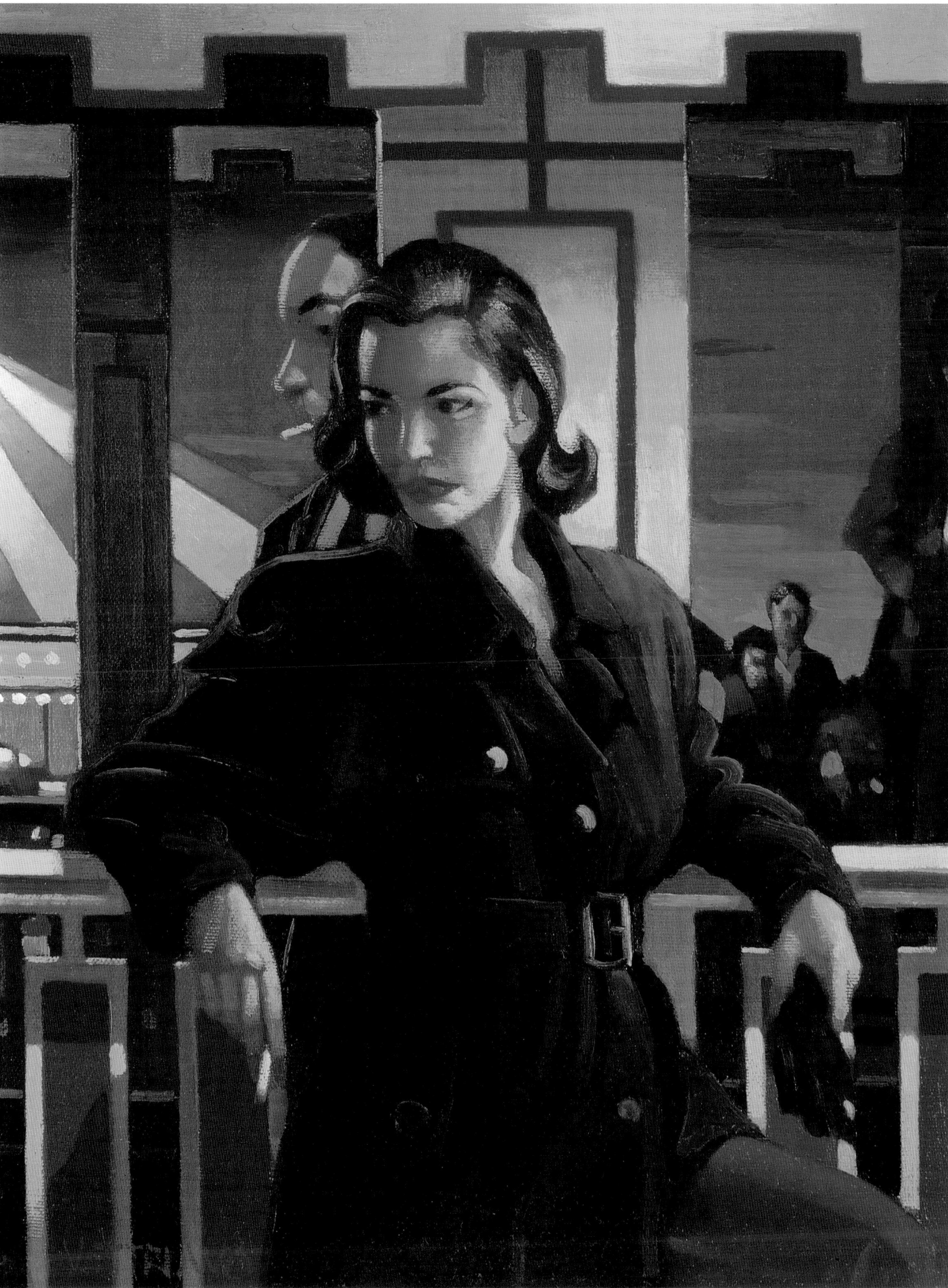

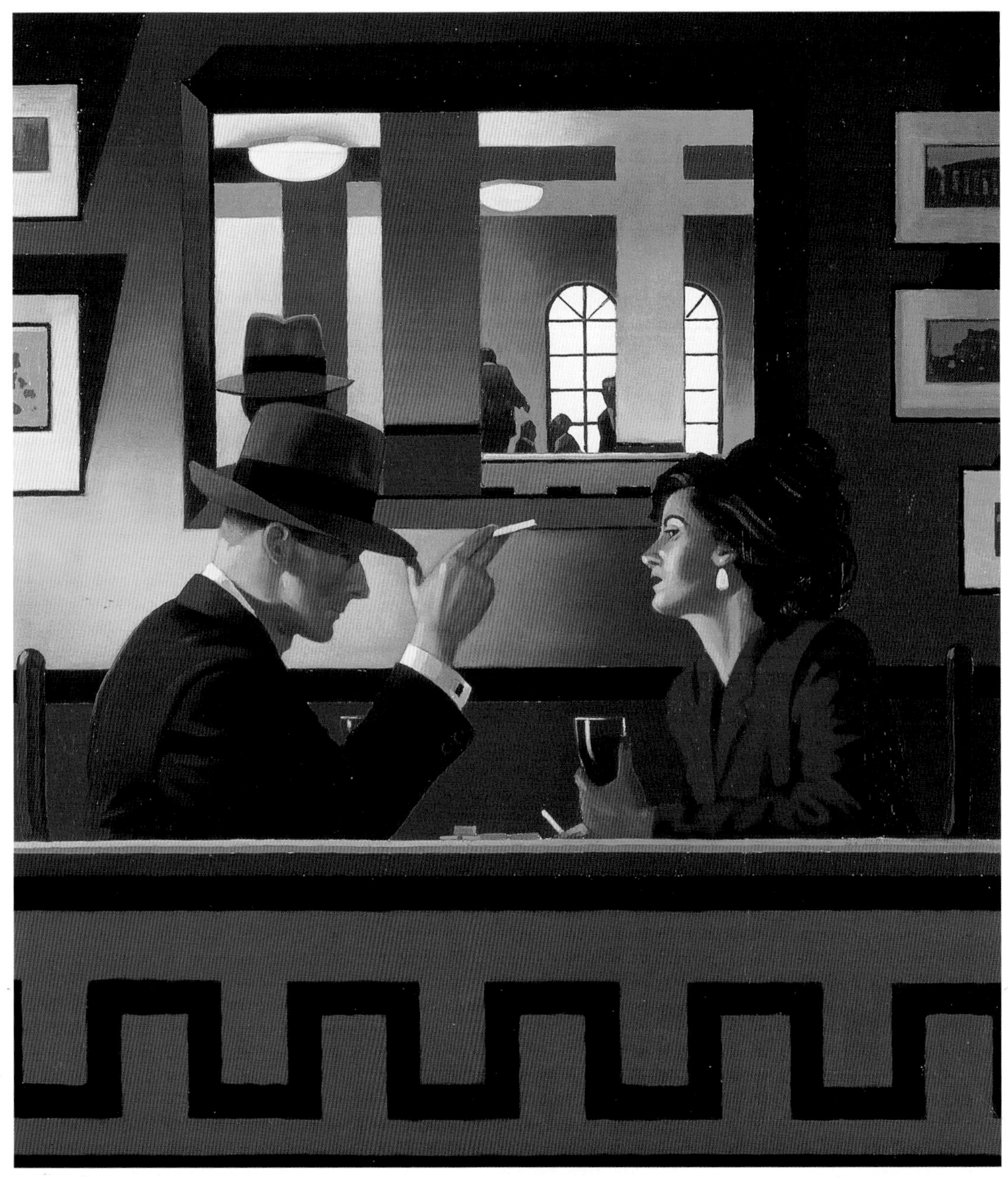

The Man in the Mirror

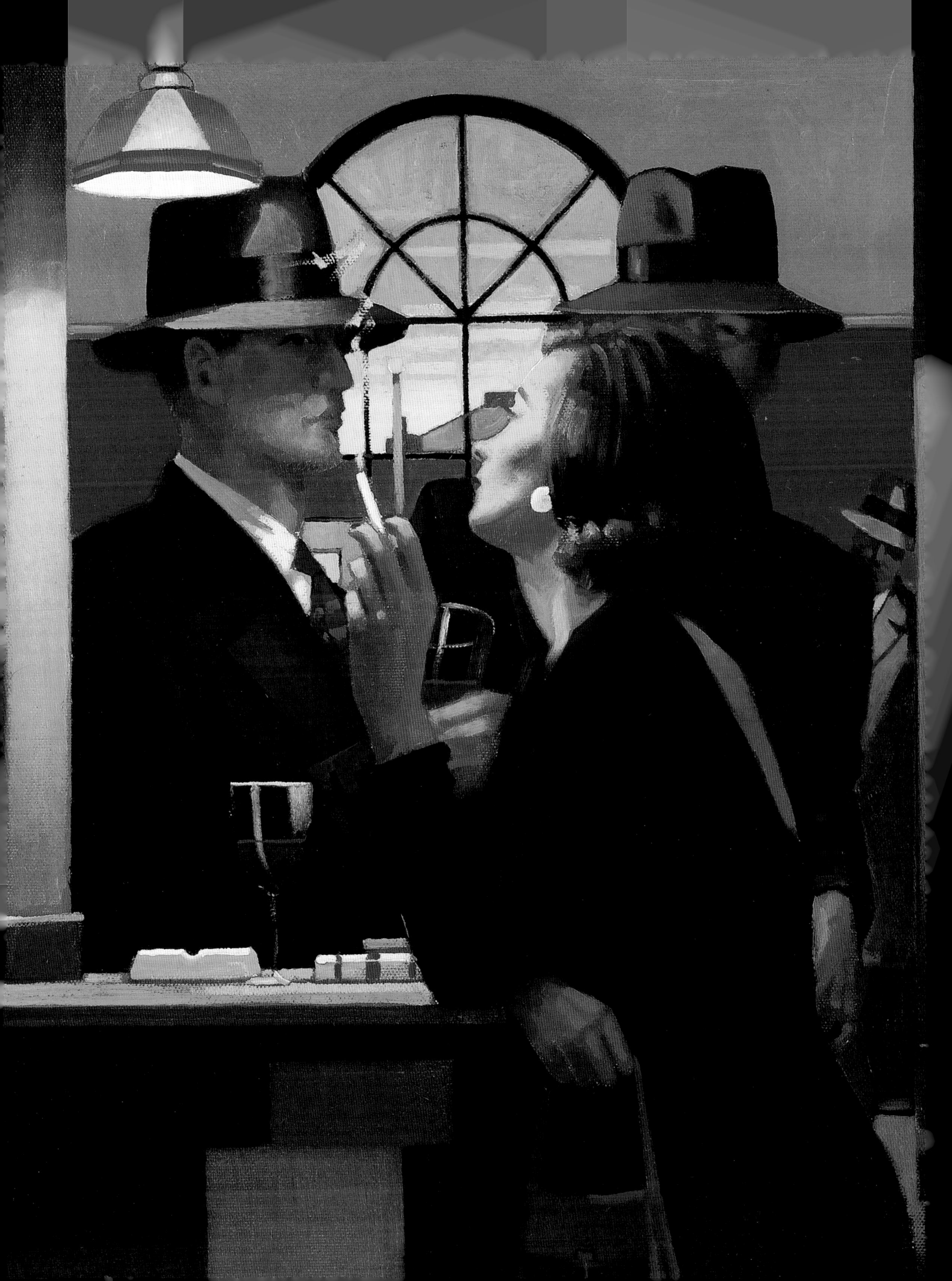

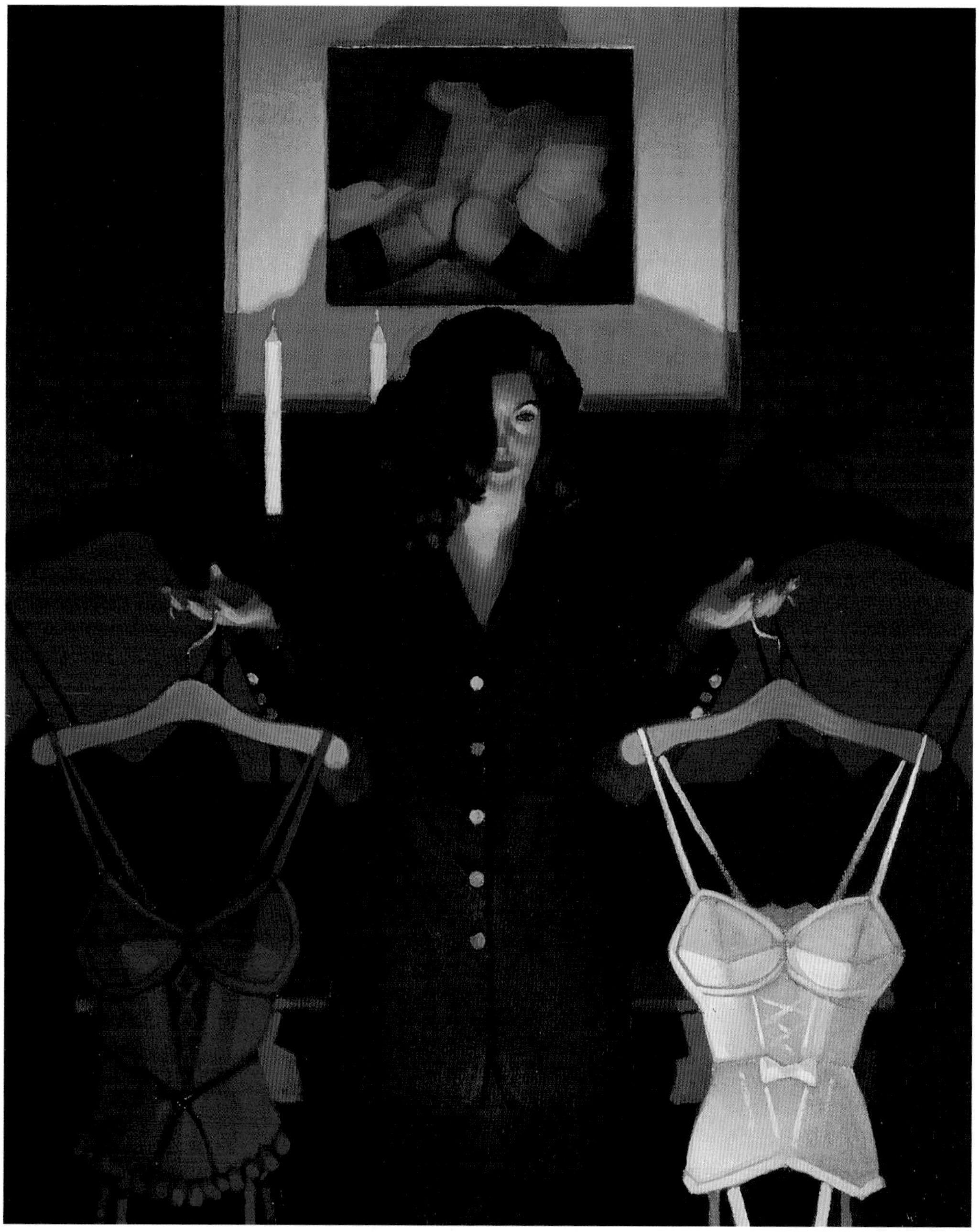

Heaven or Hell

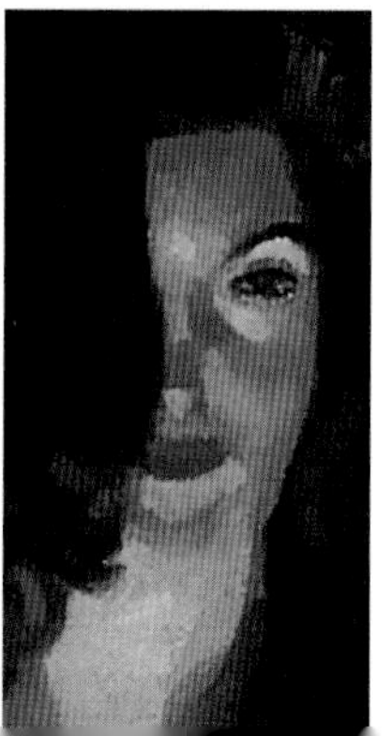

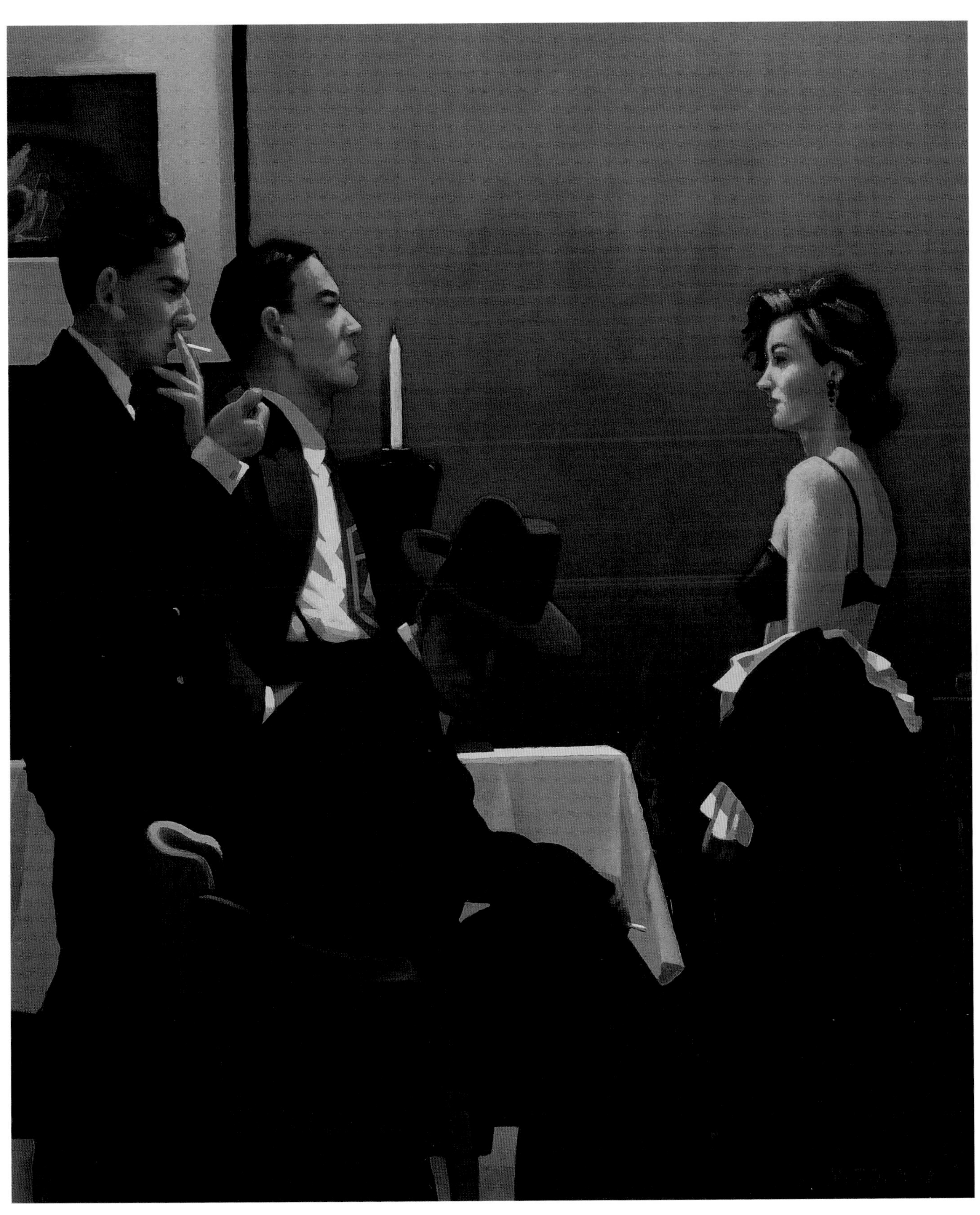

We Can't Tell Right from Wrong

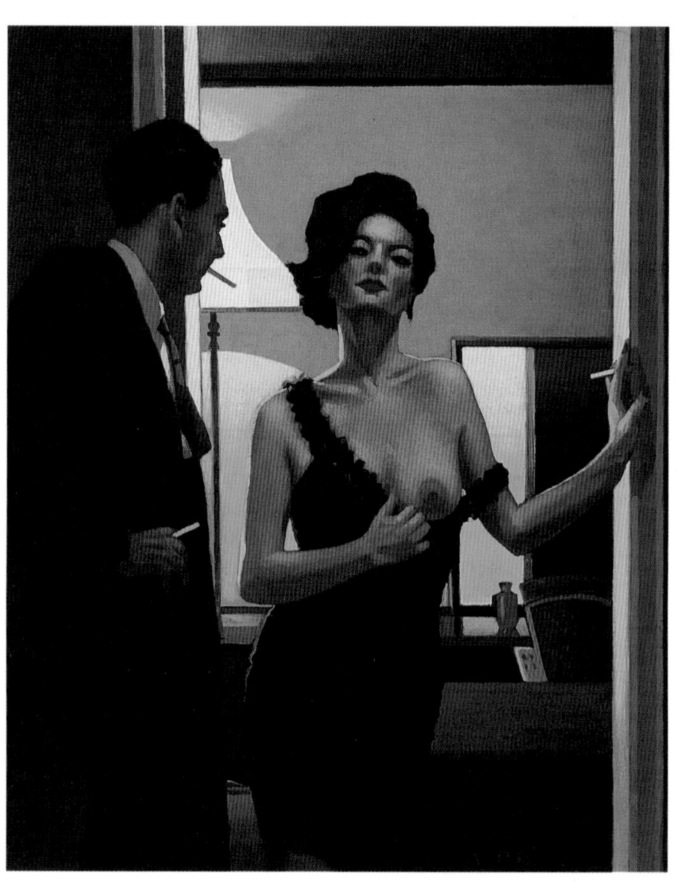

The Opening Gambit

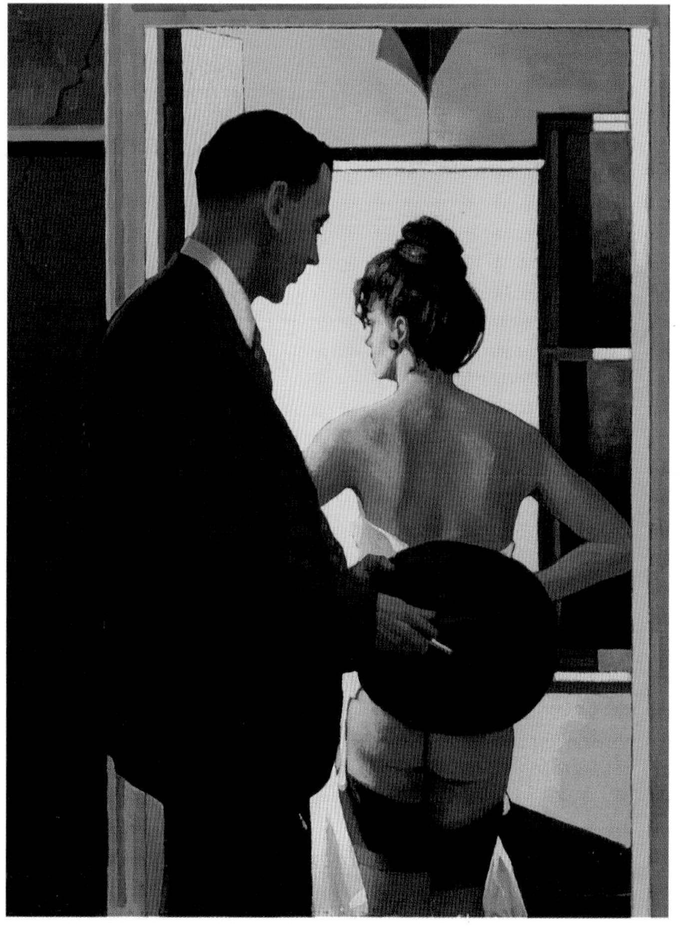

The Apprentice

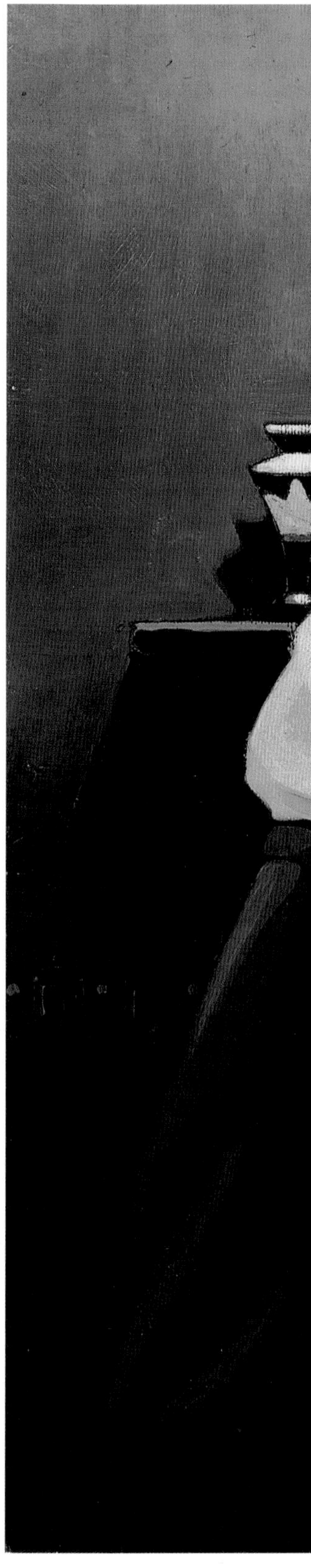

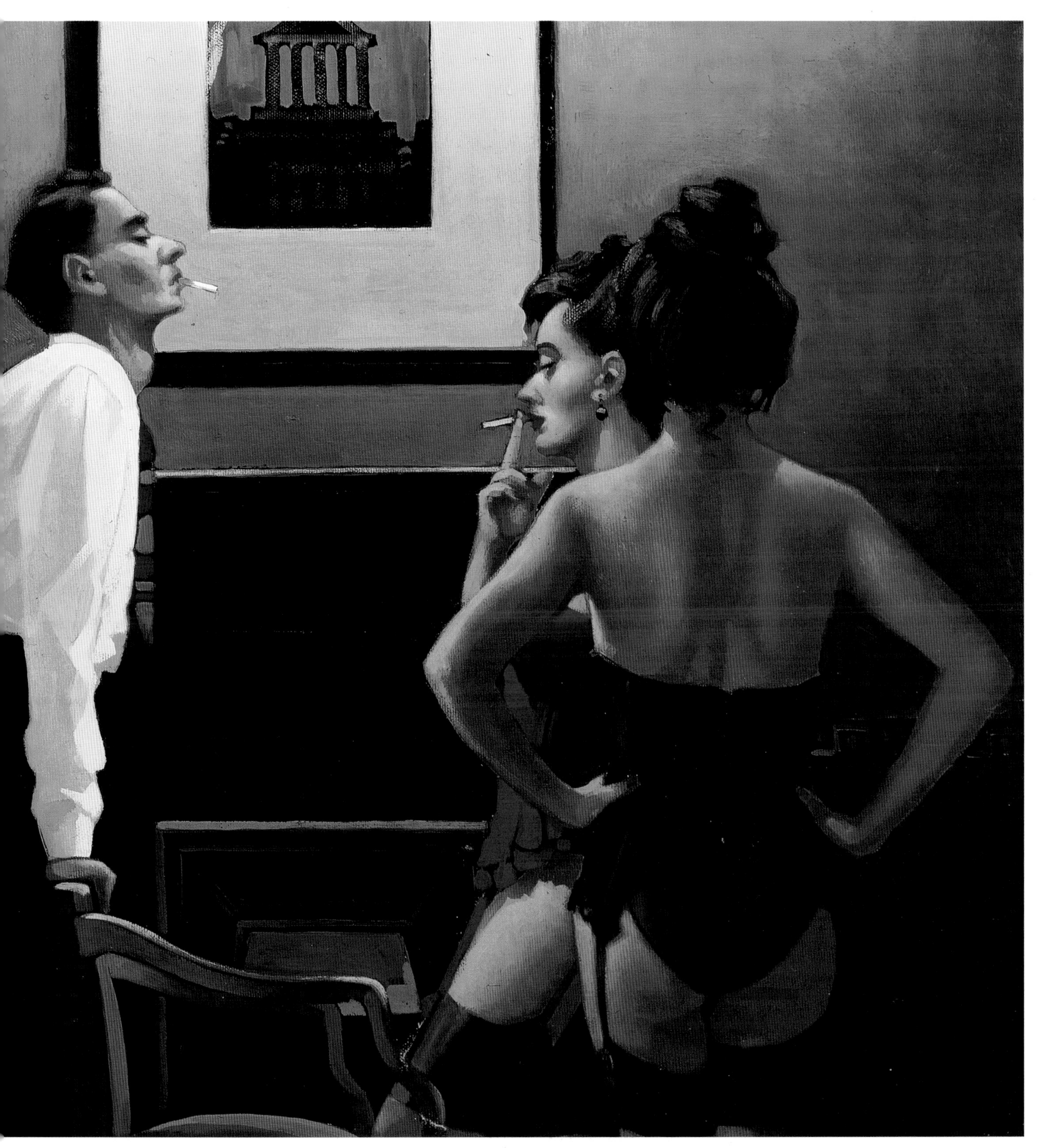

The Master of Ceremonies

The Administration of Justice

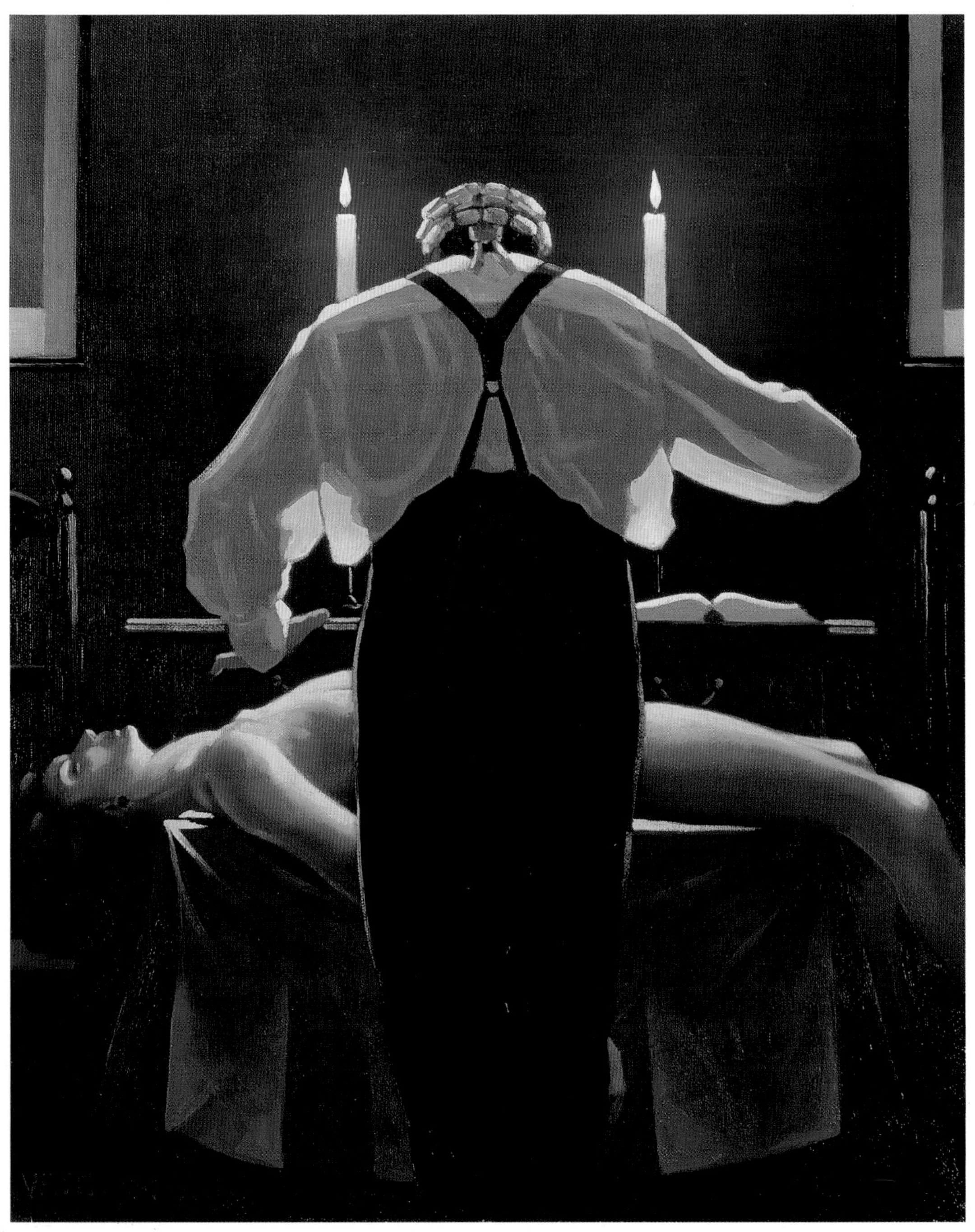

Setting New Standards

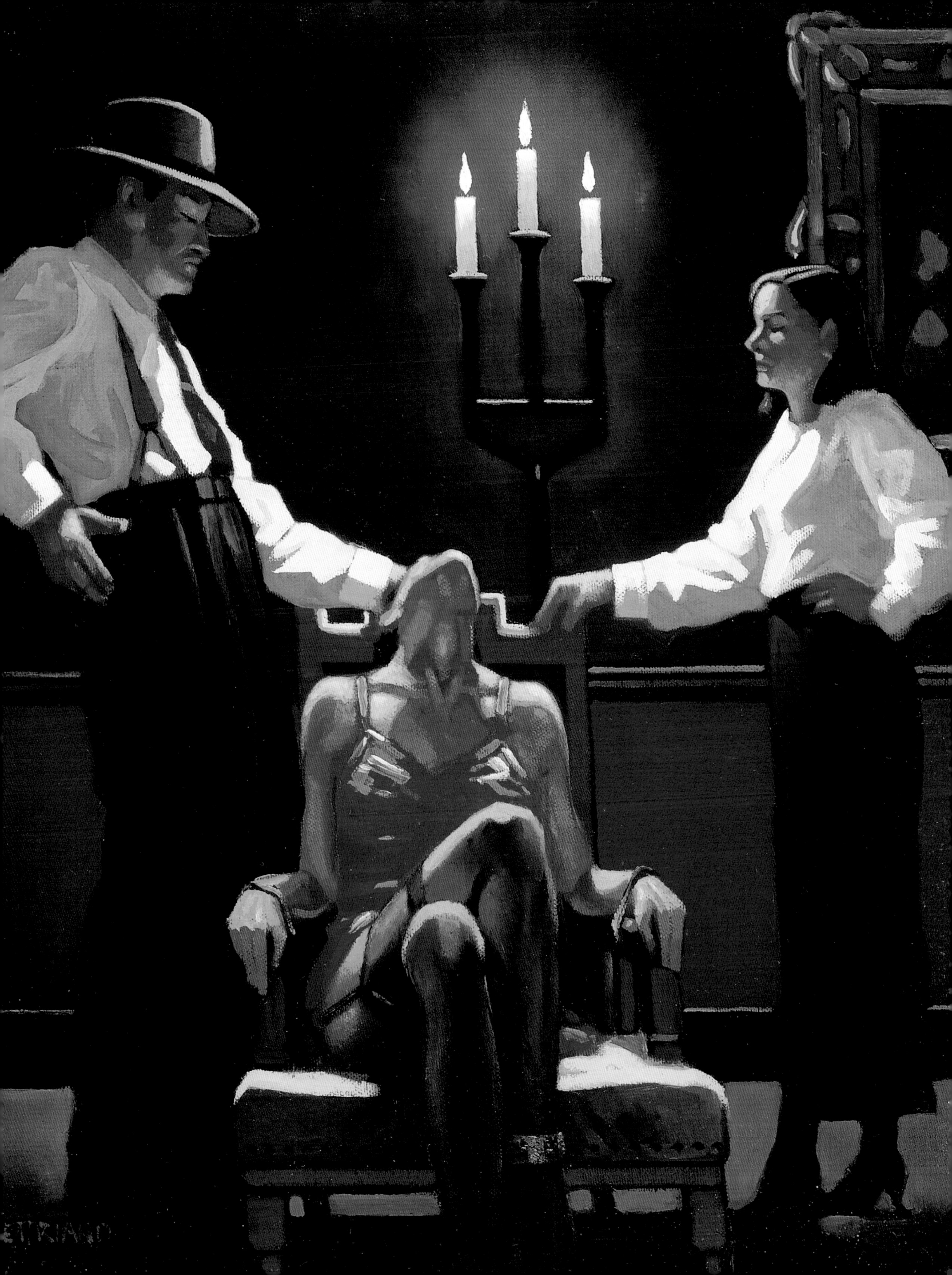

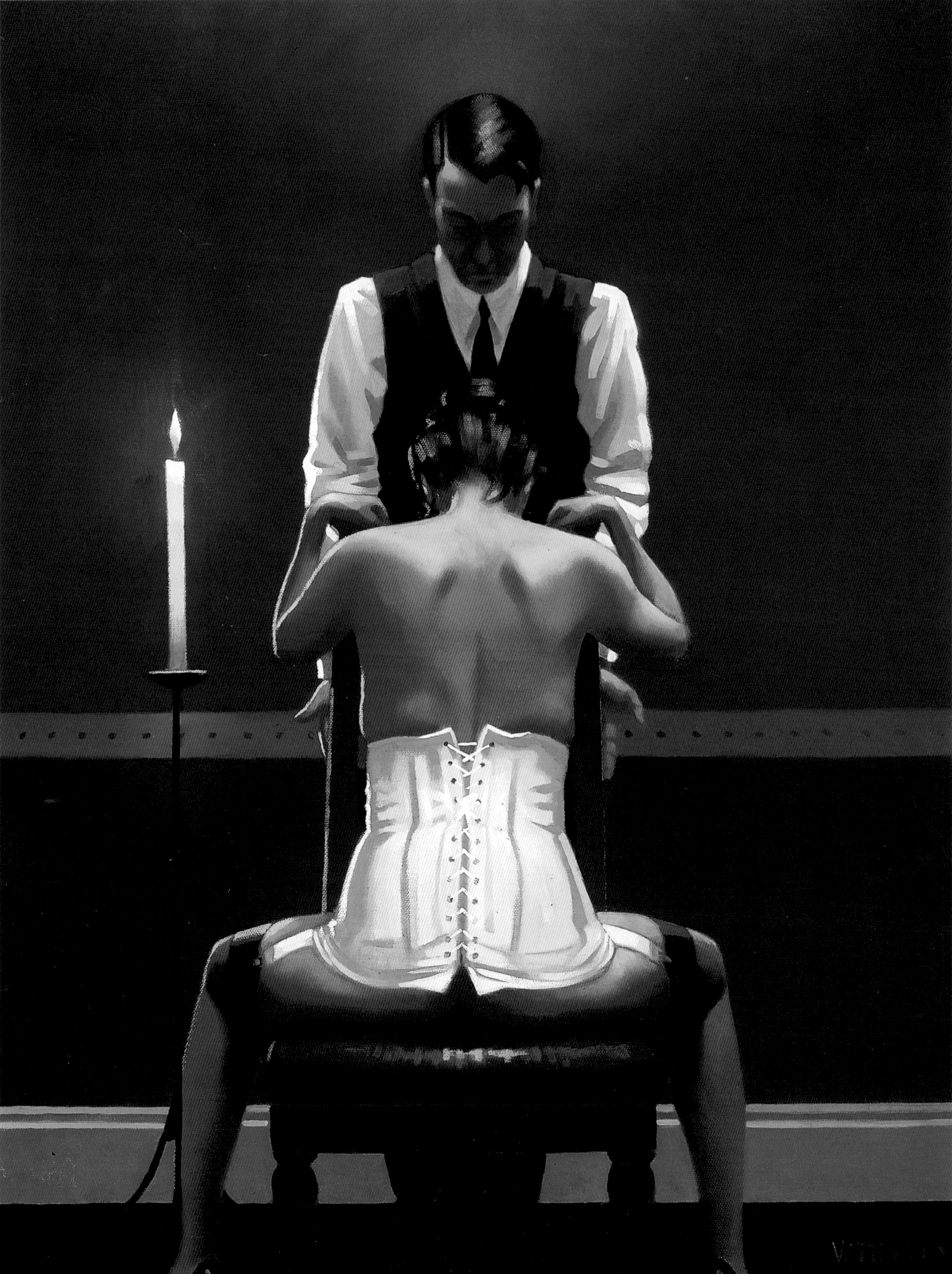

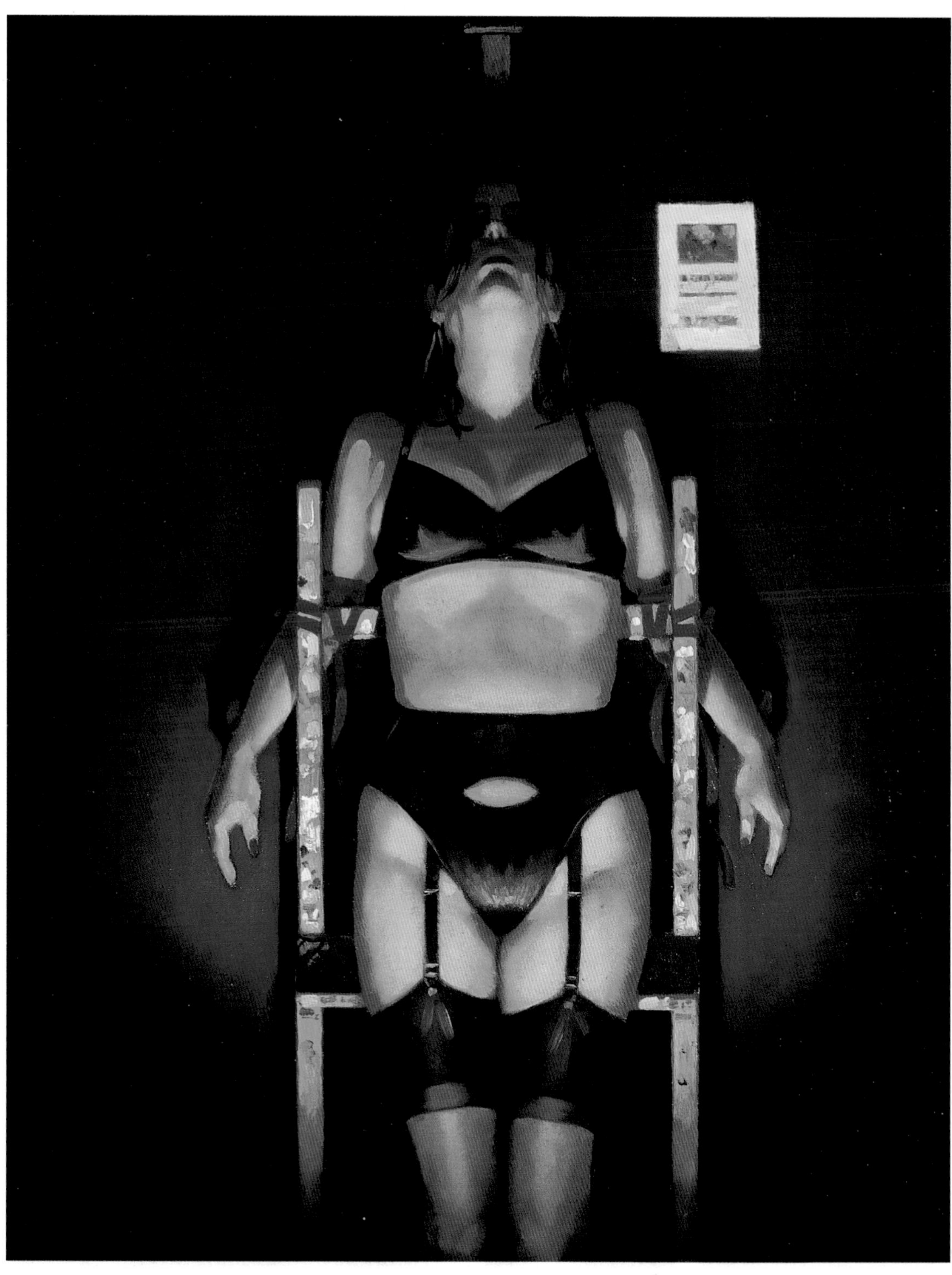

Scarlet Ribbons, Lovely Ribbons

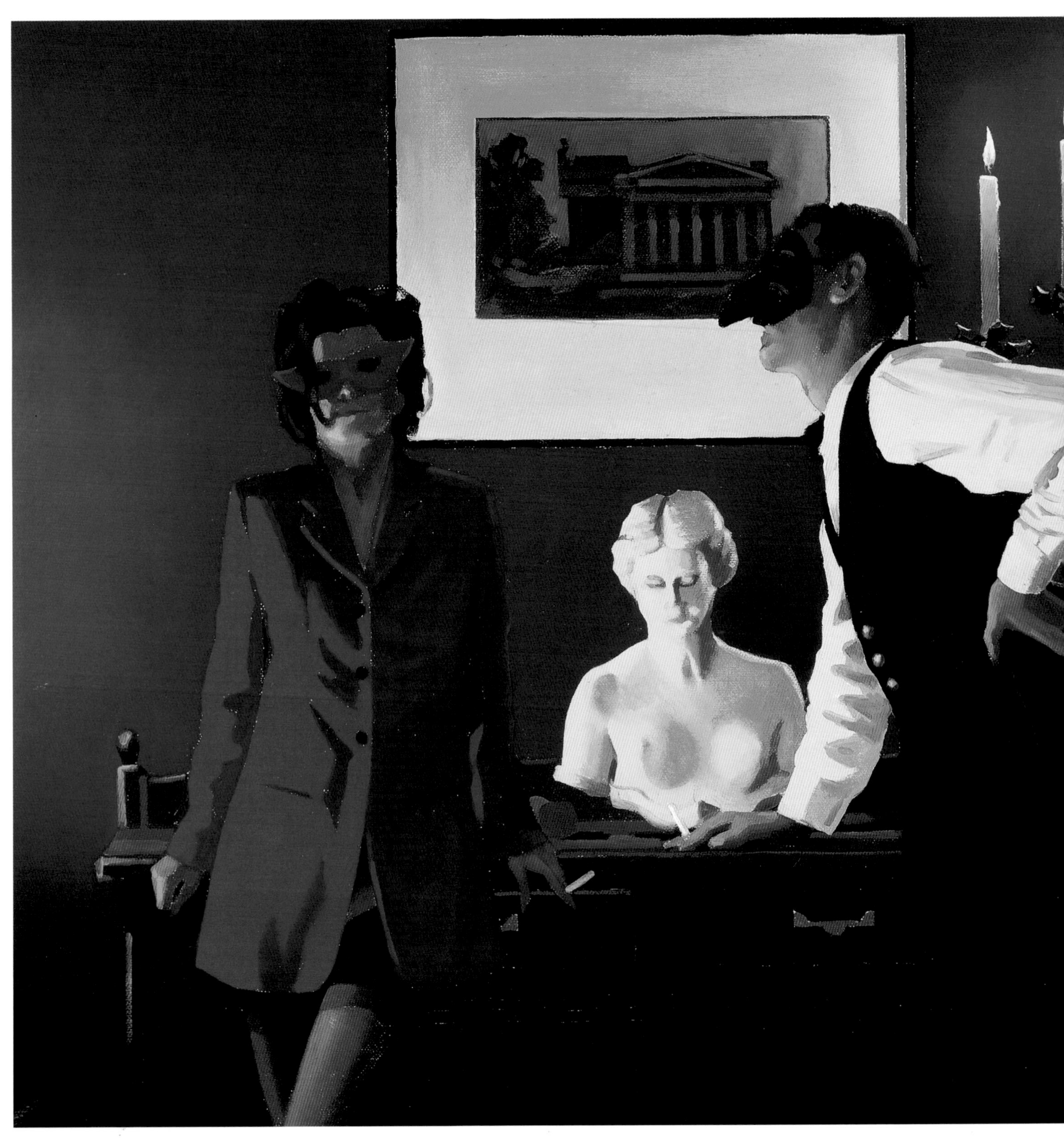

The Sparrow and the Hawk

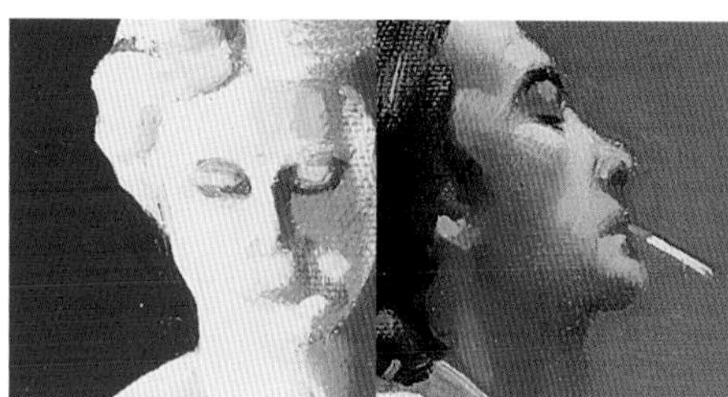

Cold Cold Hearts

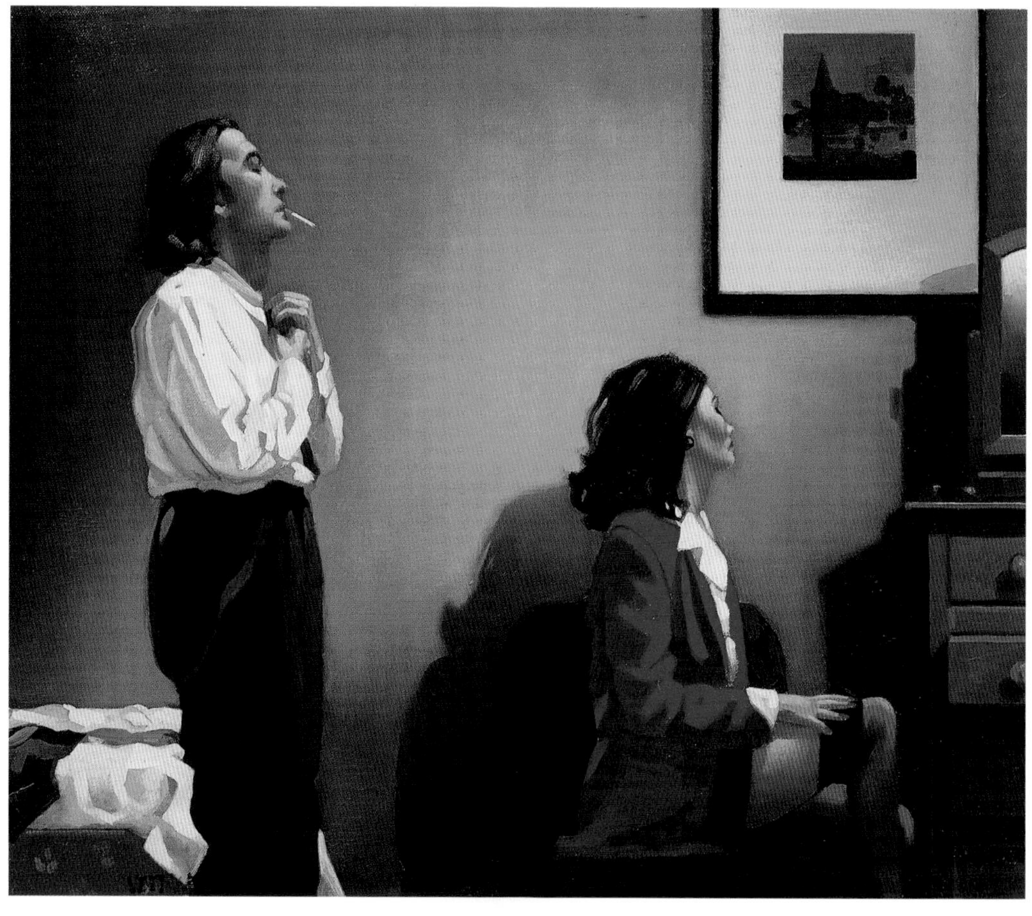

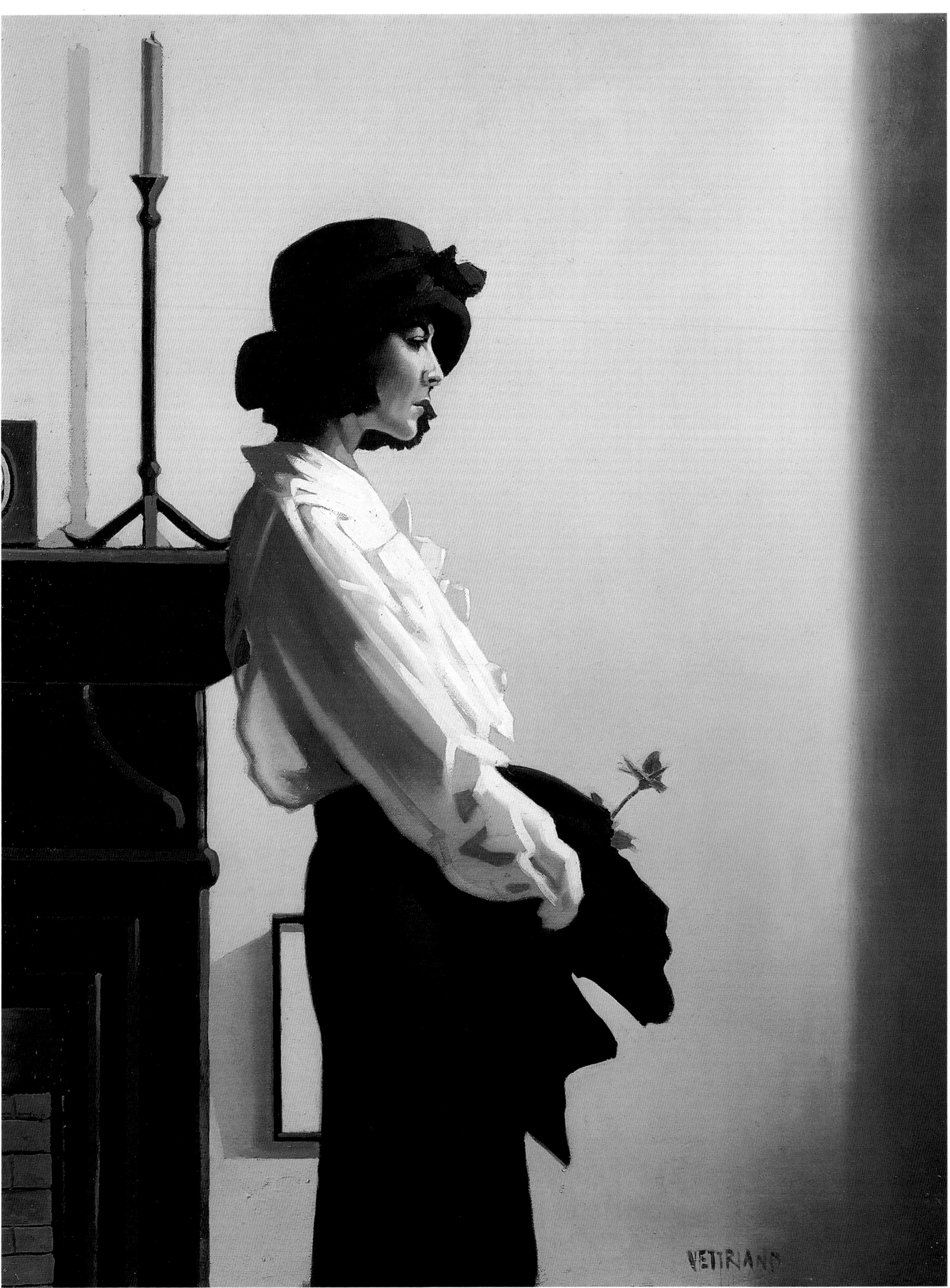
VETTRIANO

A Valentine Rose

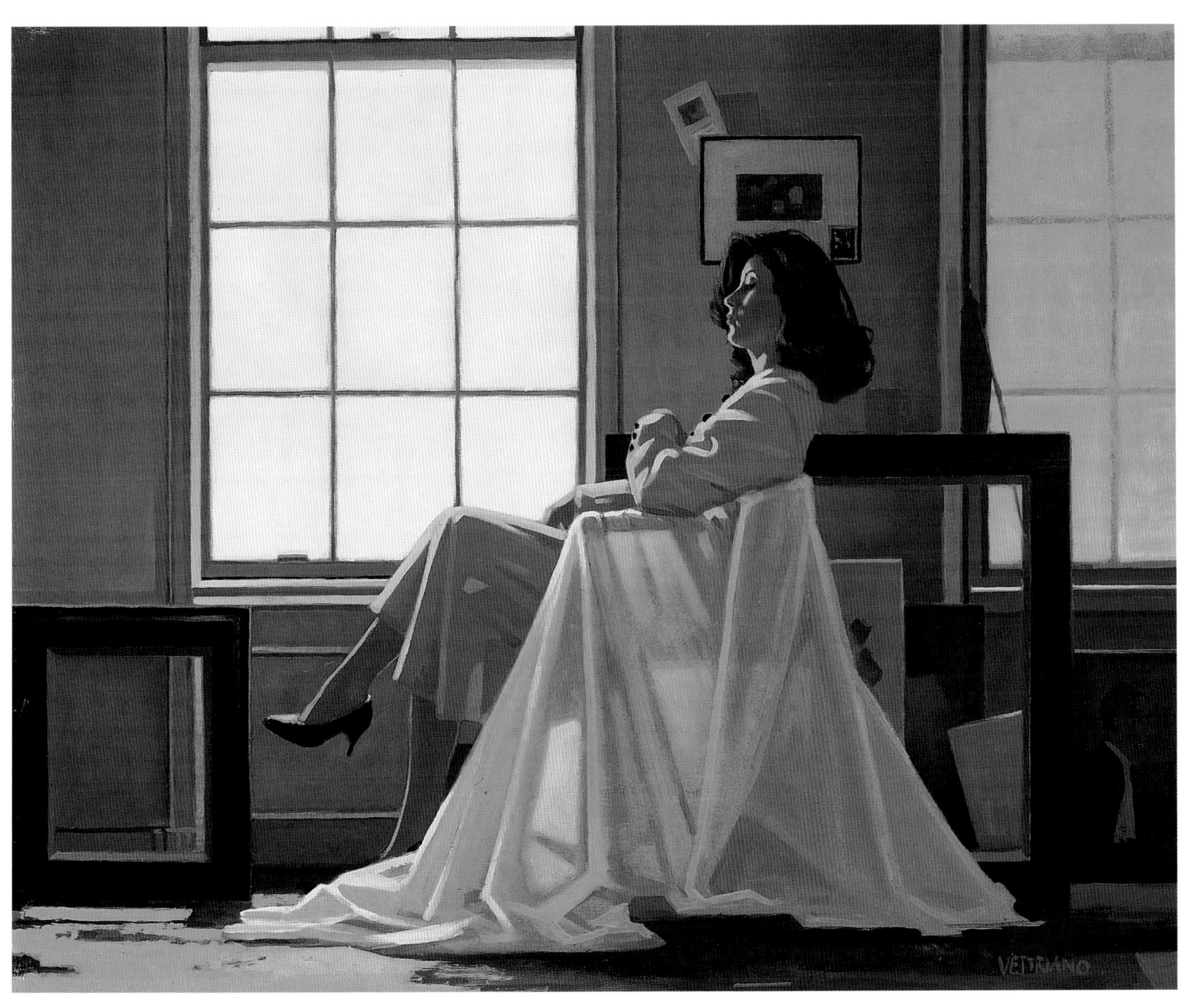

*W*inter Light and Lavender

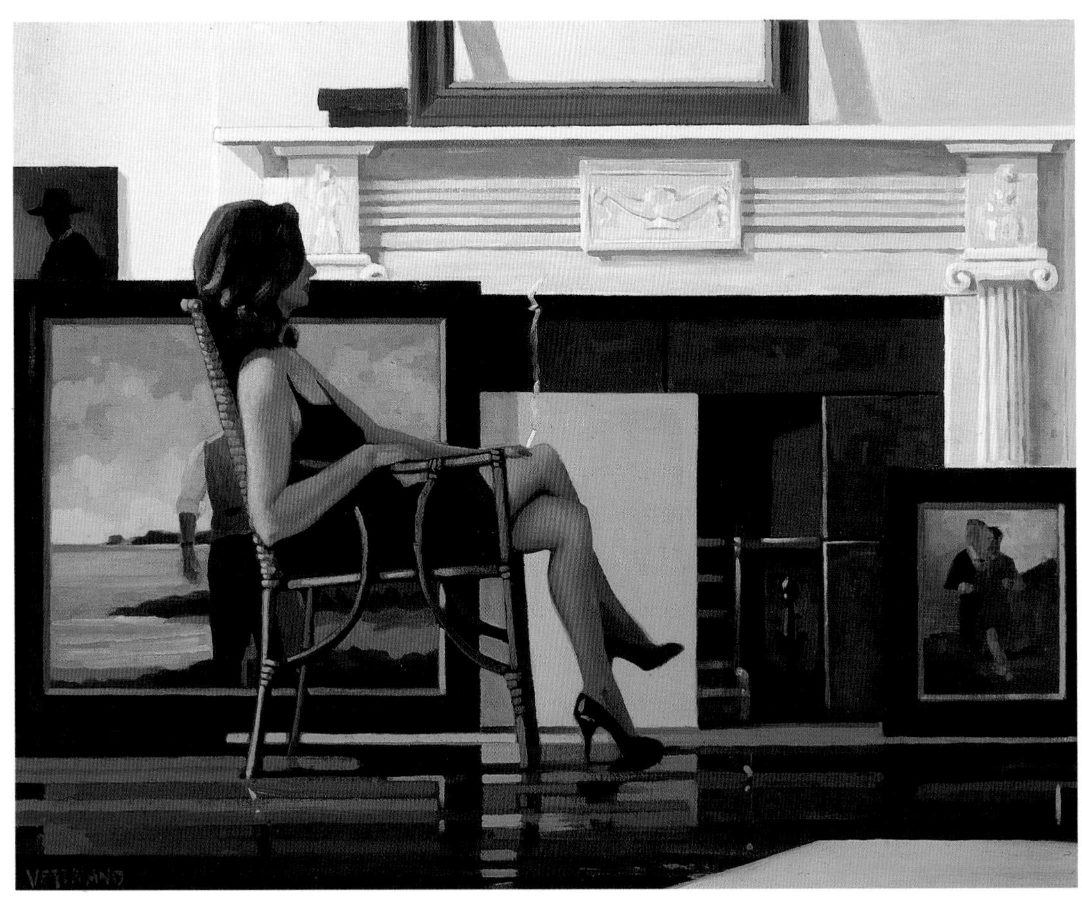

The Model and the Drifter

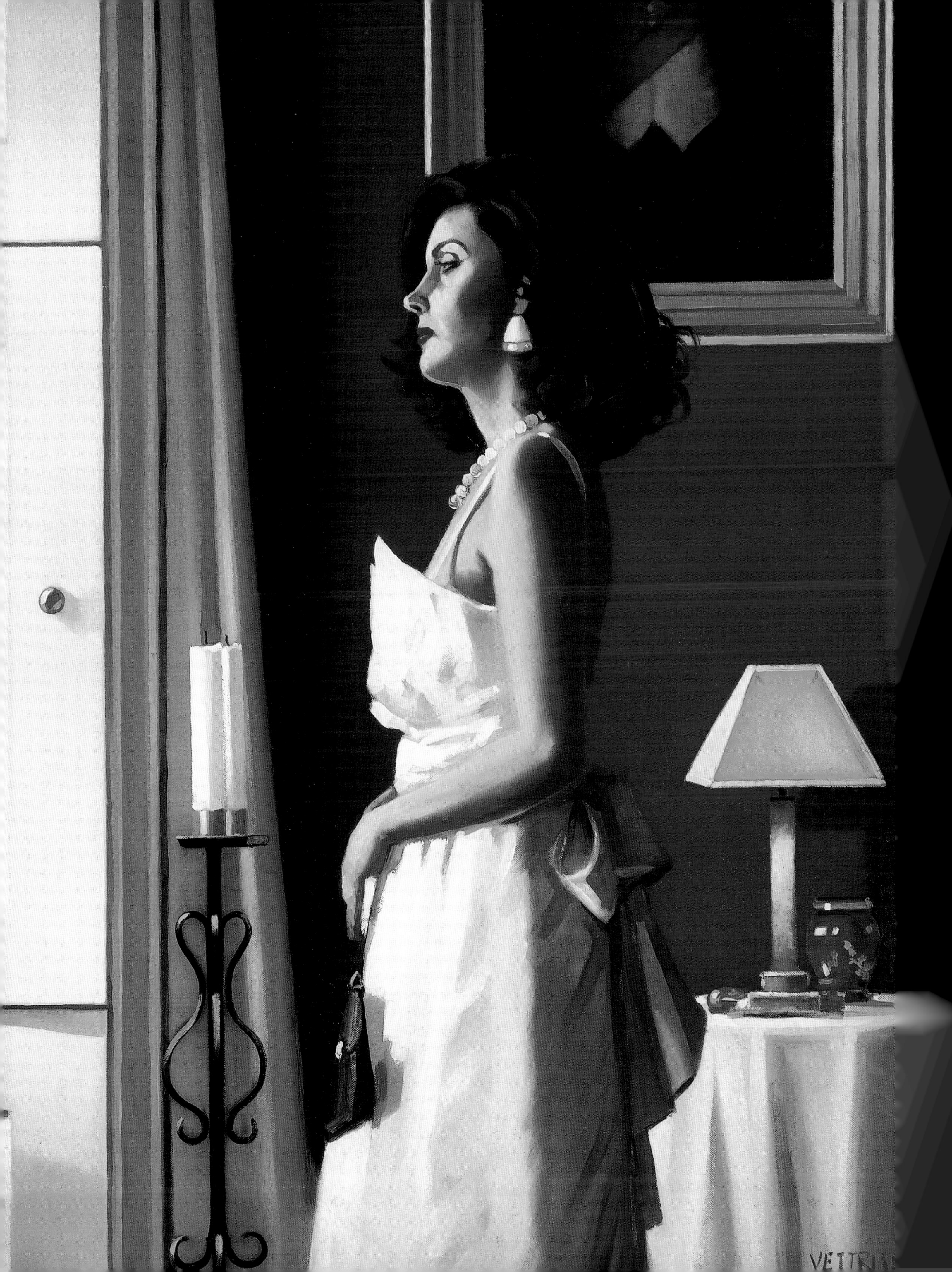

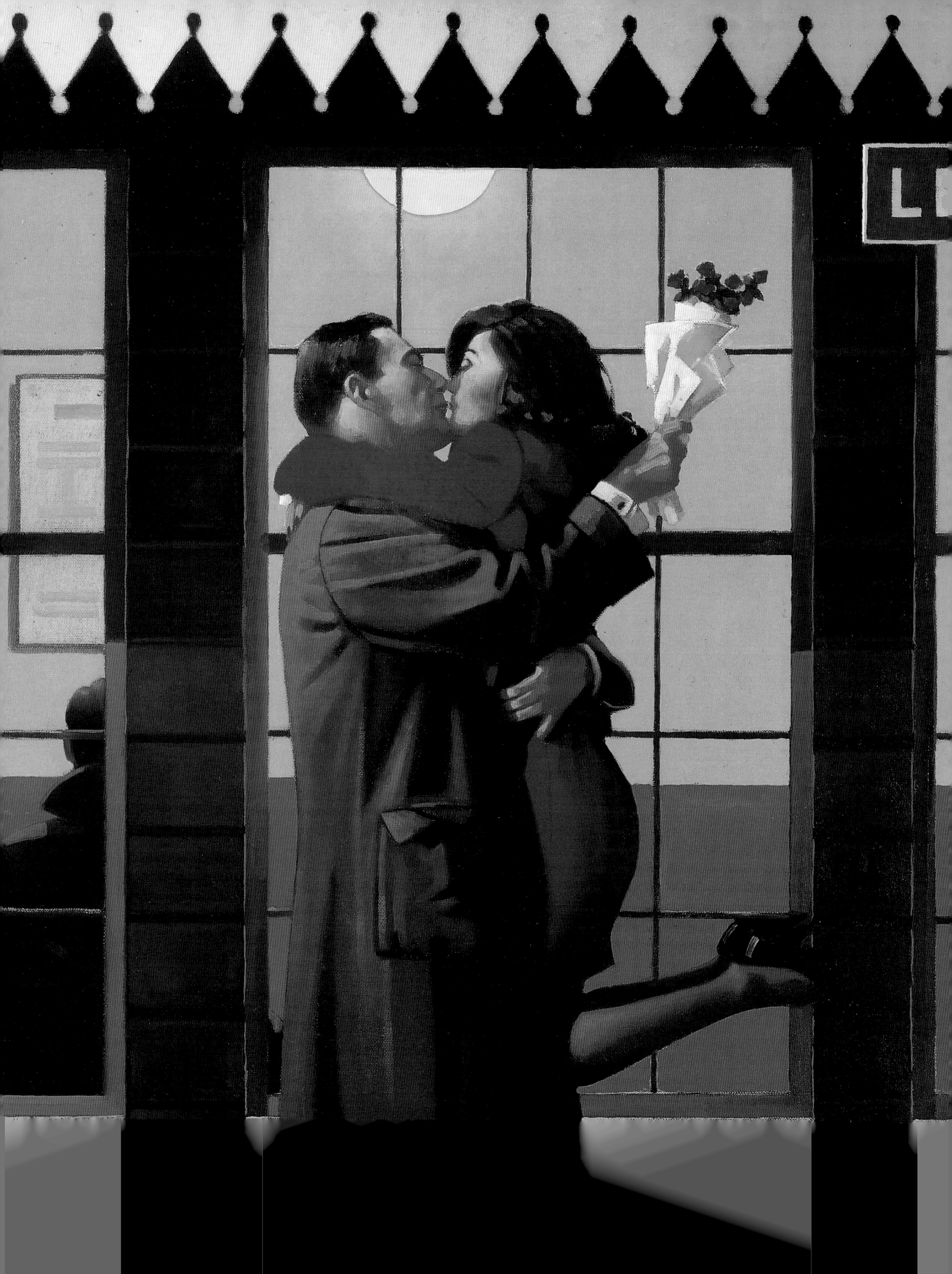

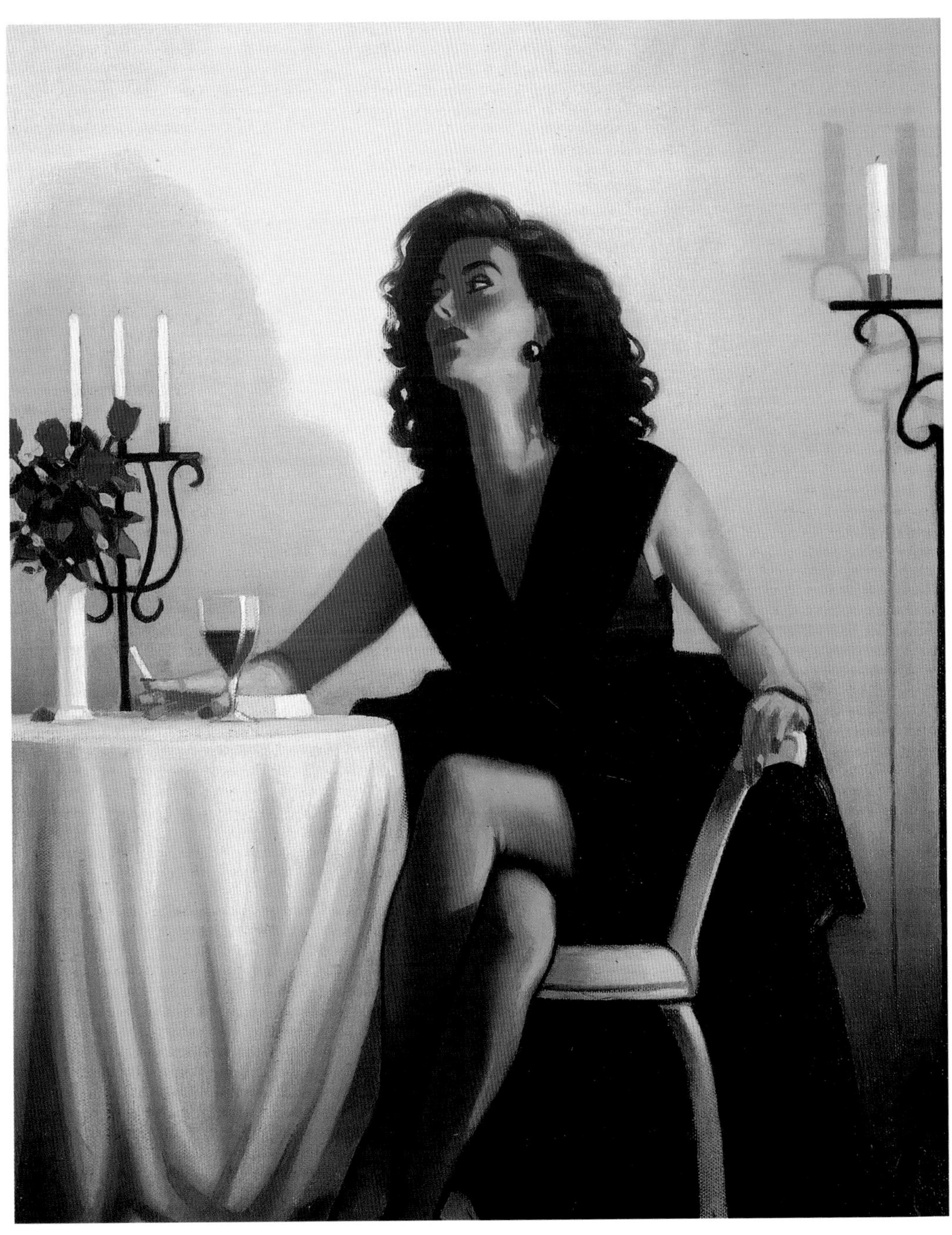

Table for One

Dressing to Kill

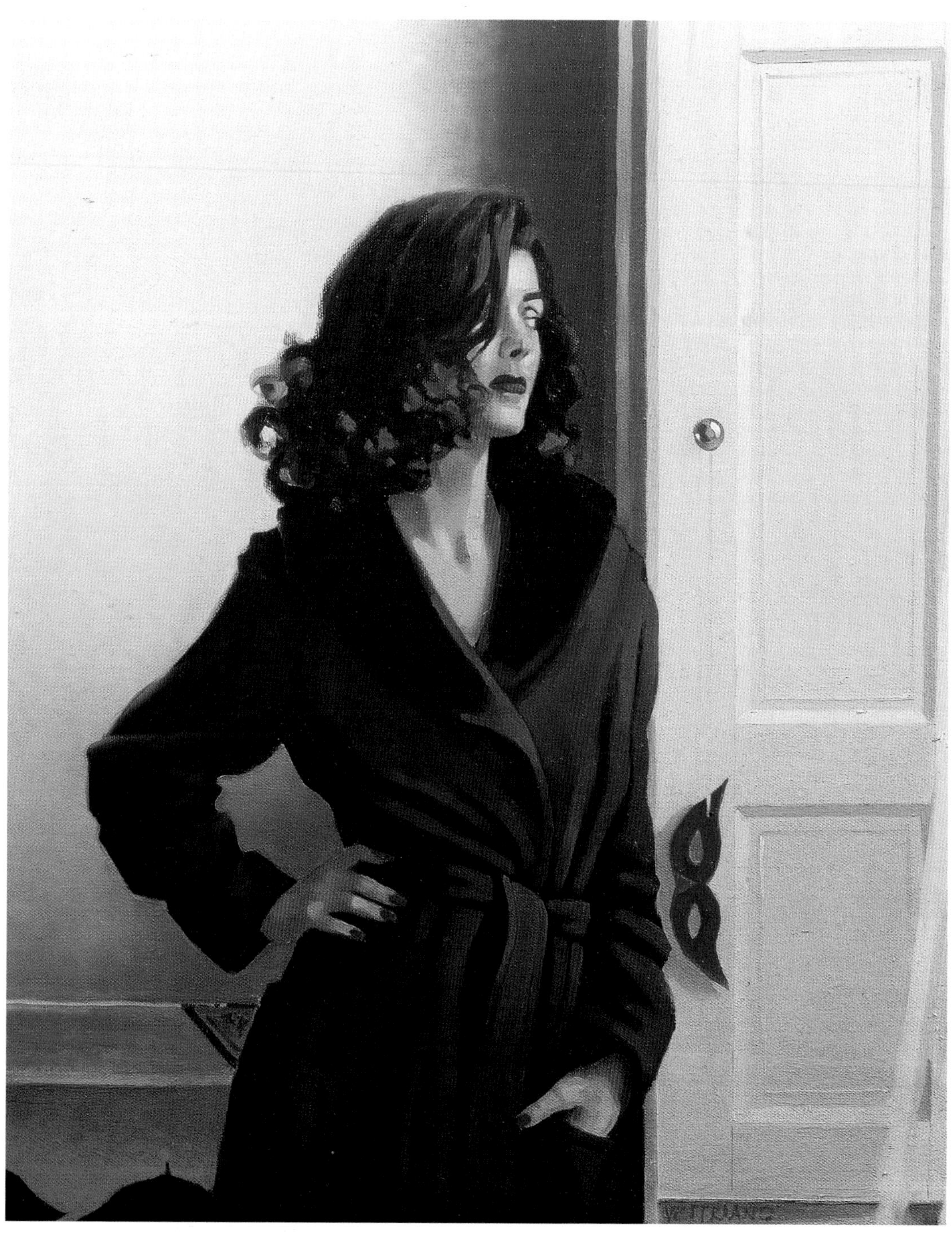

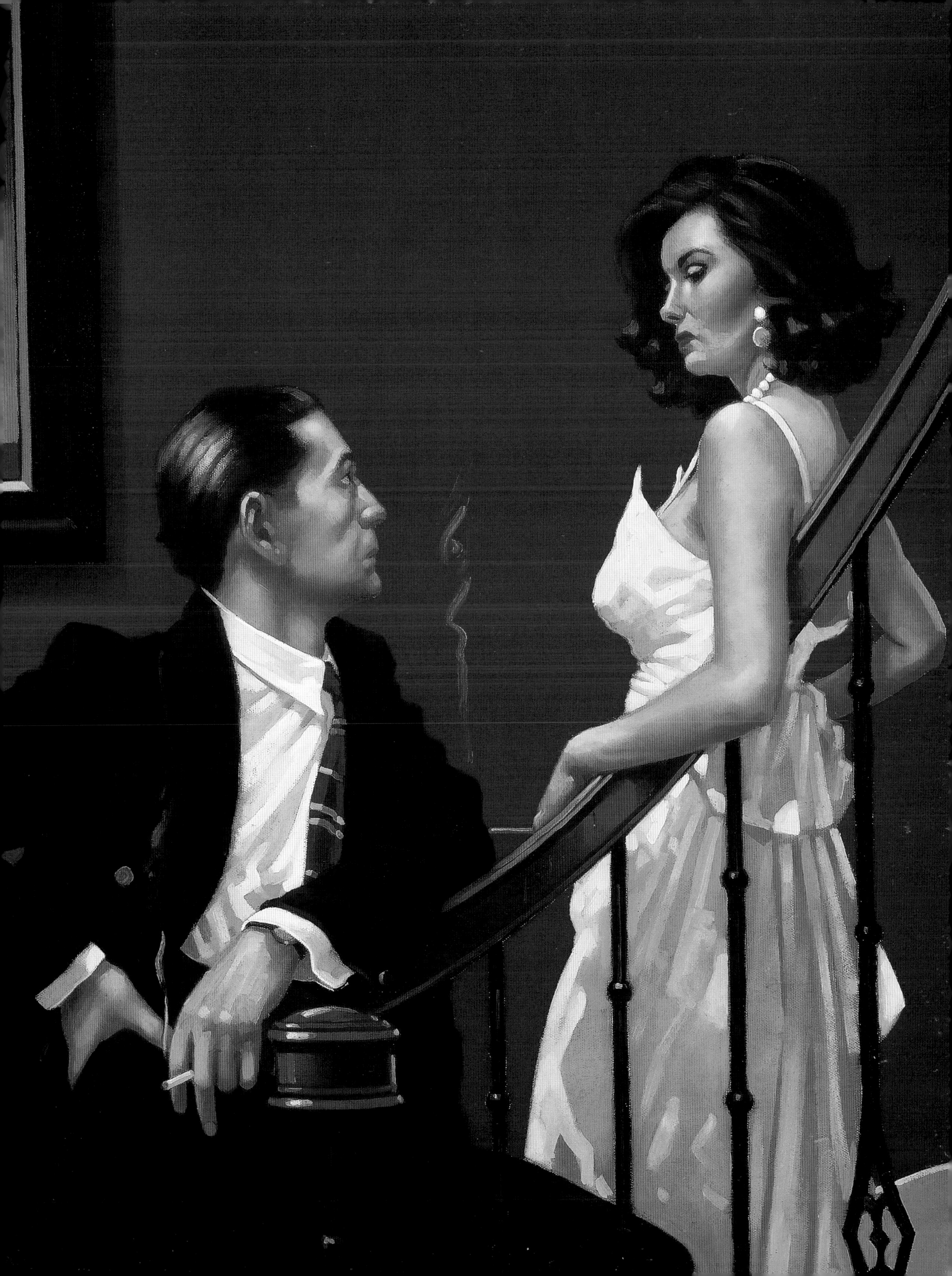

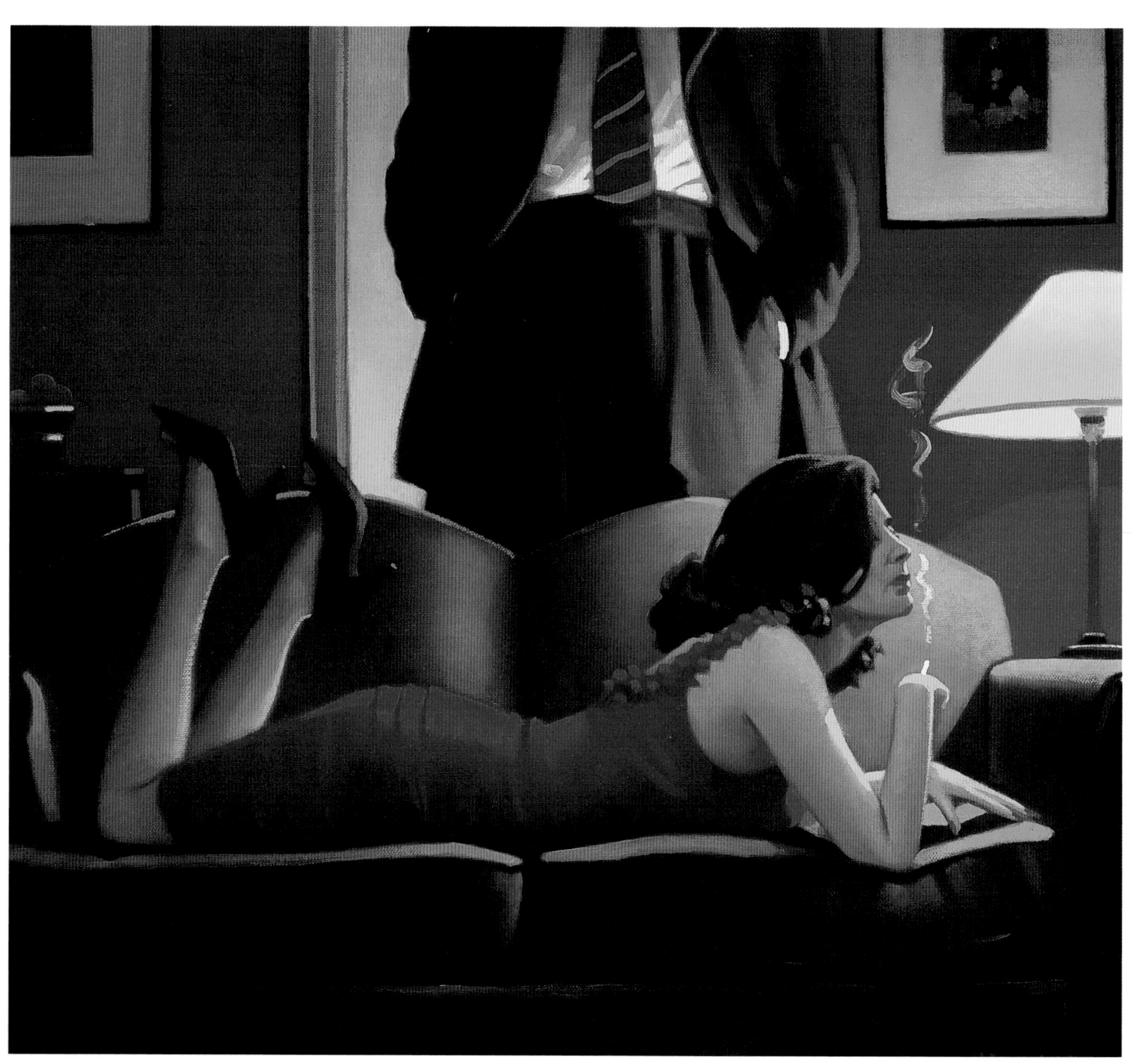

The Parlour of Temptation

After Midnight

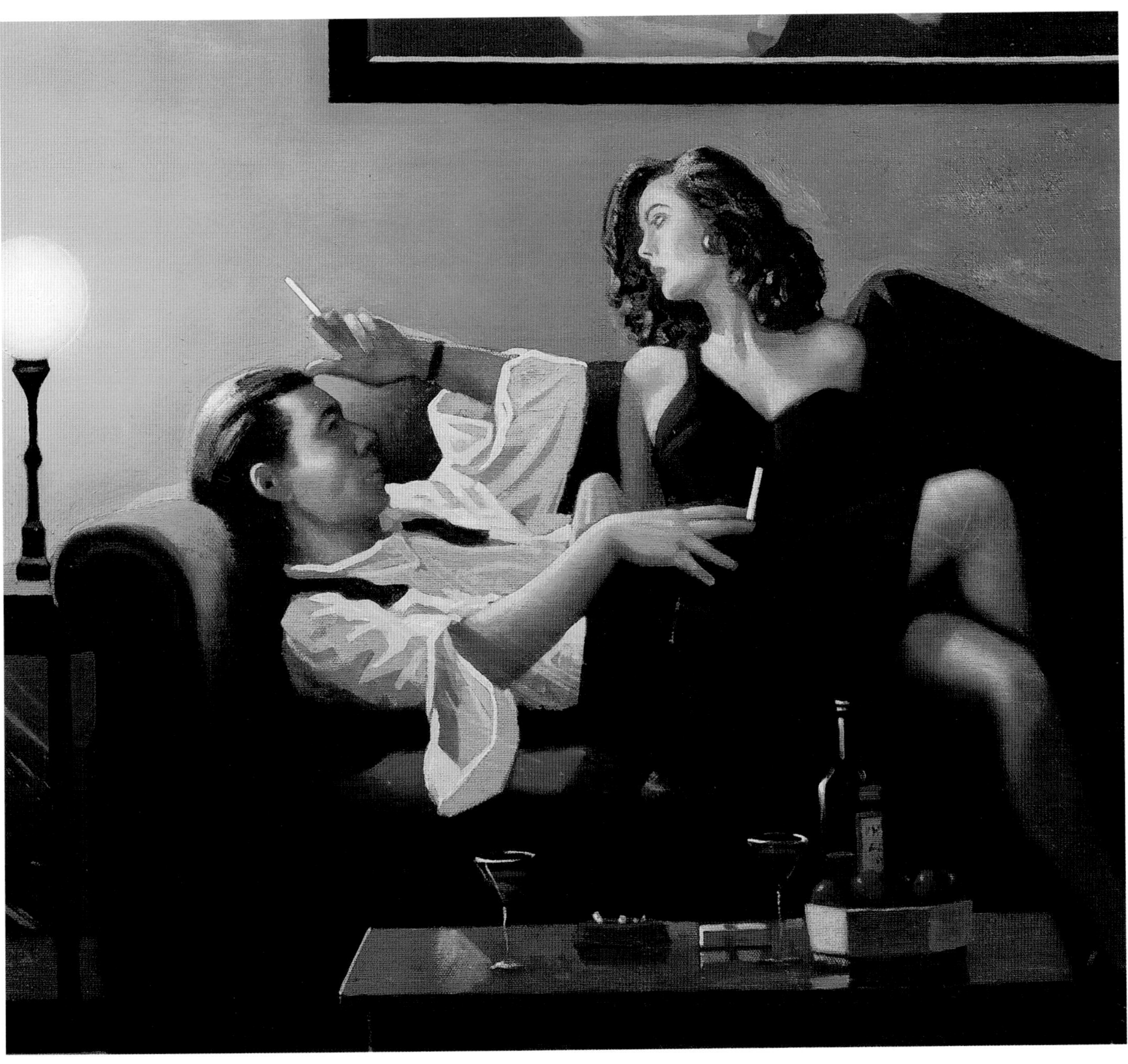

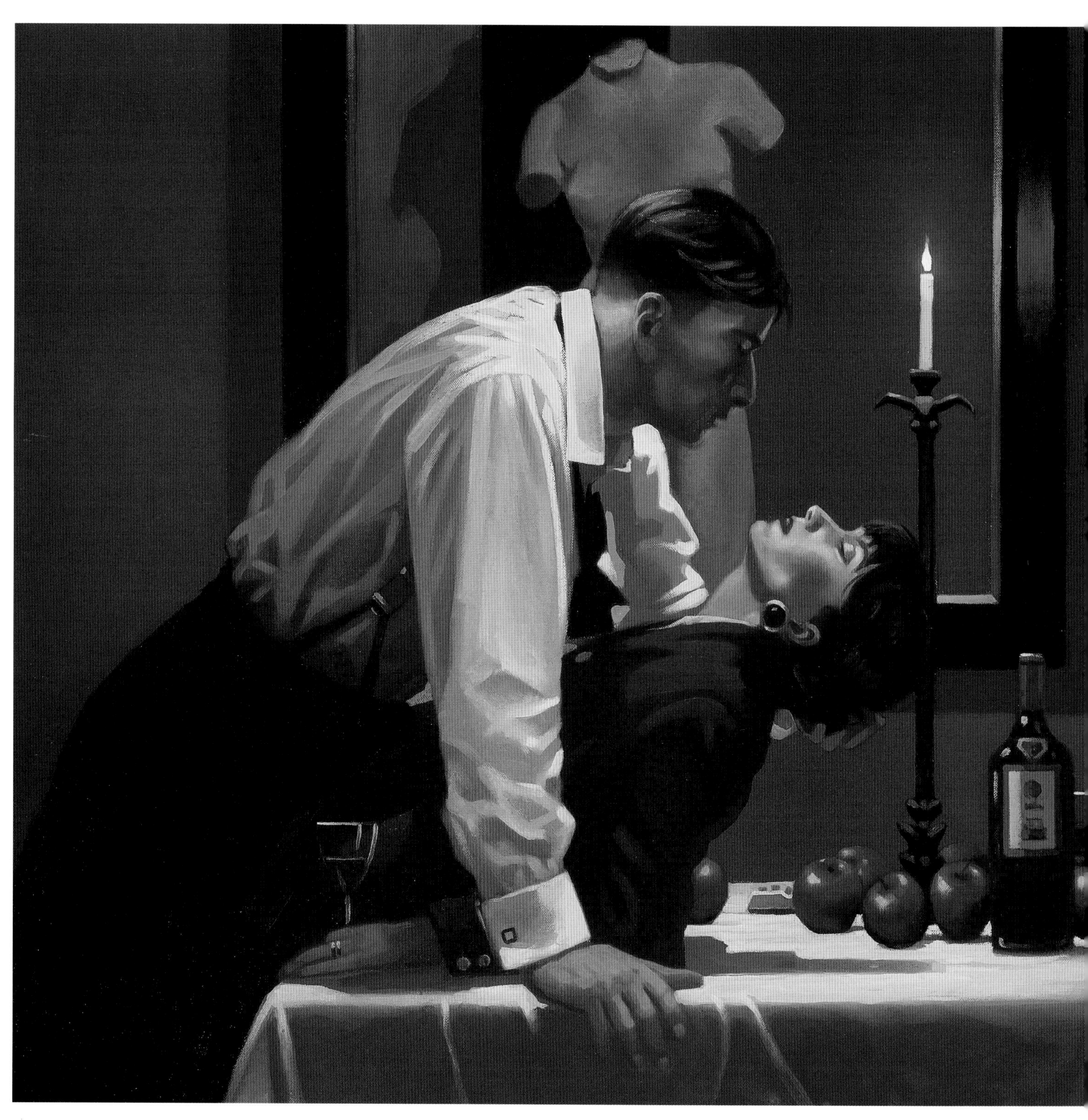

The Party's Over

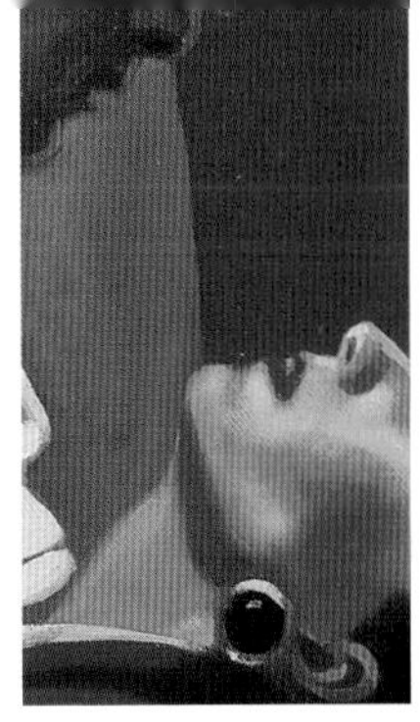

Rooms of a Stranger

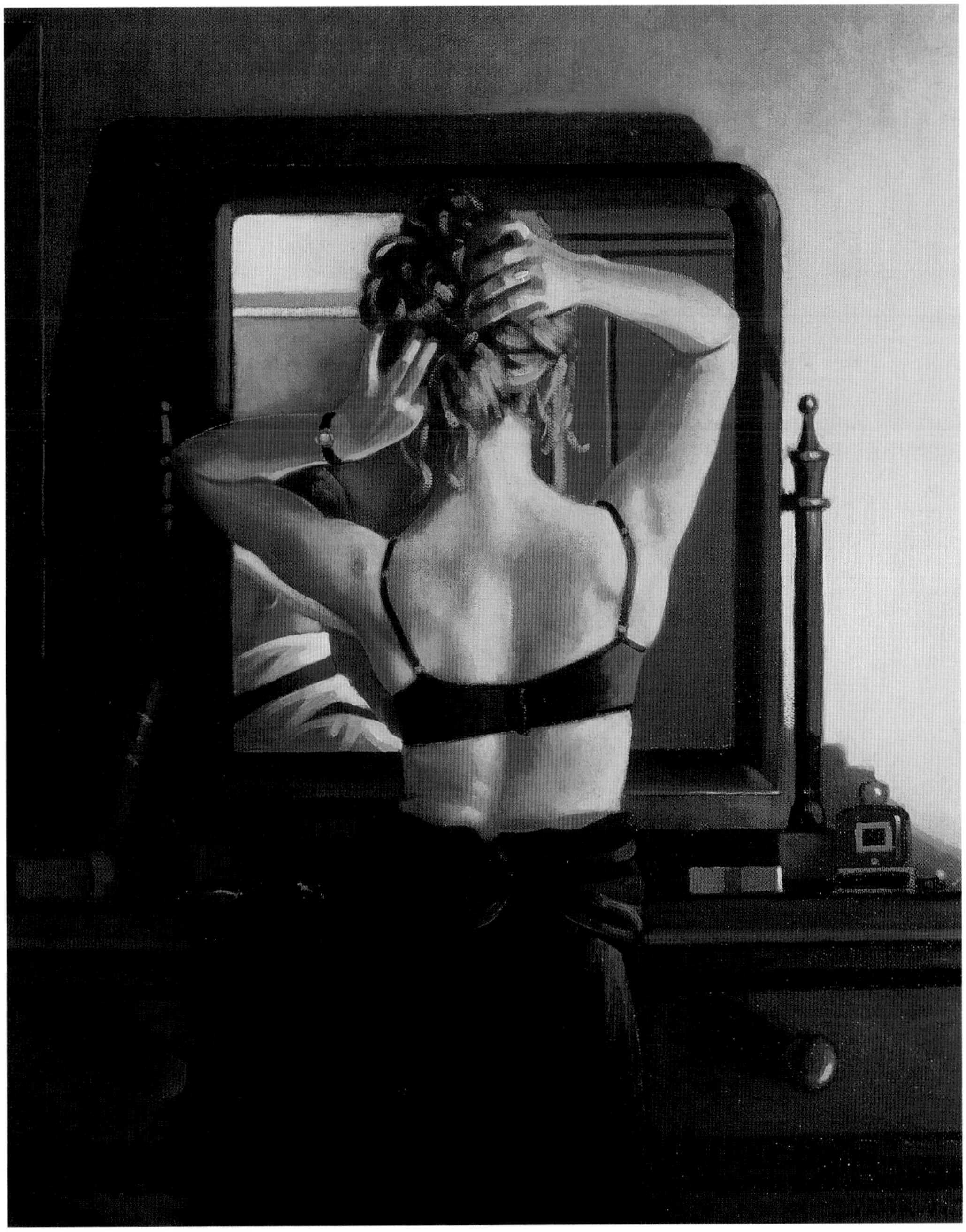

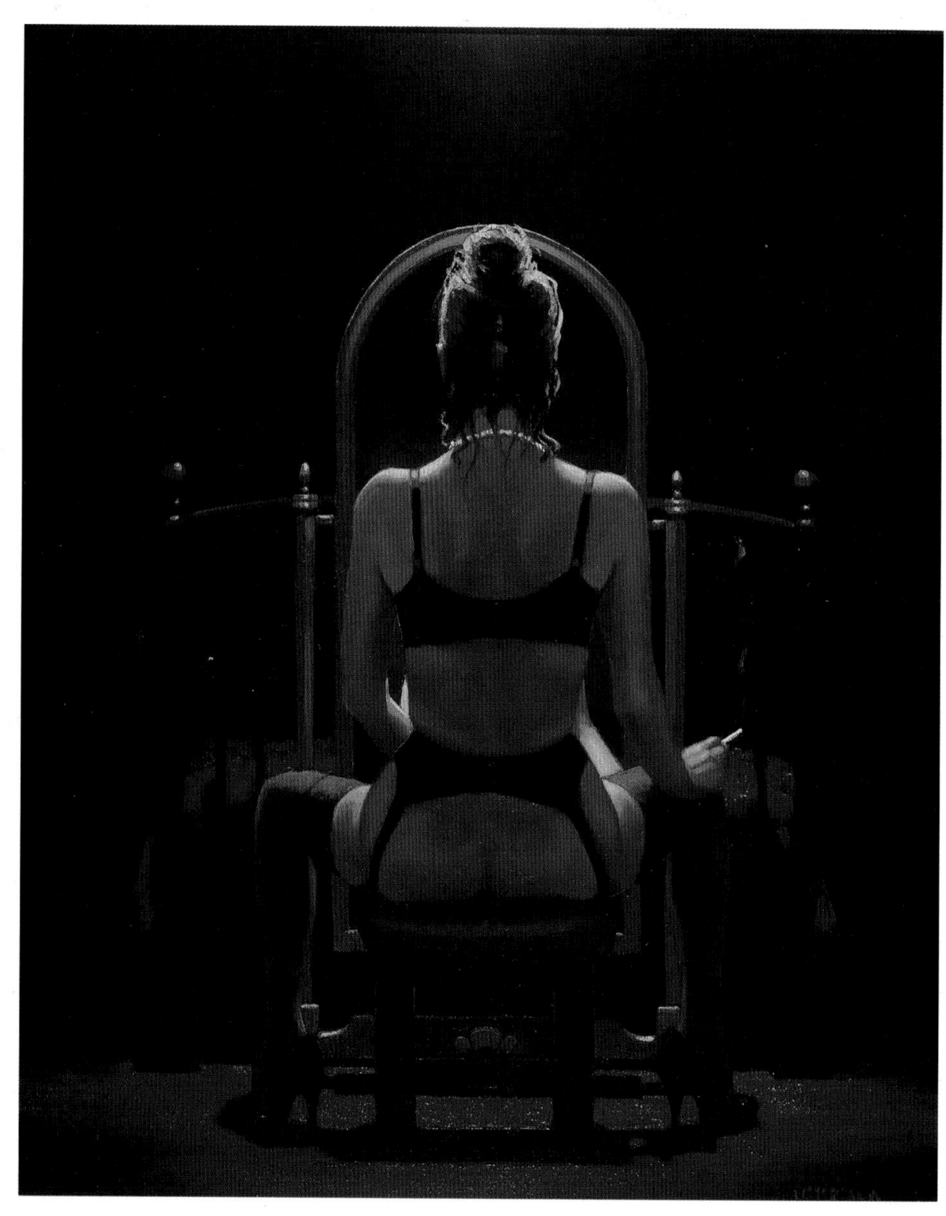

Mirror, Mirrorr

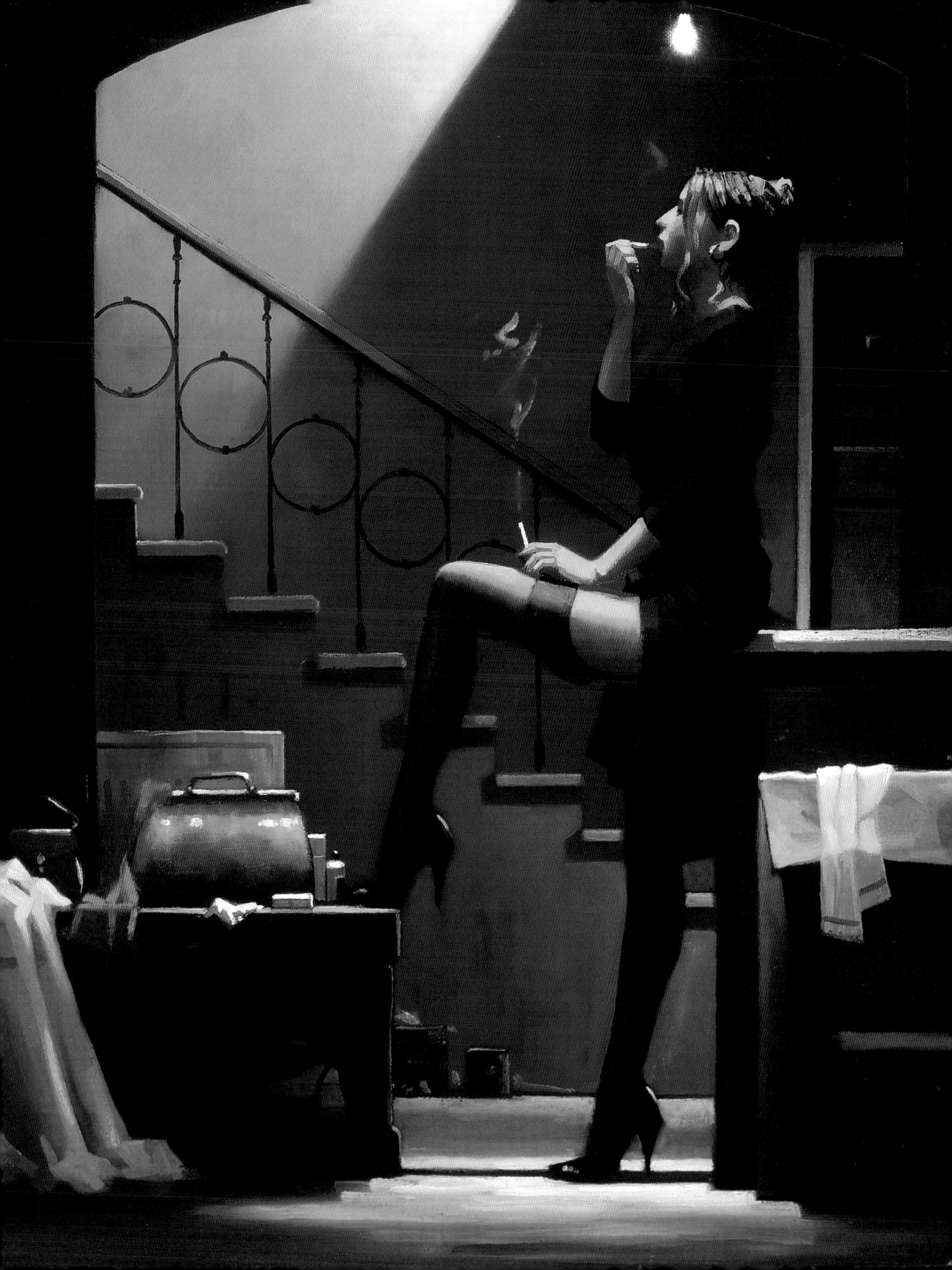

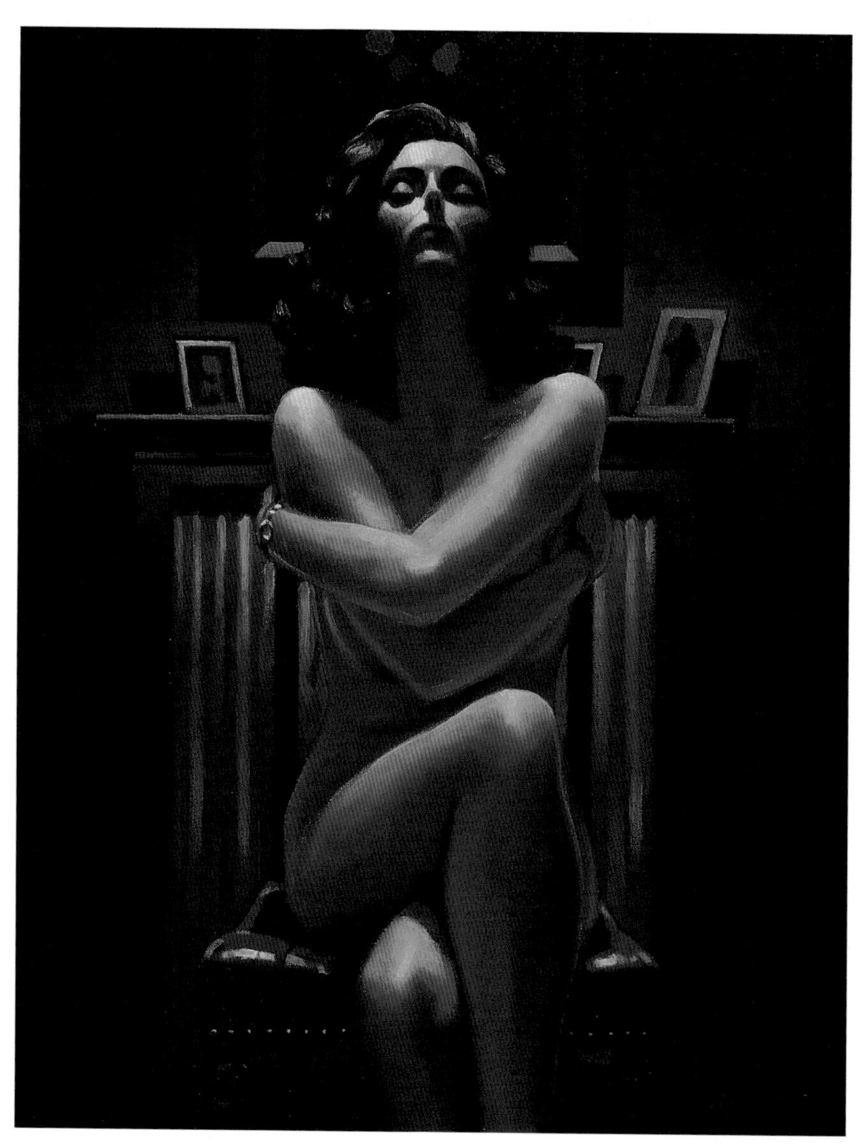

Just The Way It Is

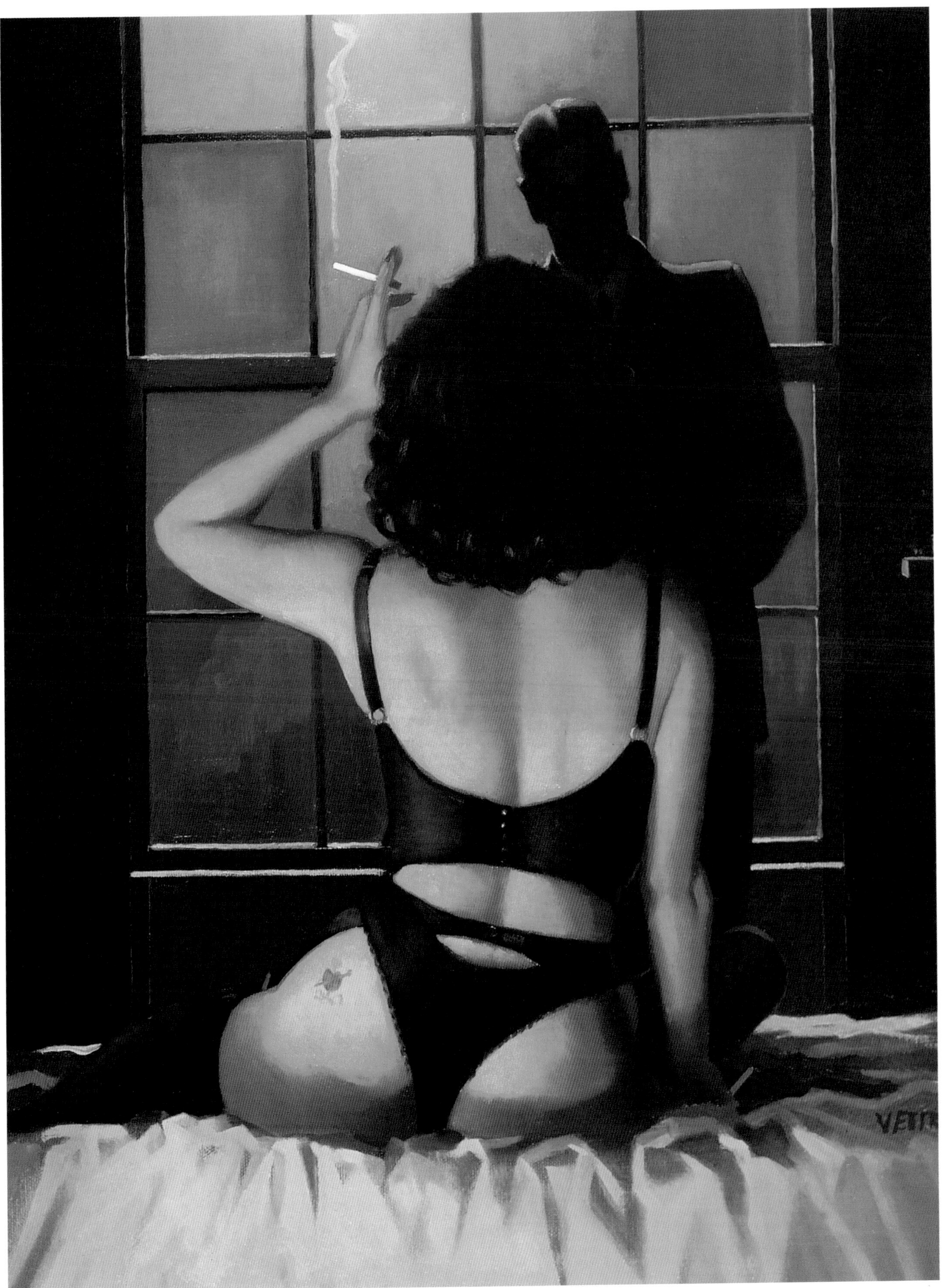

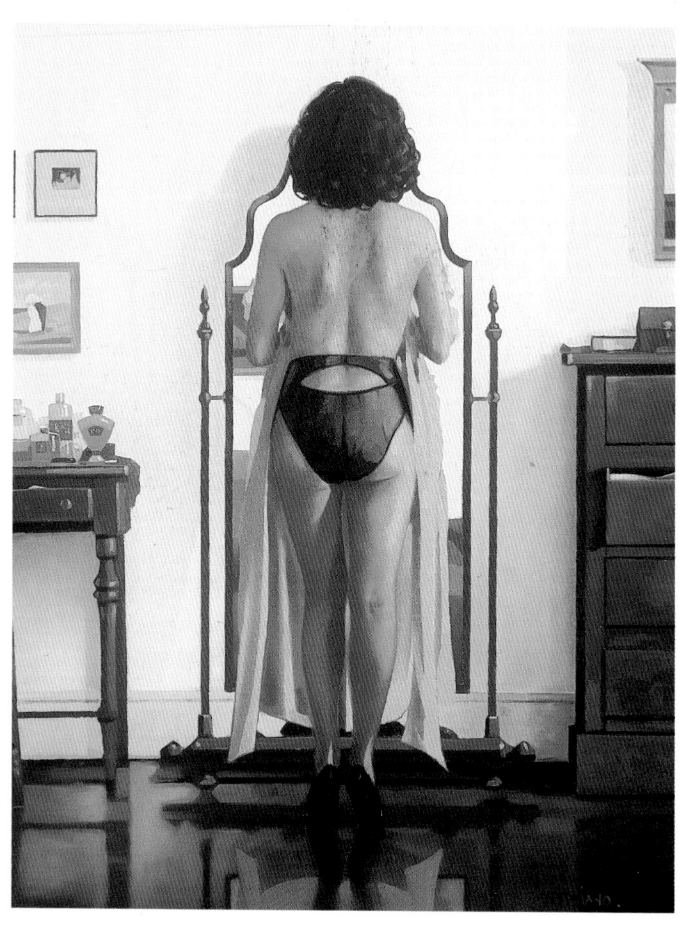

The Blue Gown

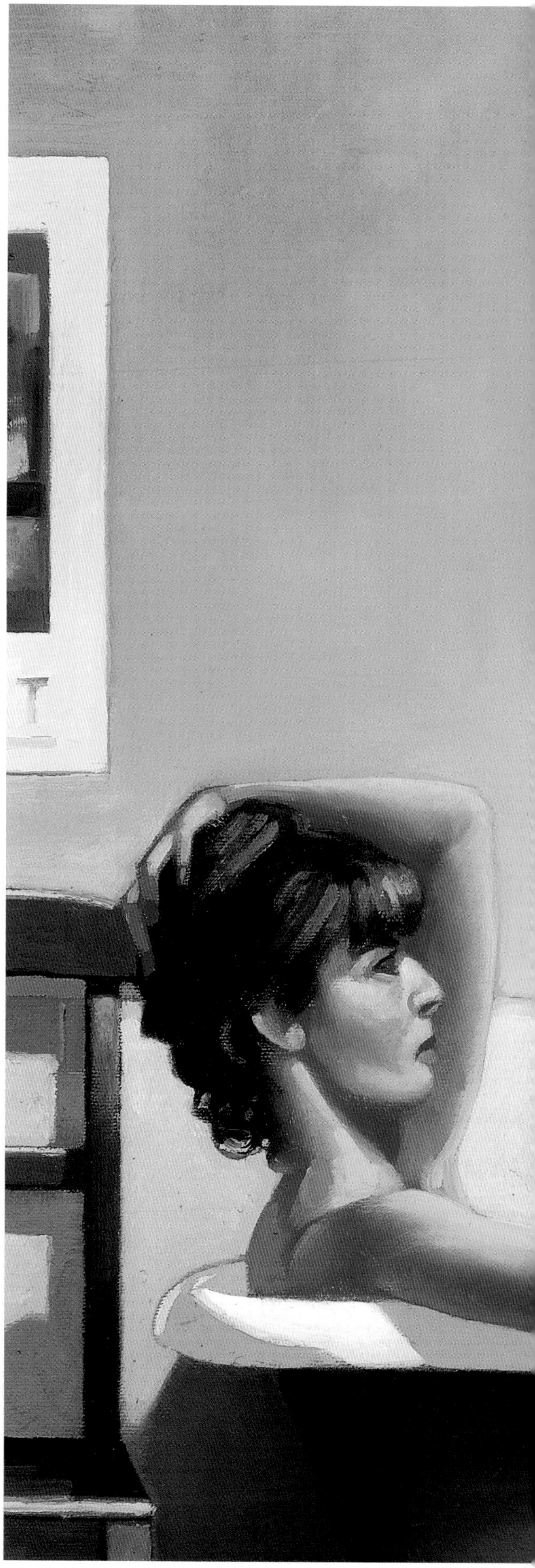

Bad Boy Blues

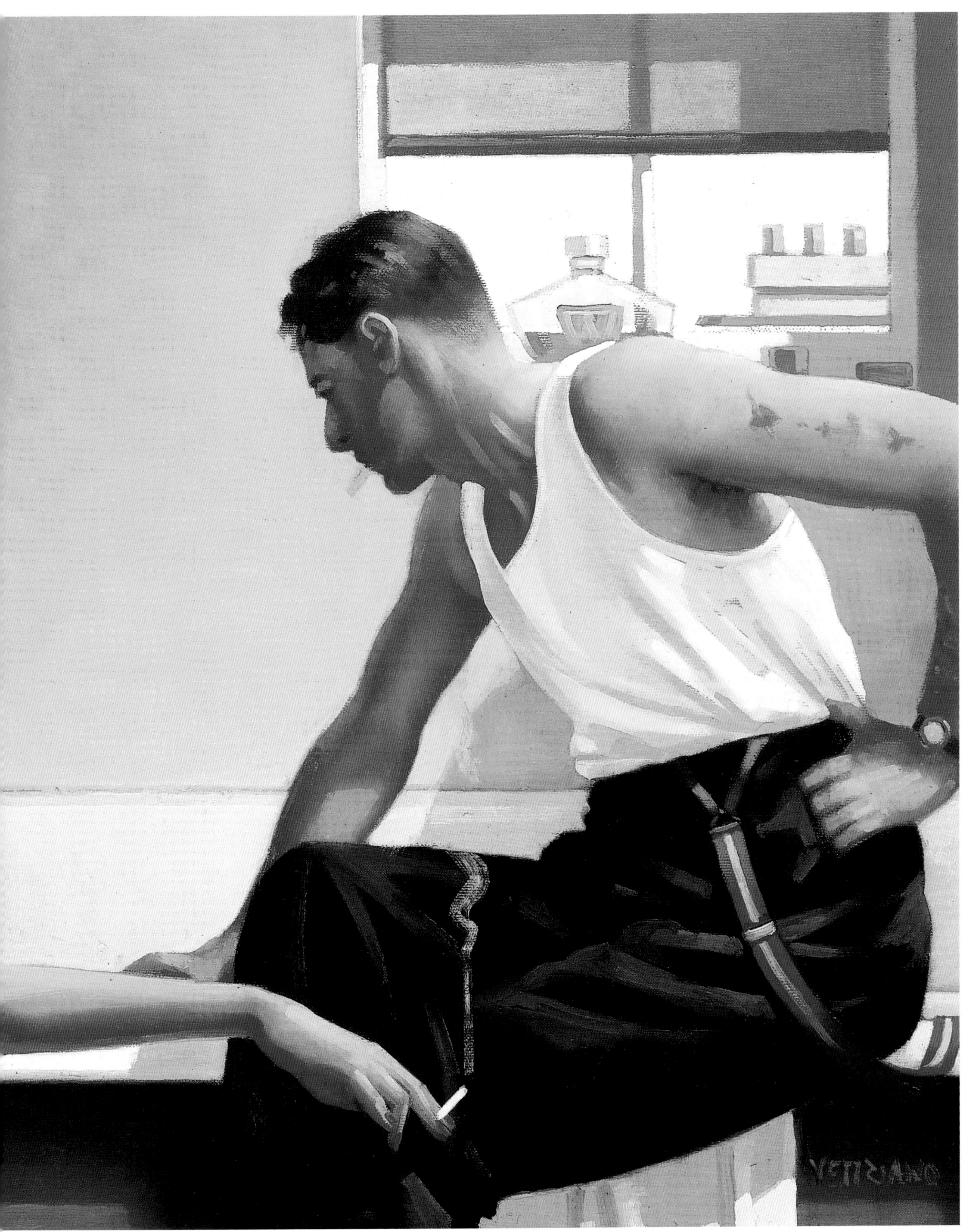
VETTRIANO

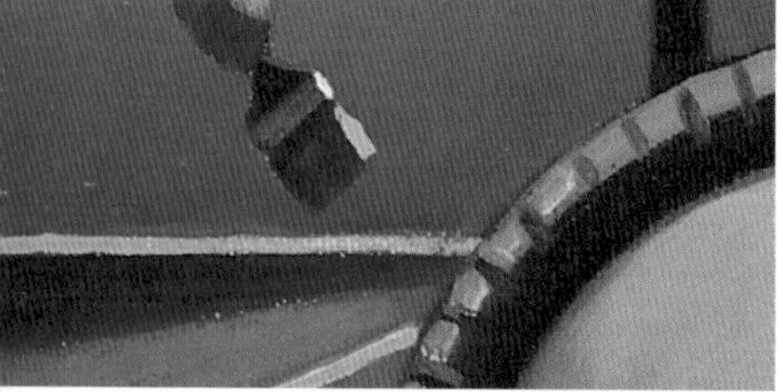

Birth of a Dream

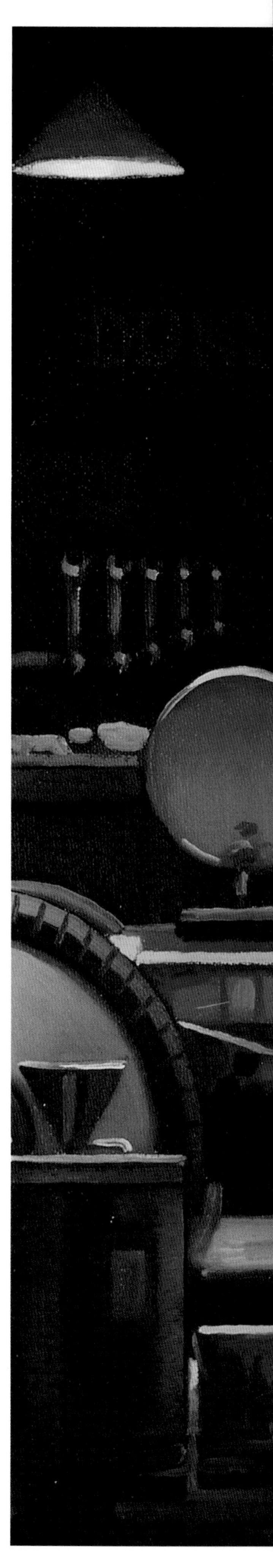

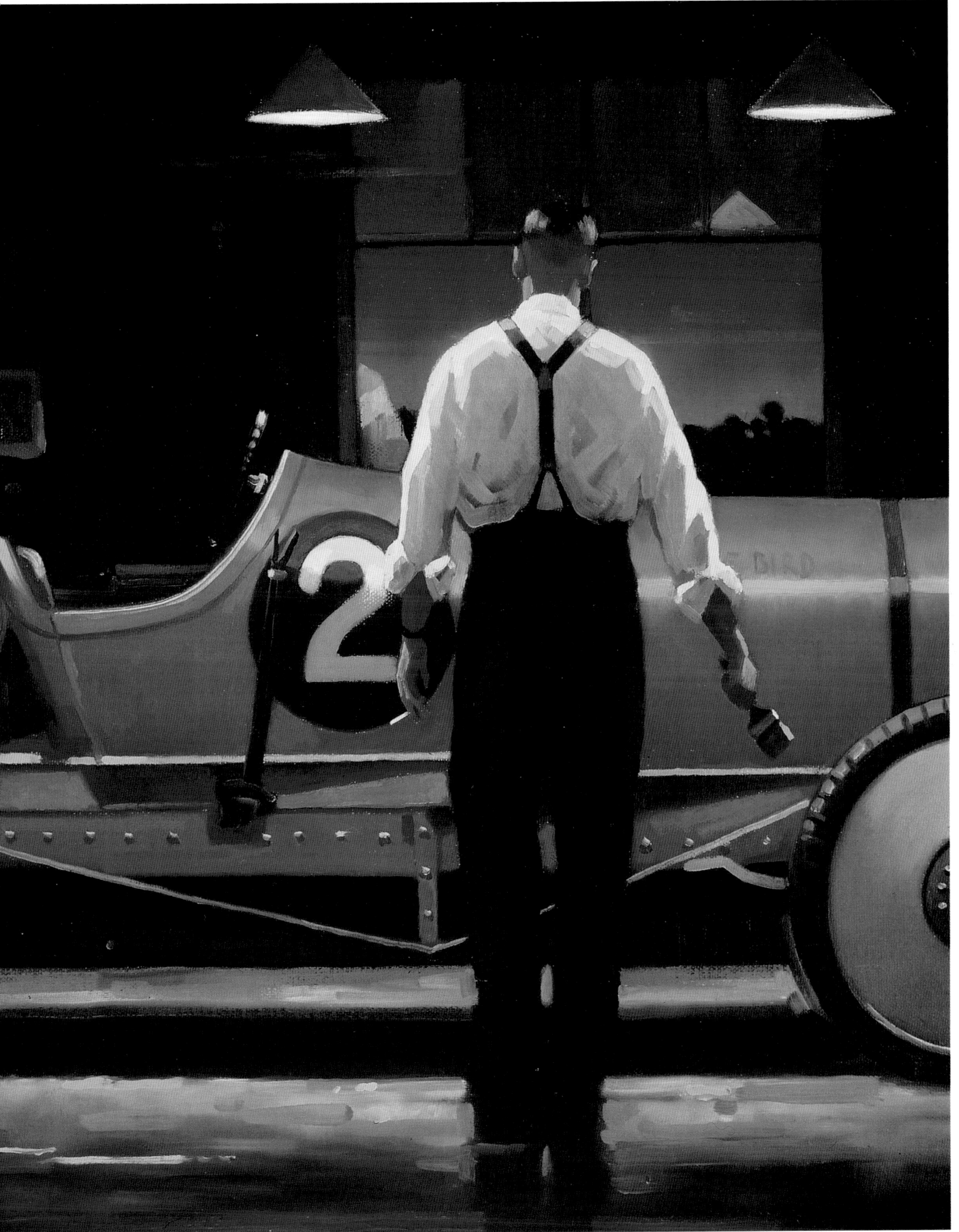

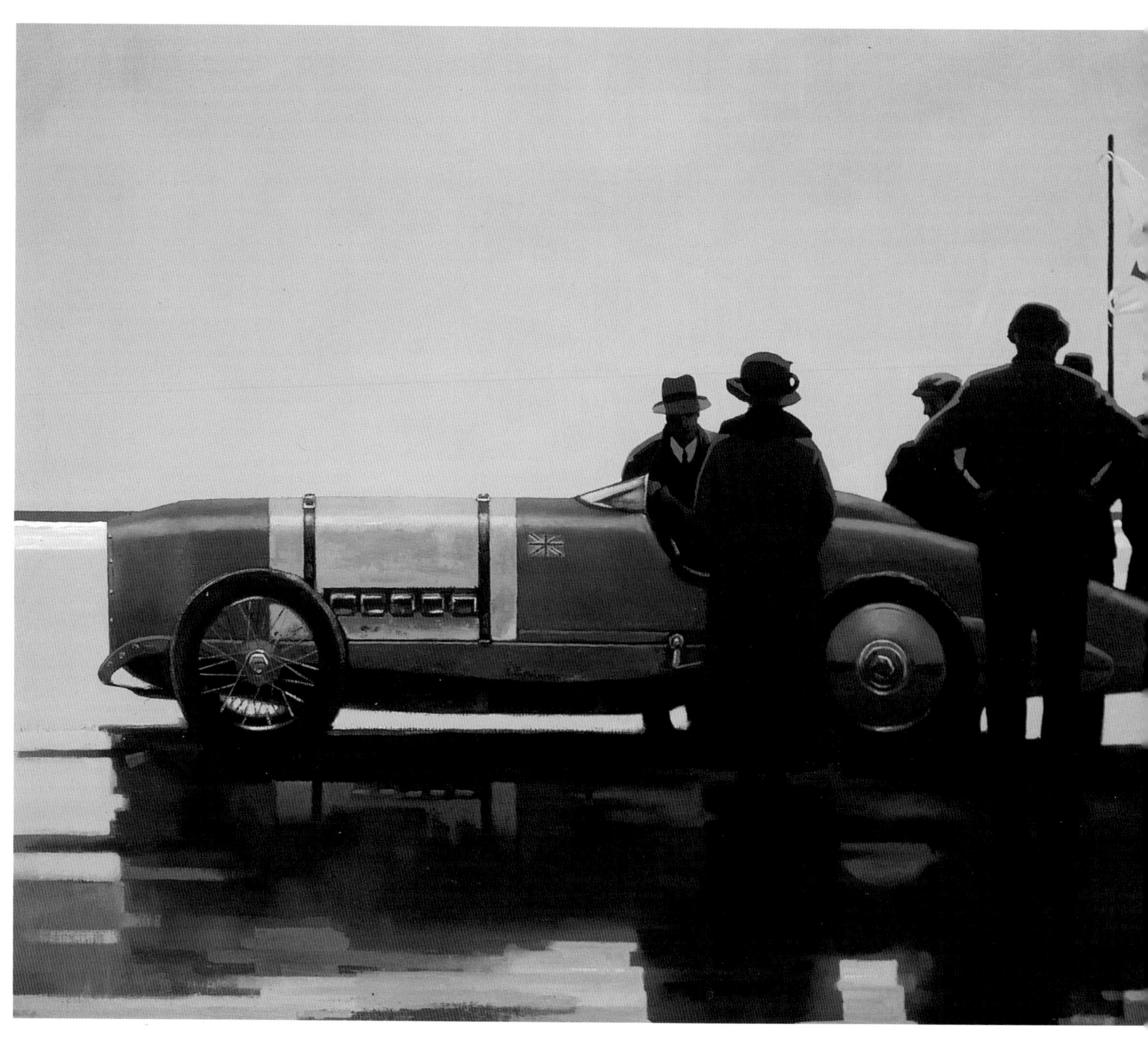

Pendine Beach

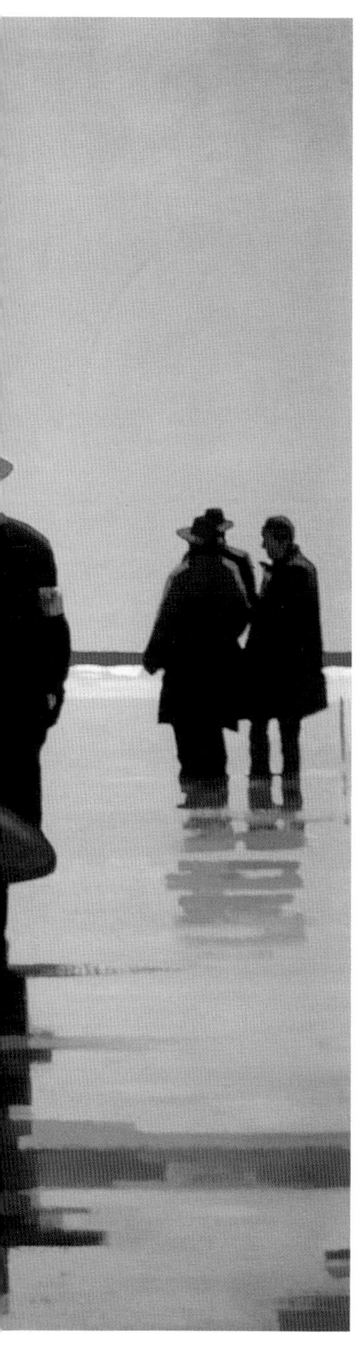

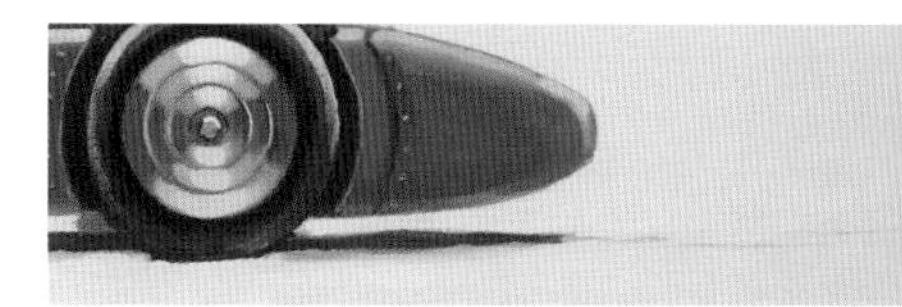

Bluebird at Bonneville

(Following pages)

The British are Coming

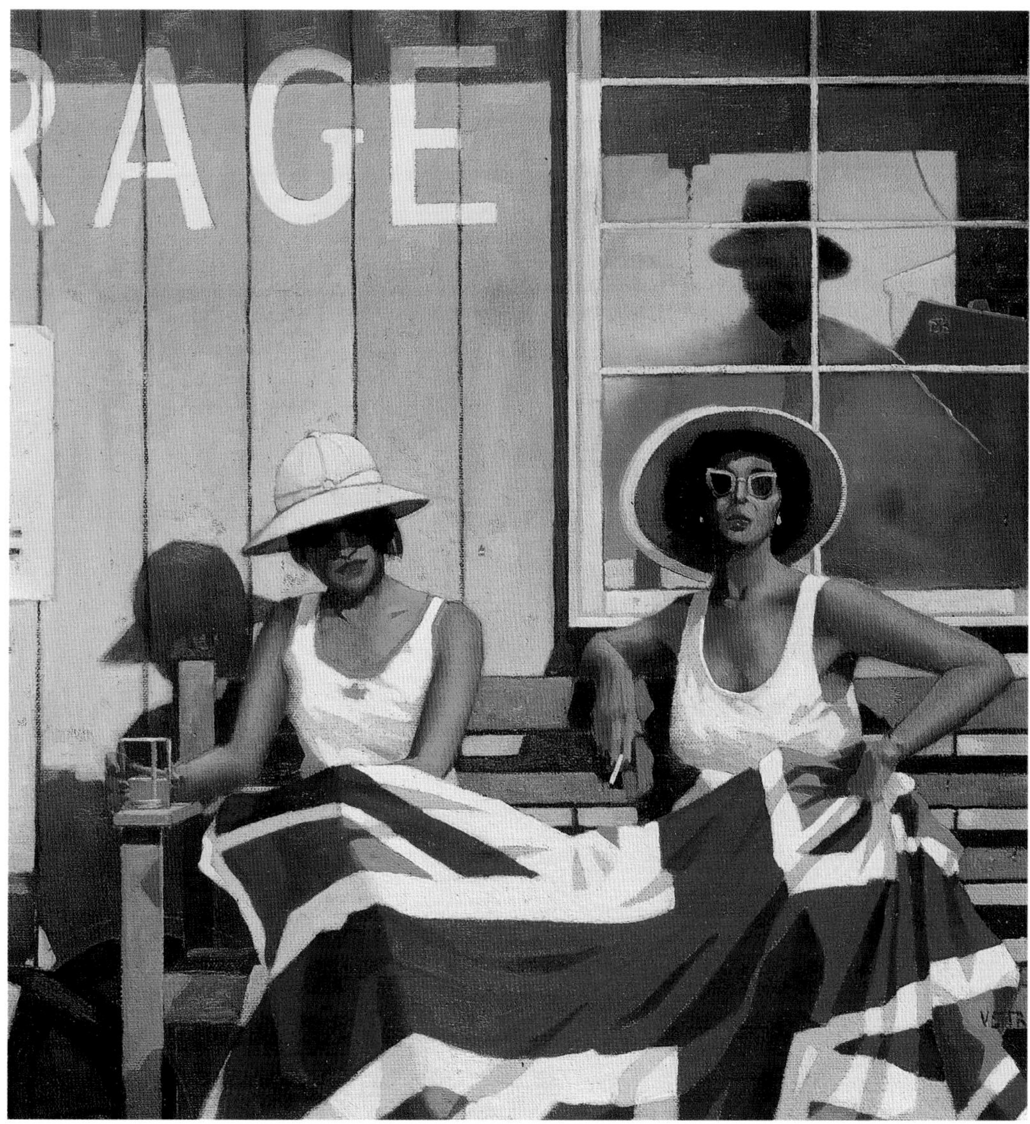

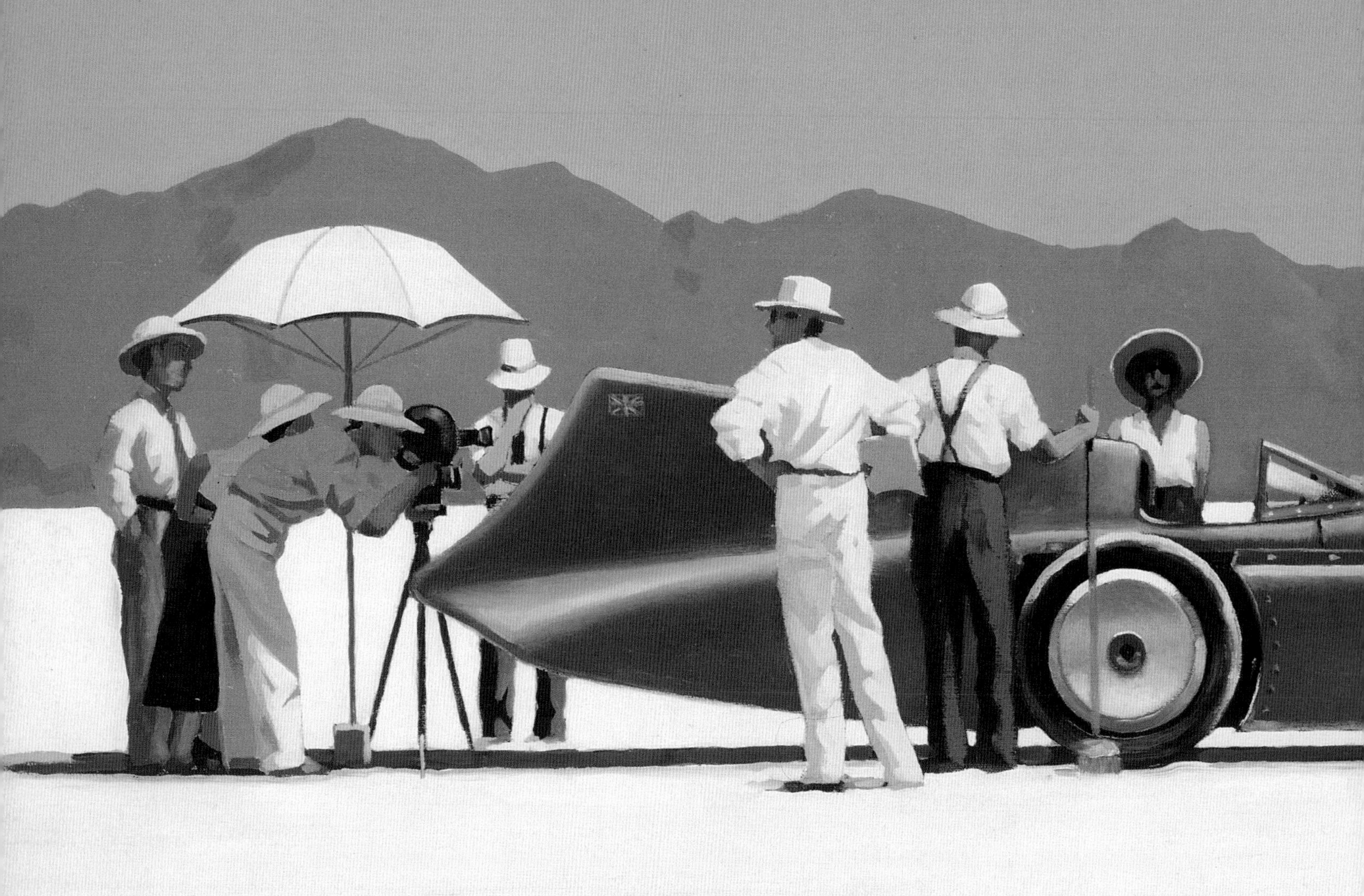

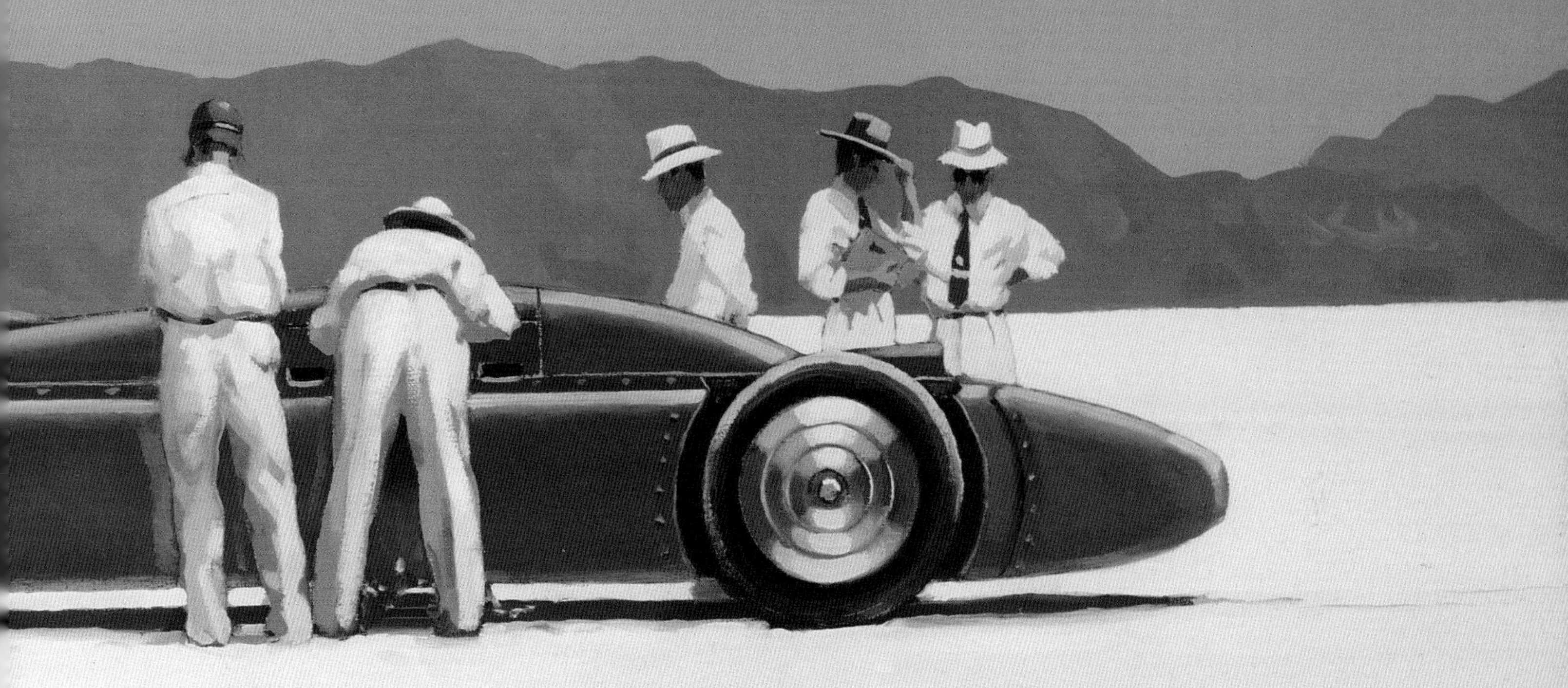

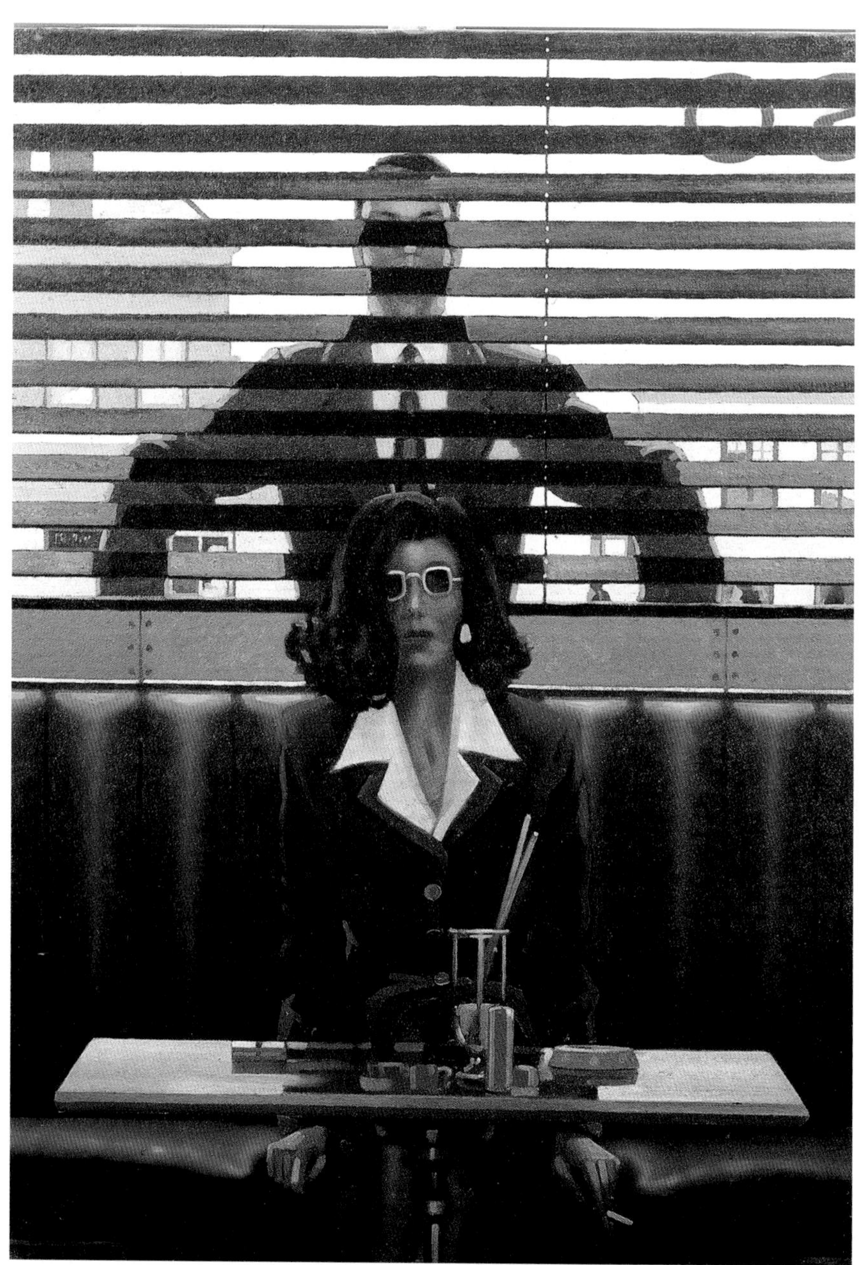

There's Always Someone Watching You

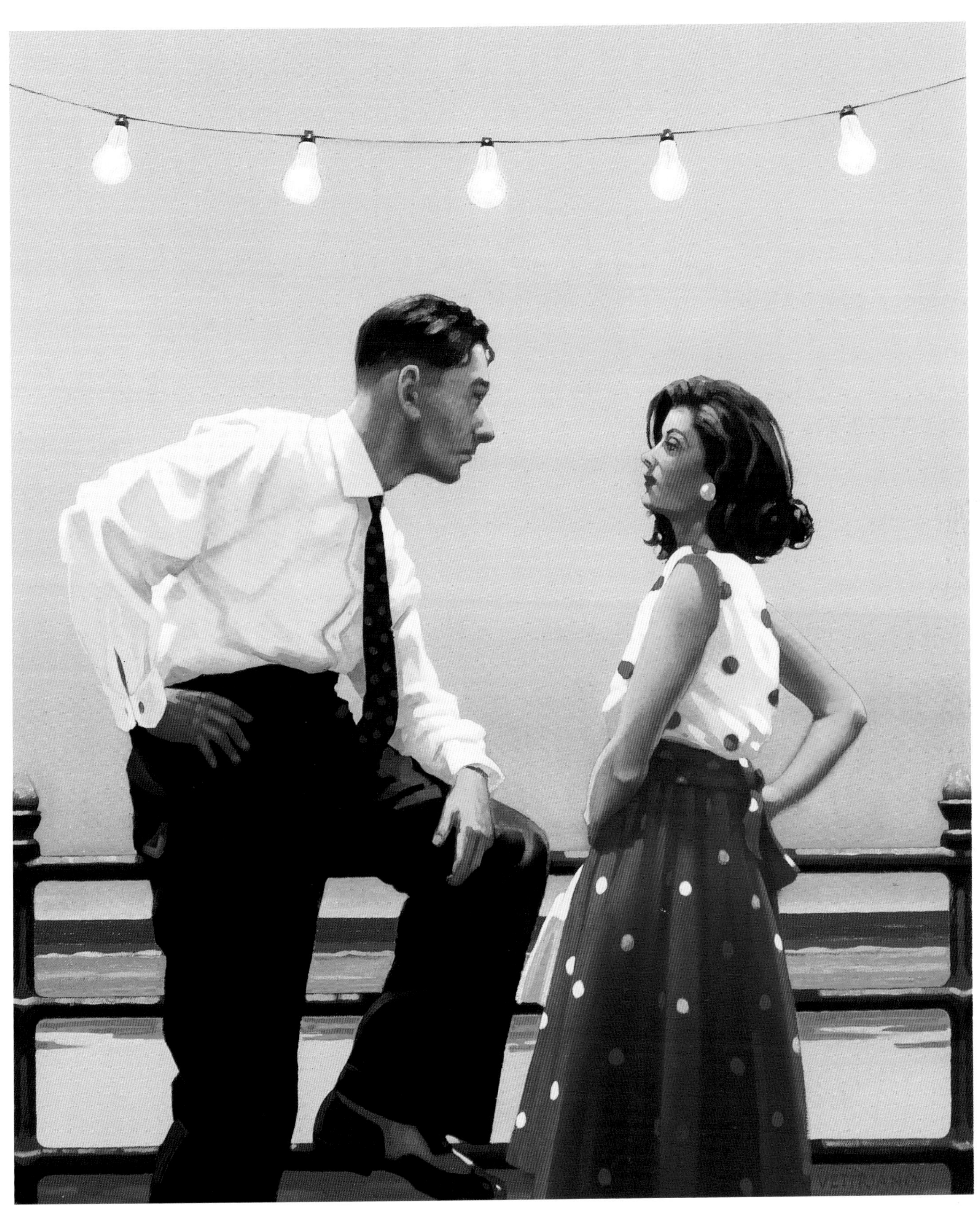

The Big Tease

The Missing Man II

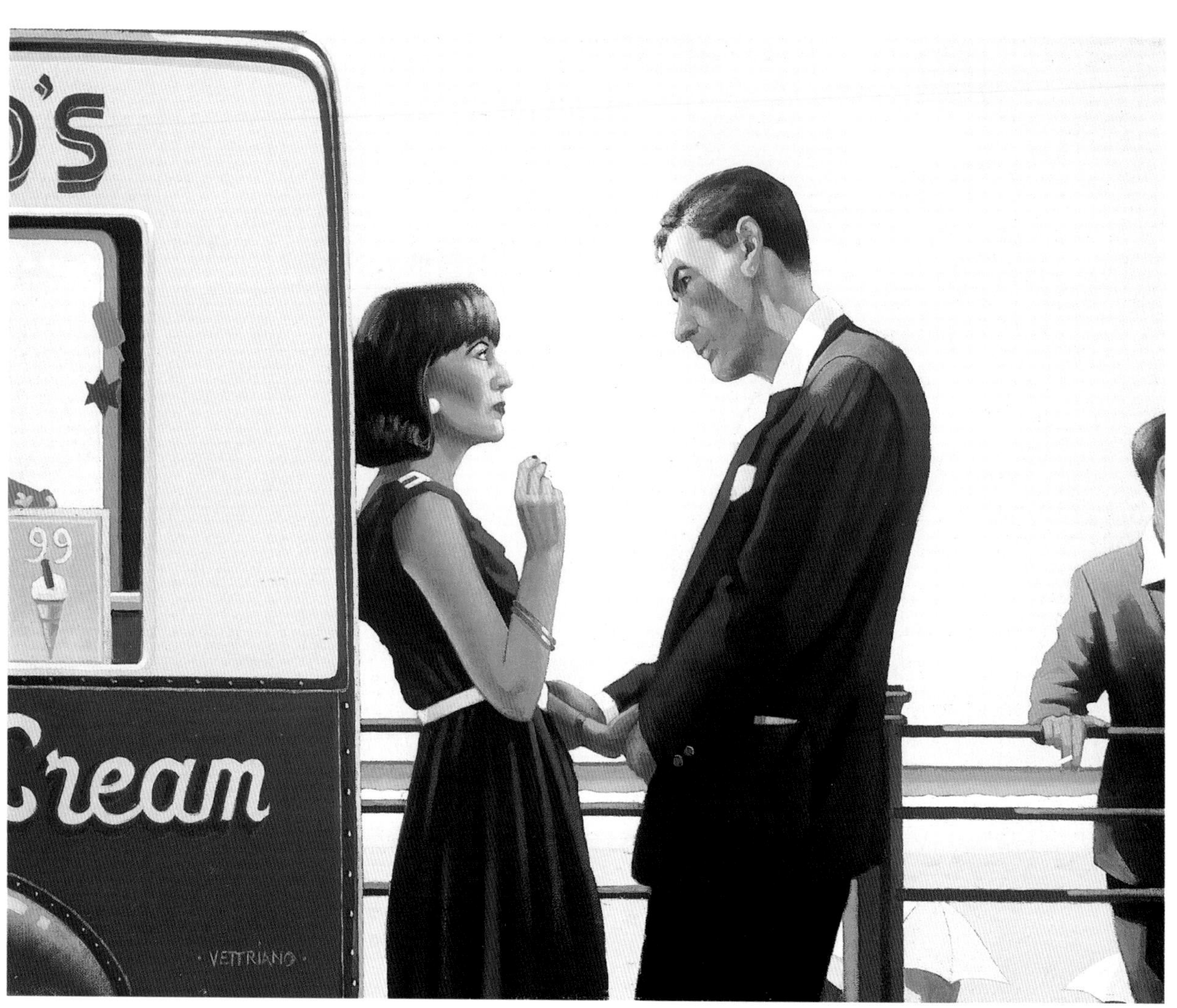

The Lying Game

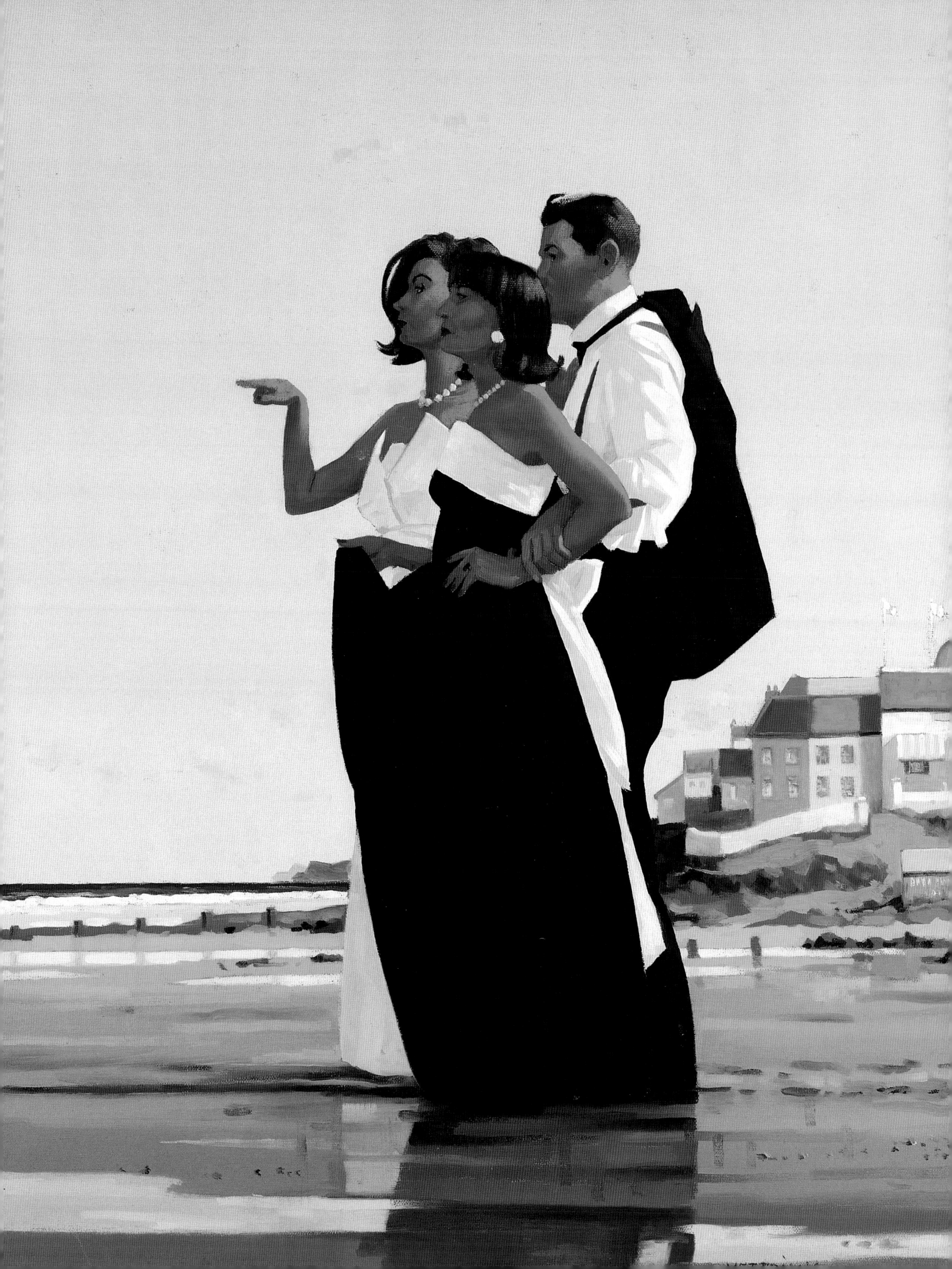

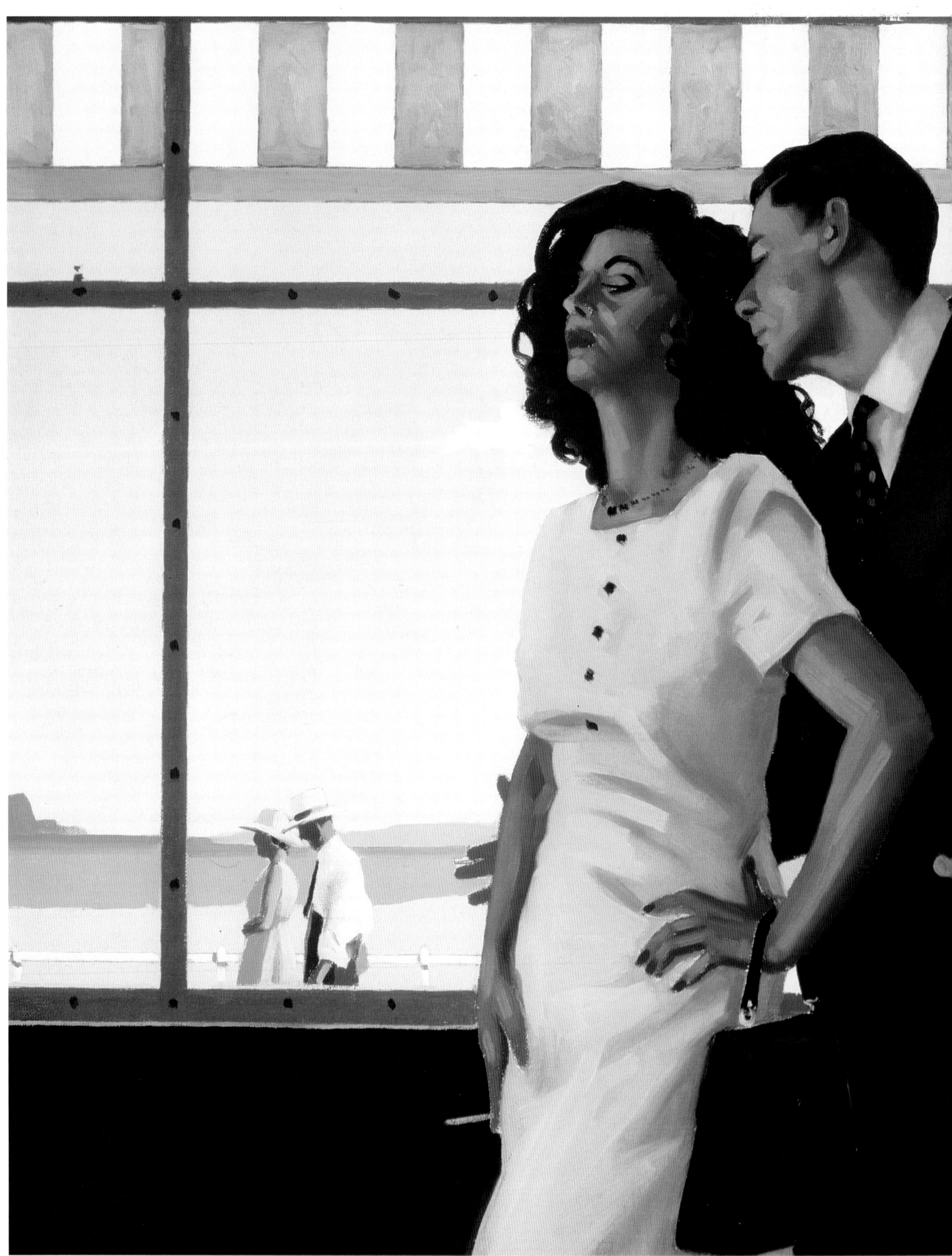

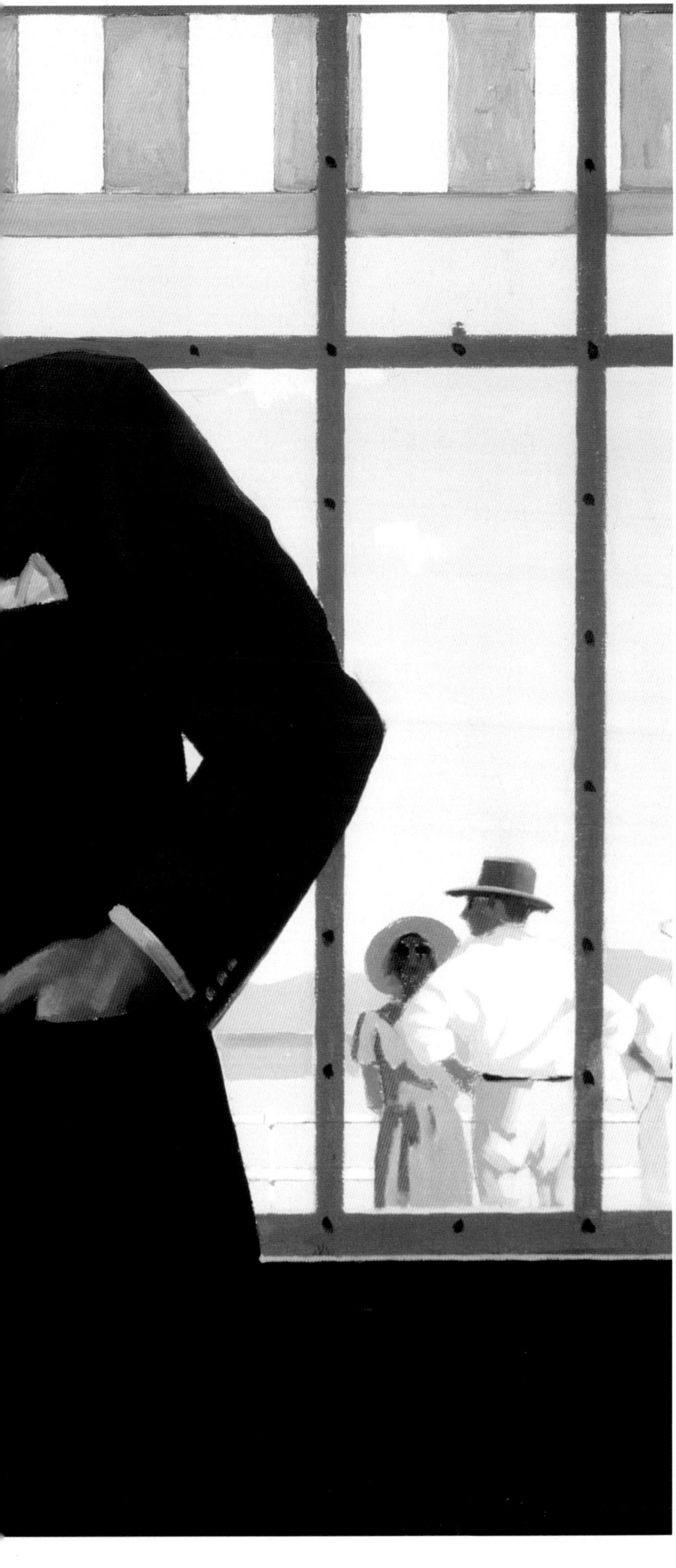

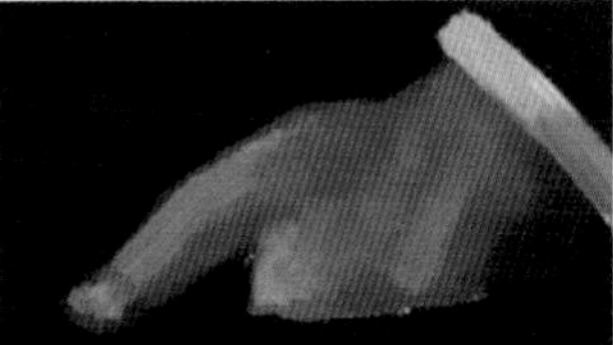

The Man in the Navy Suit

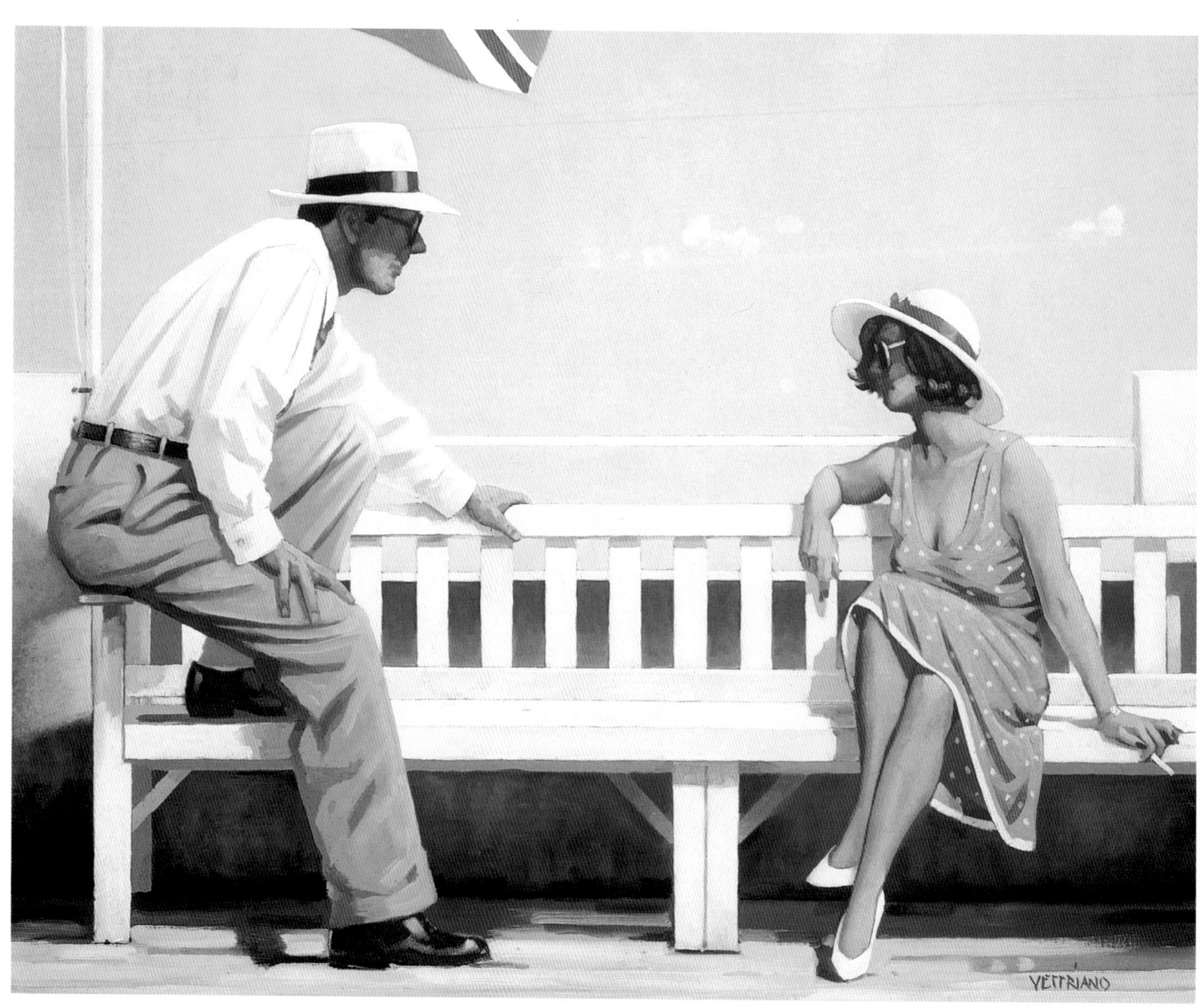

Mr Cool

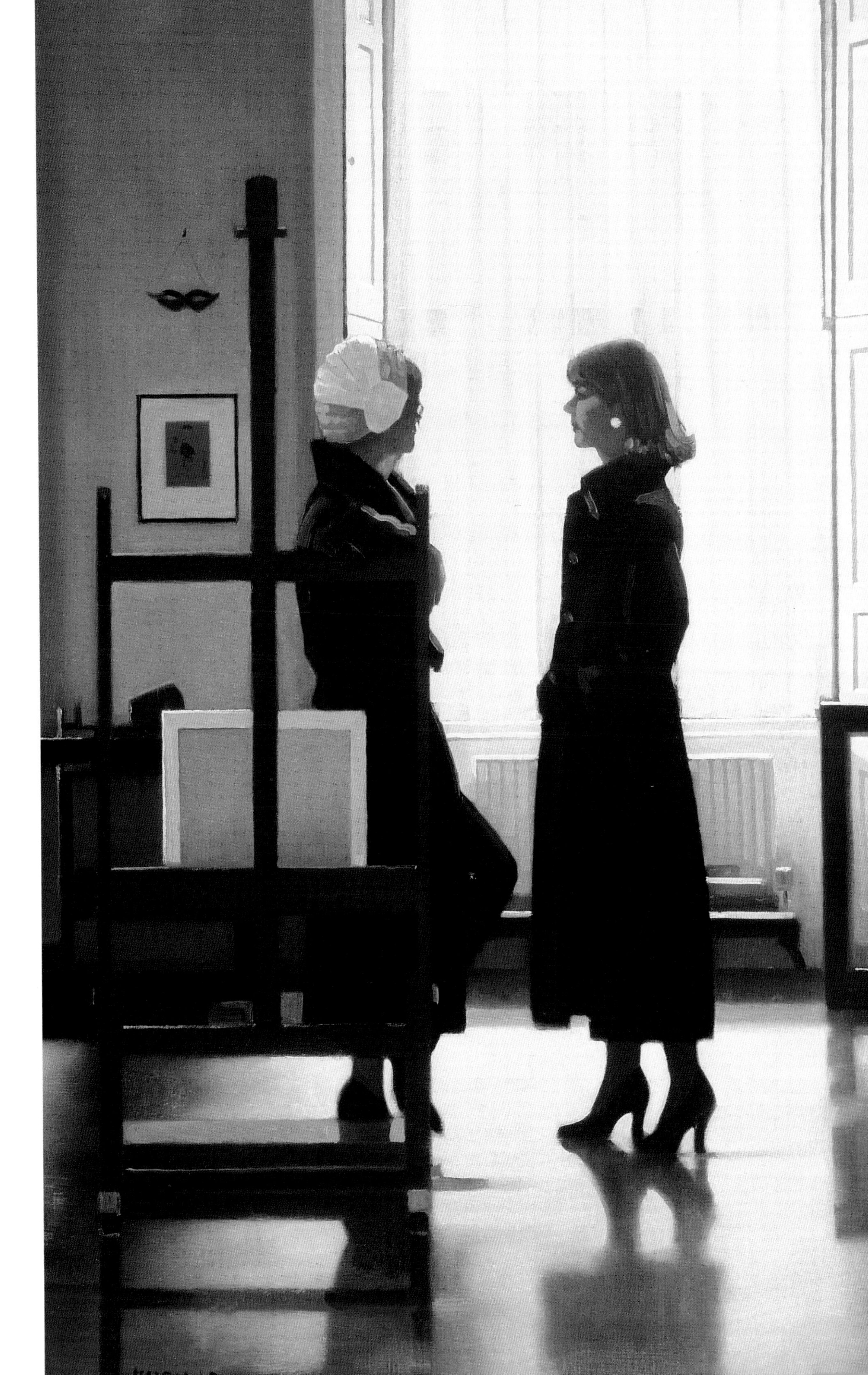

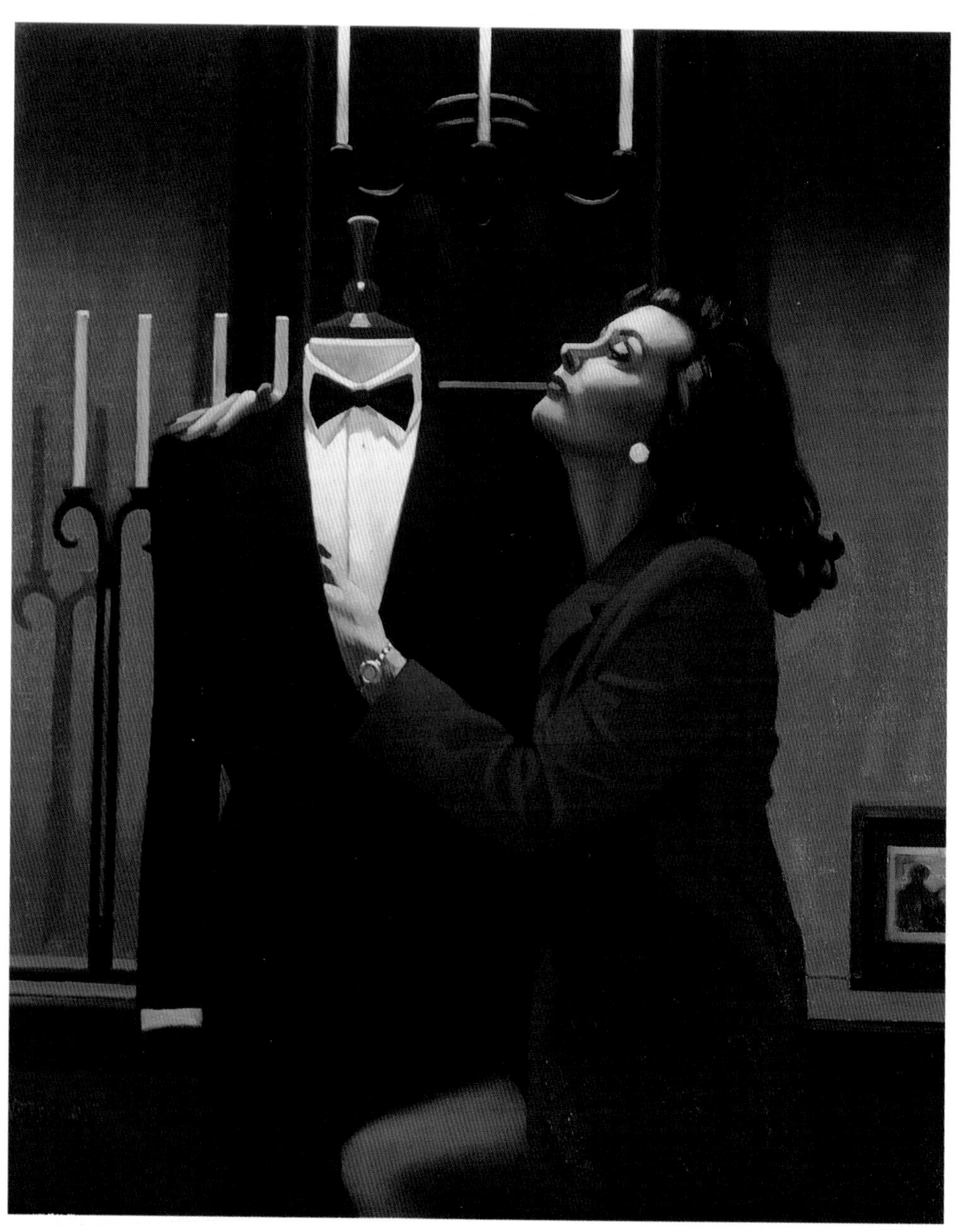

Another Kind of Love

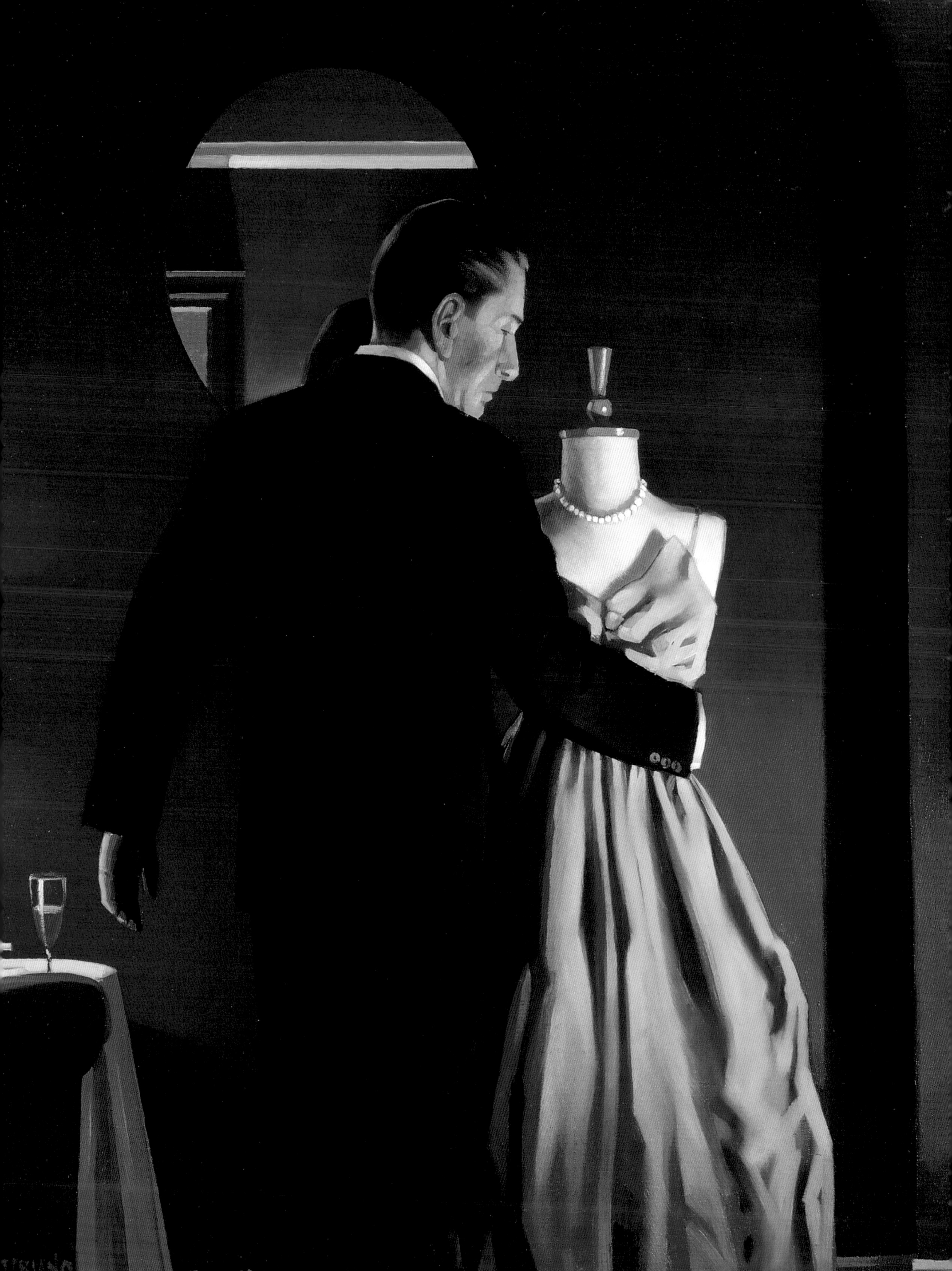

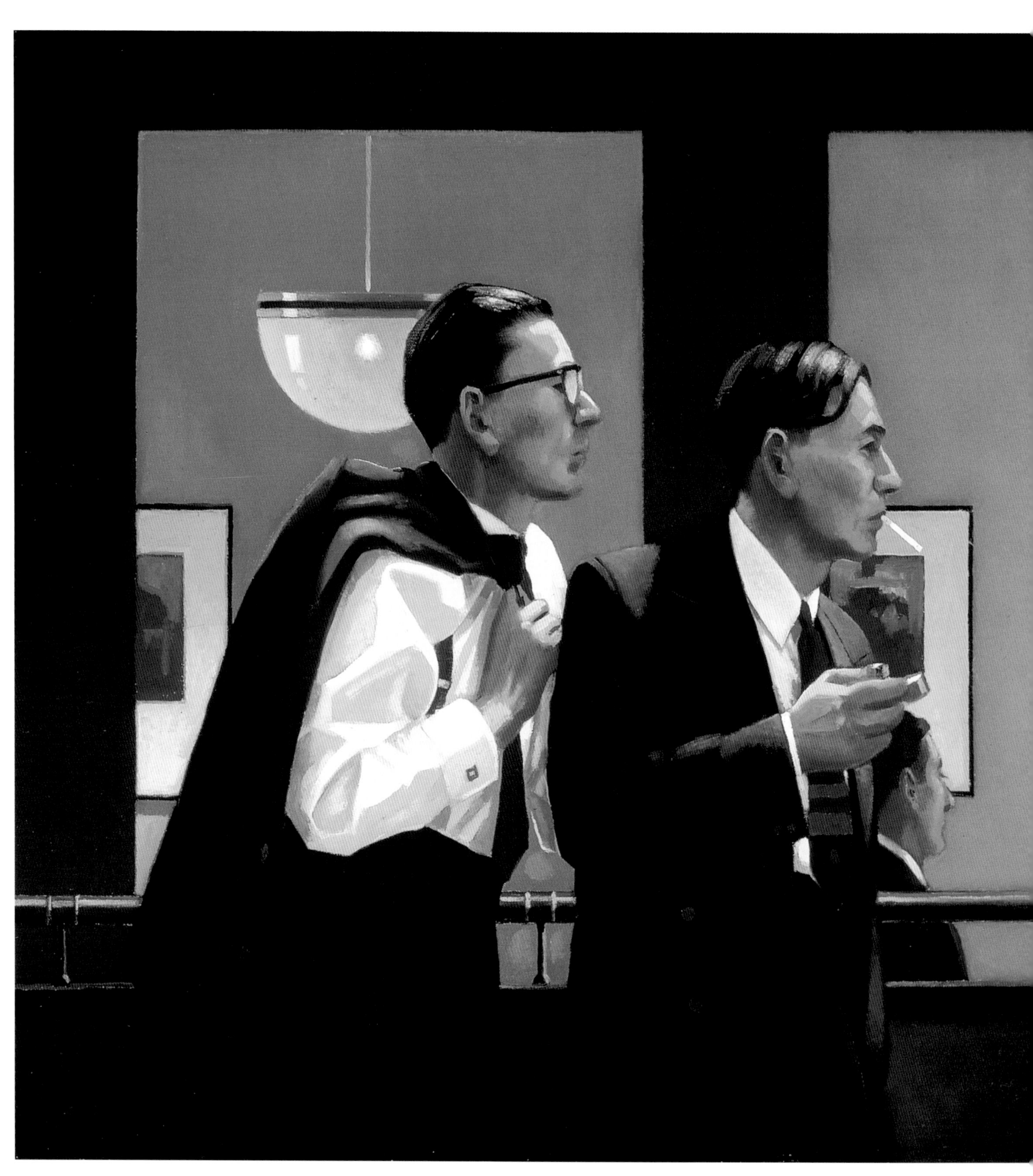

Men in White Shirts

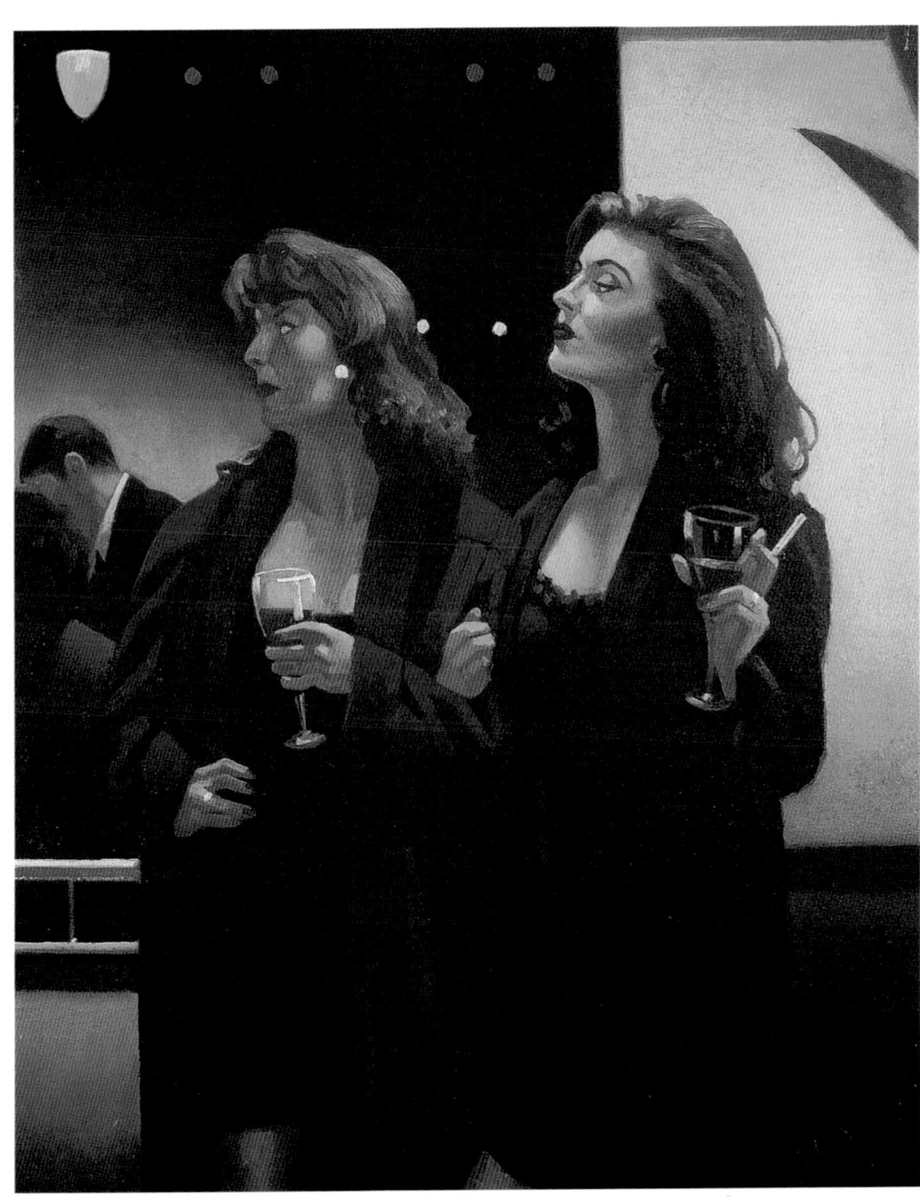

Girls' Night

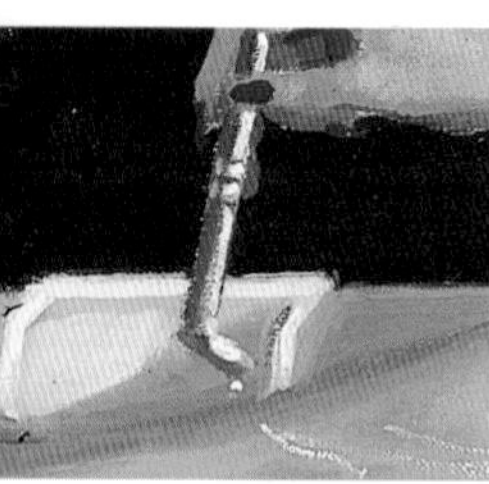

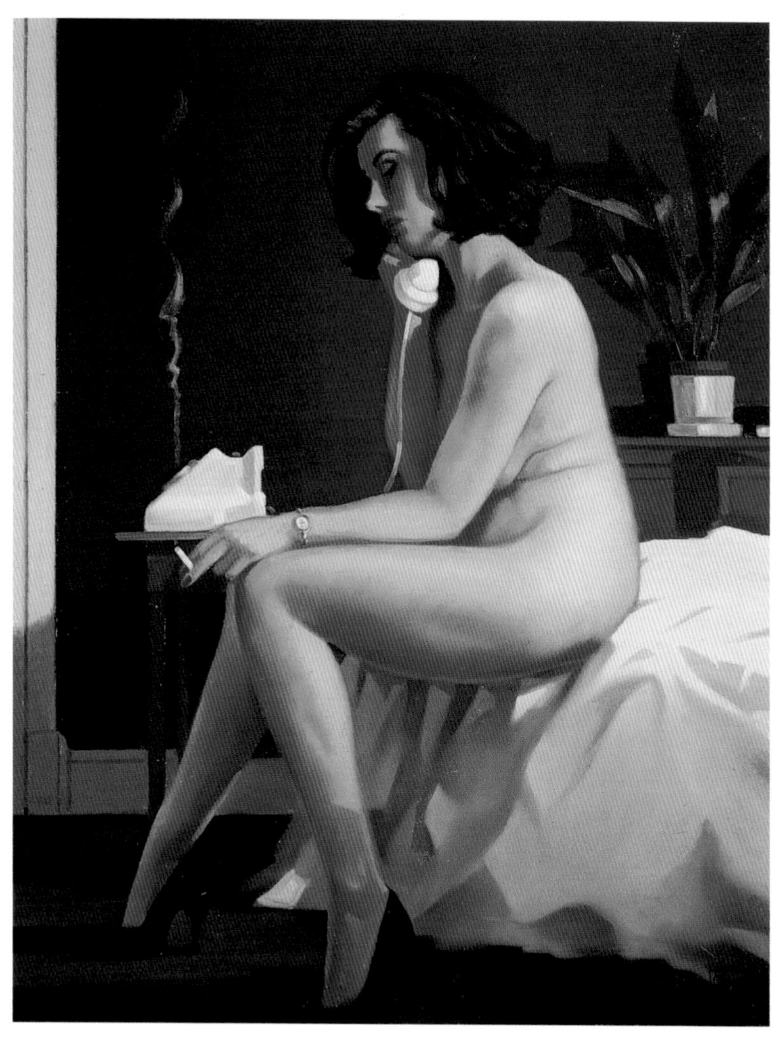

The Arrangement

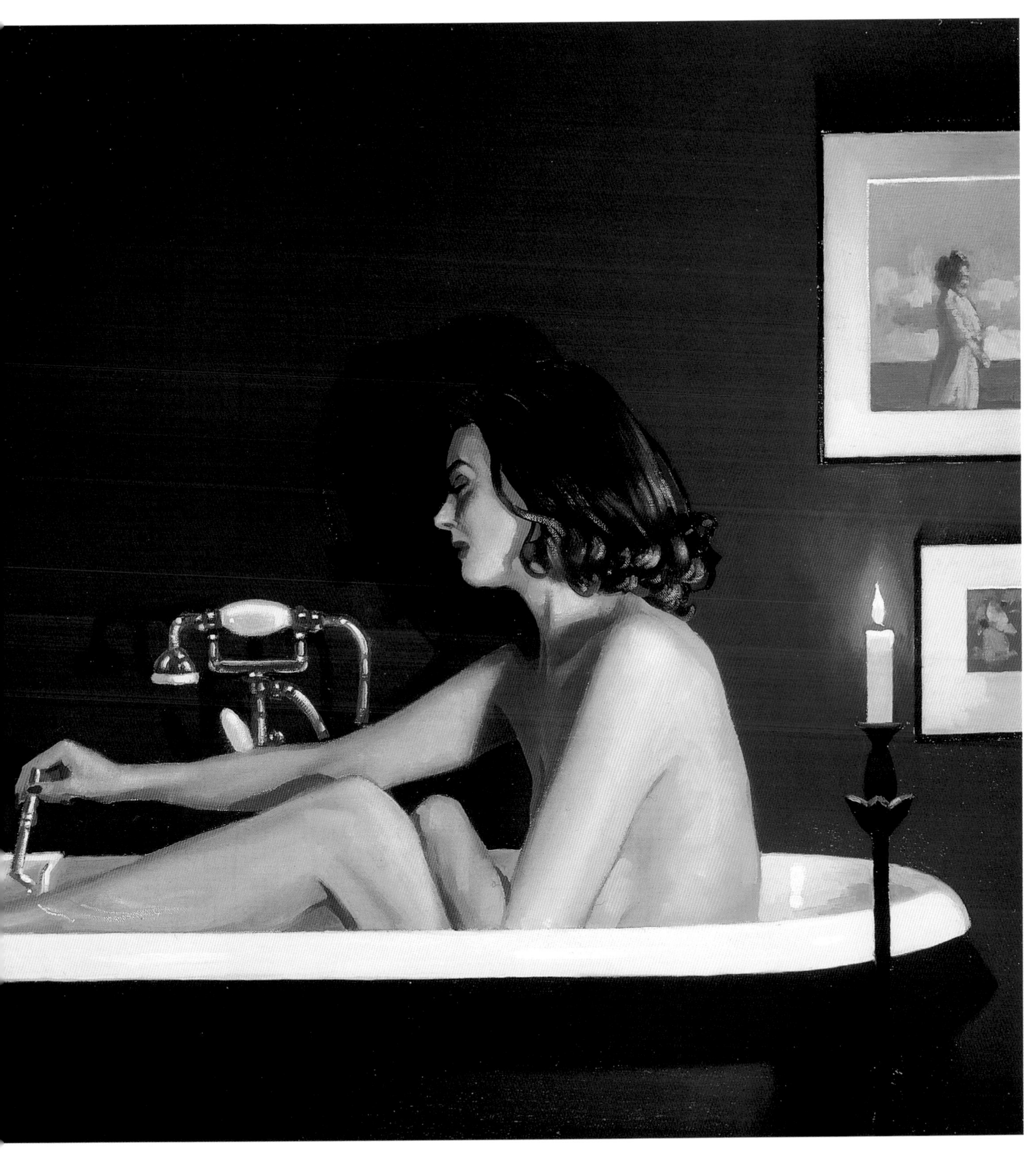

Night Preparations

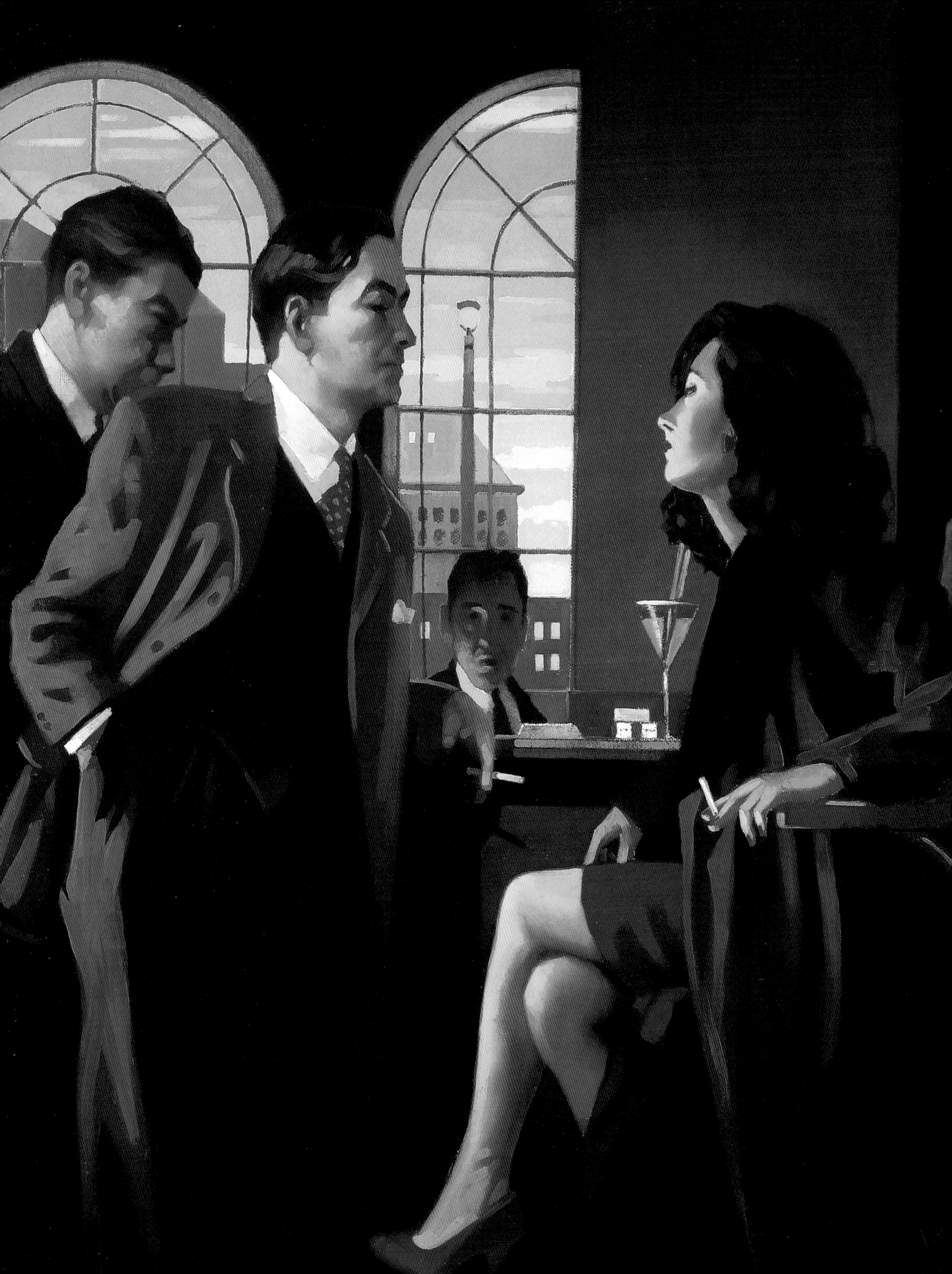

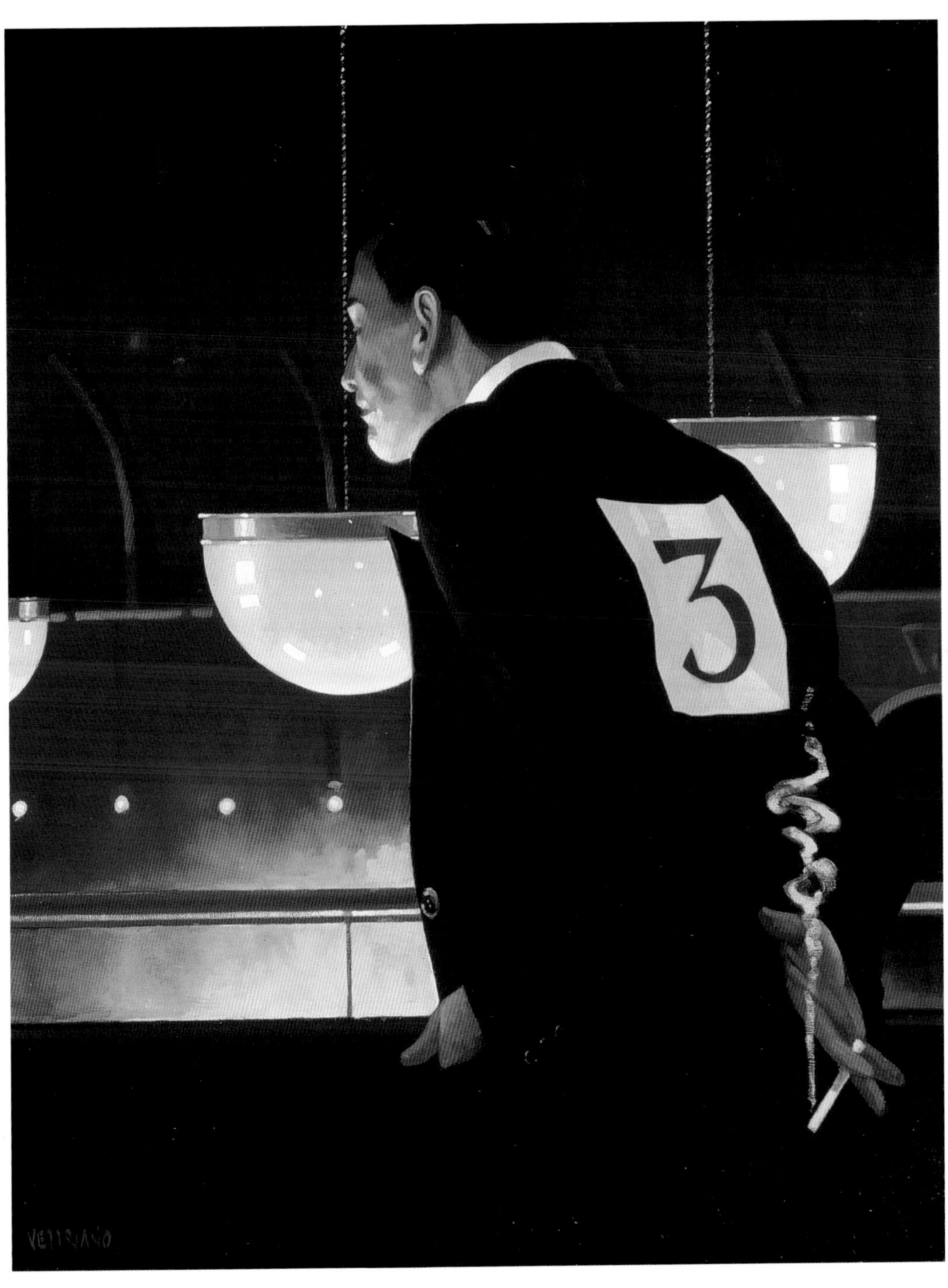

Ballroom Spy

Private Dancer

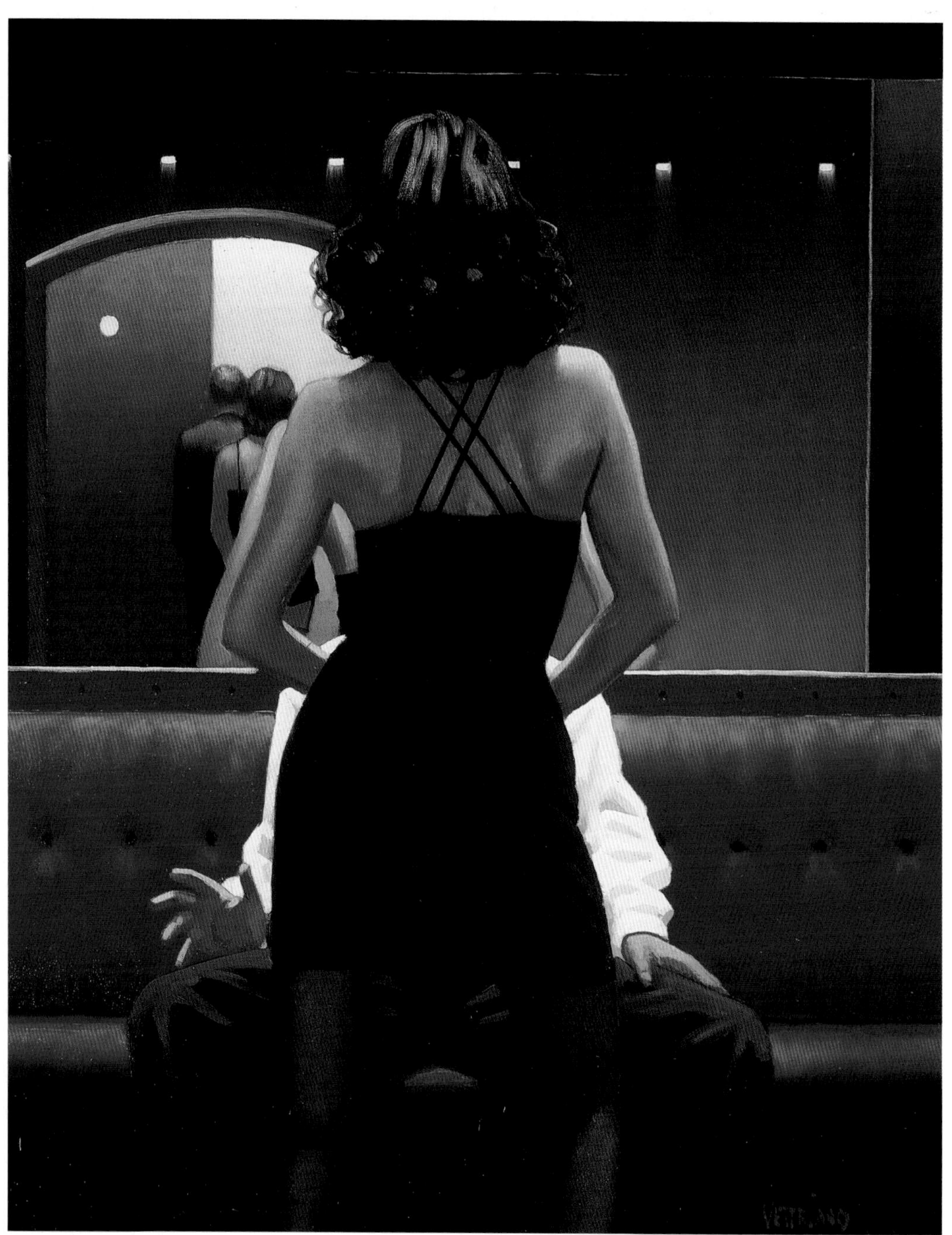

The Purple Cat

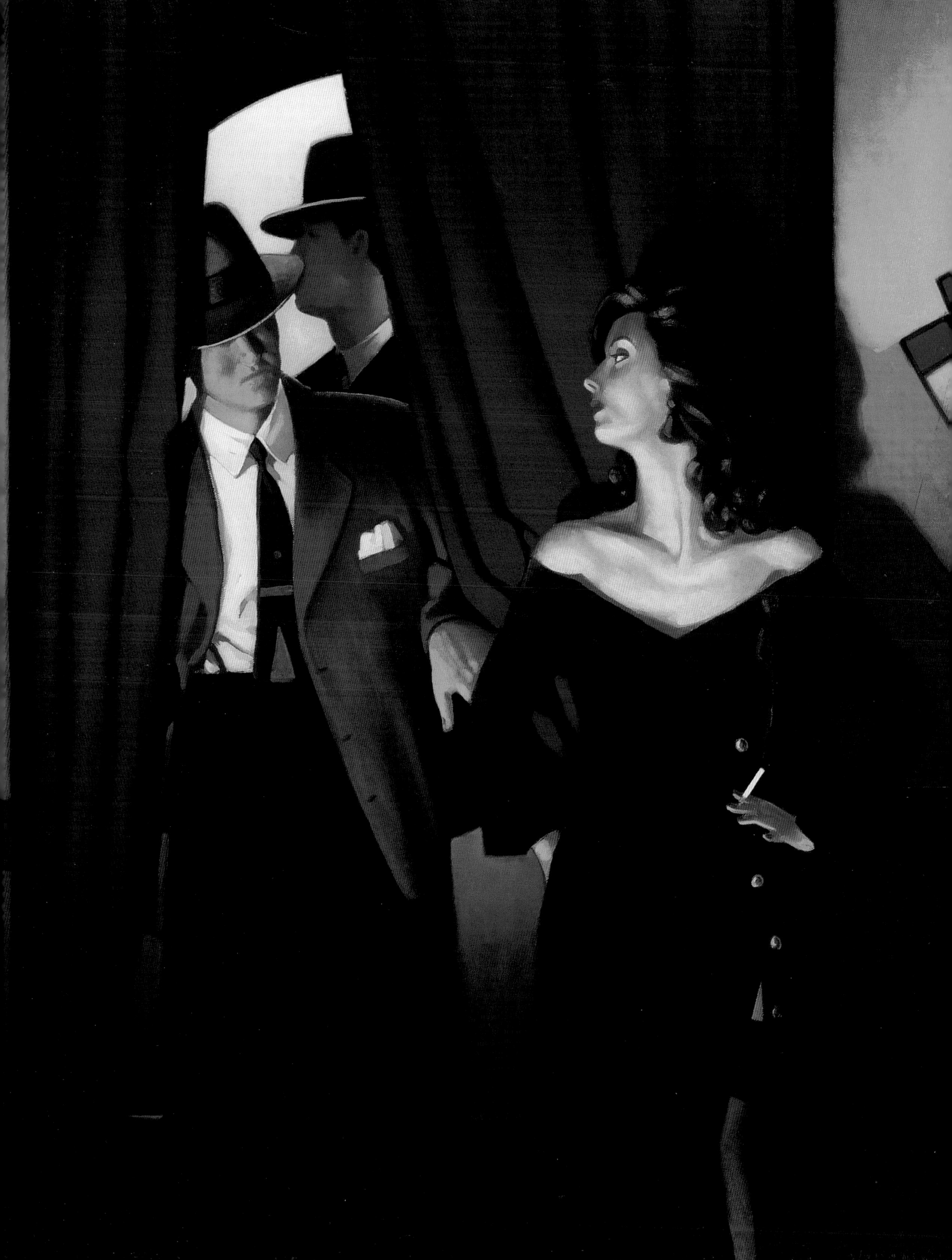

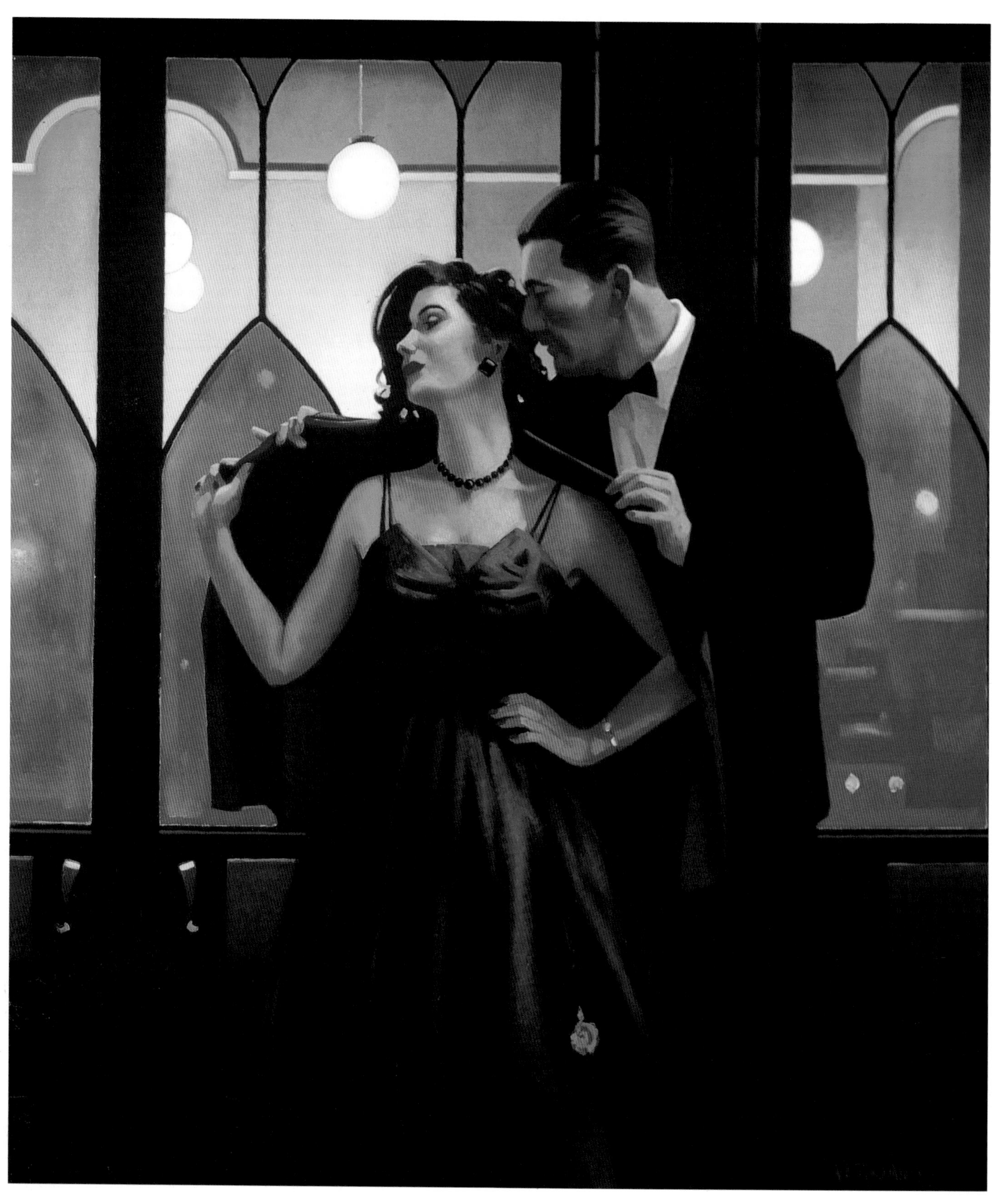

Words of Wisdom

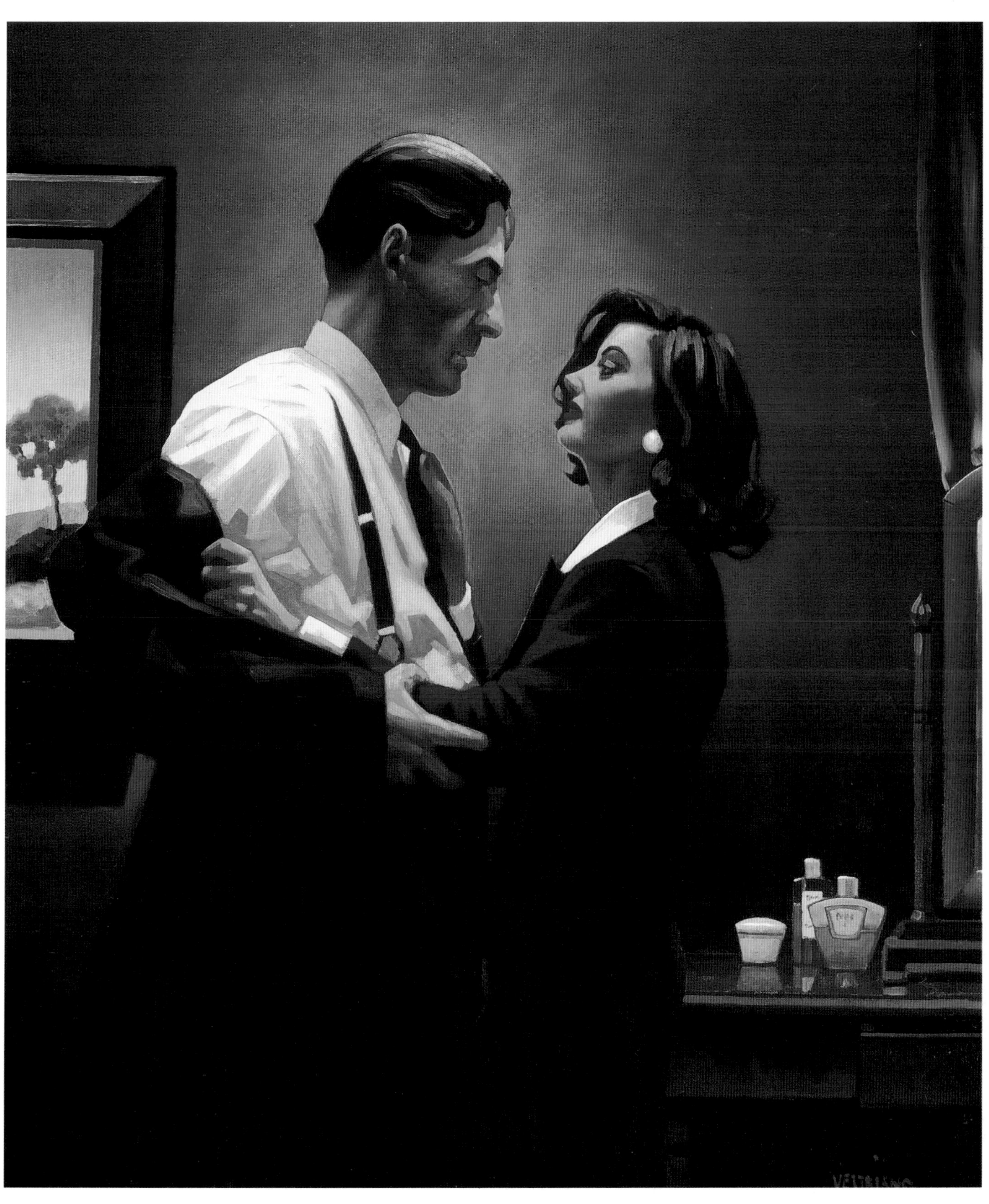

Welcome to My World

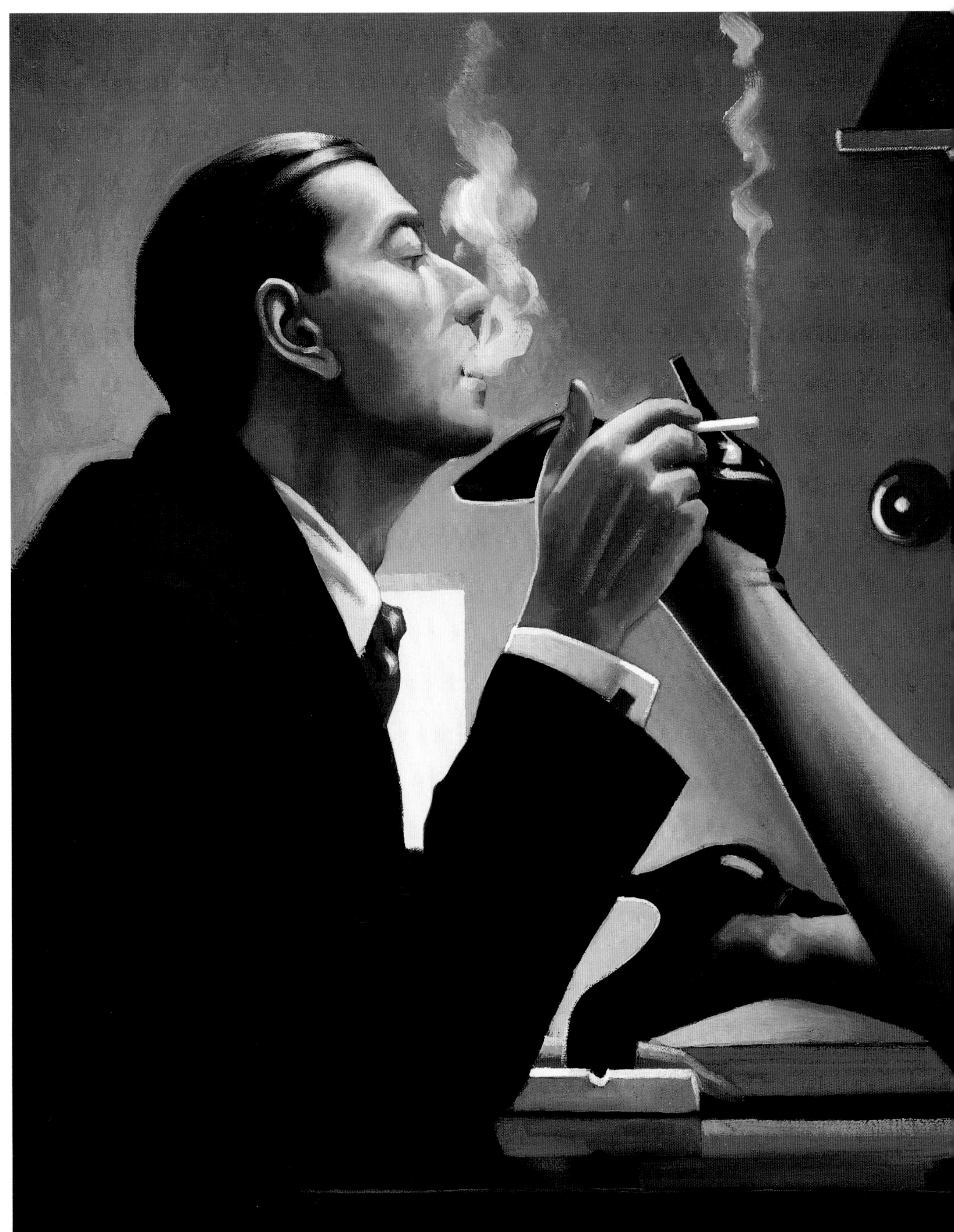

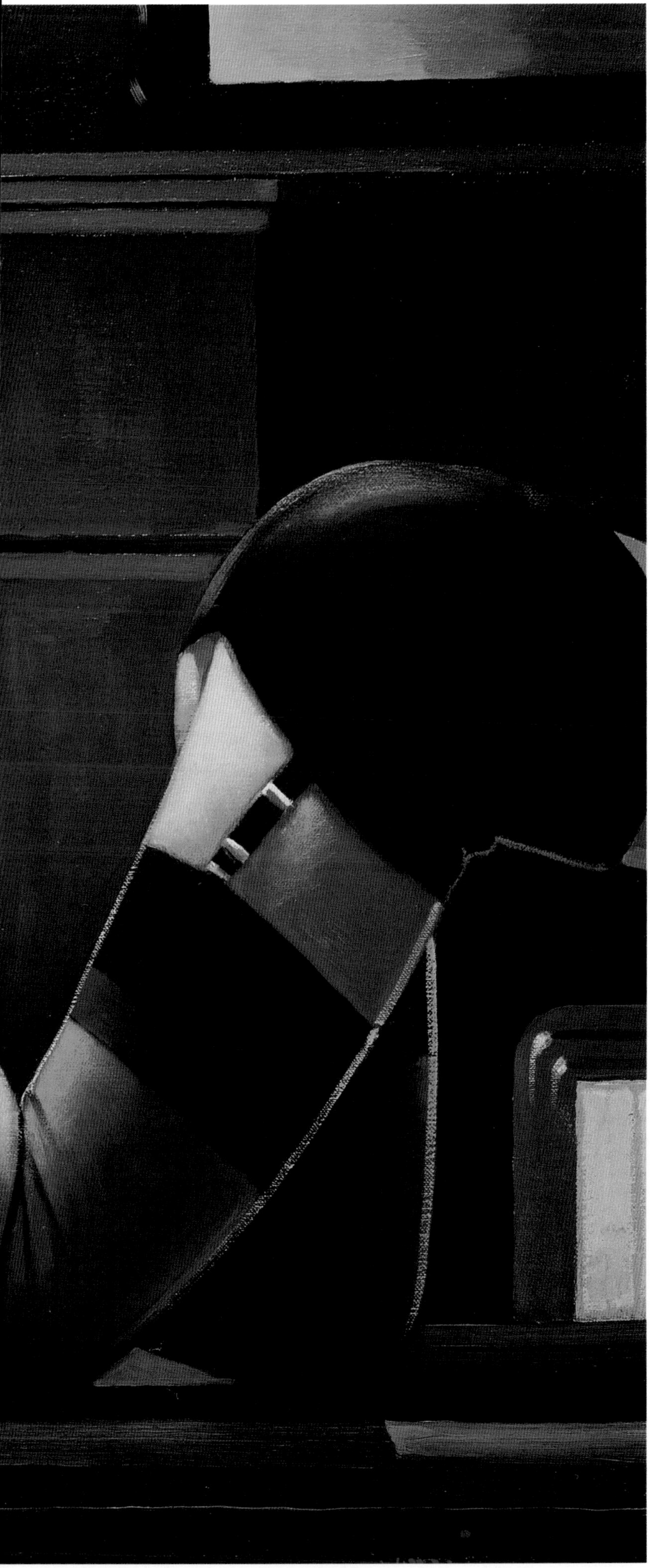

Fetish

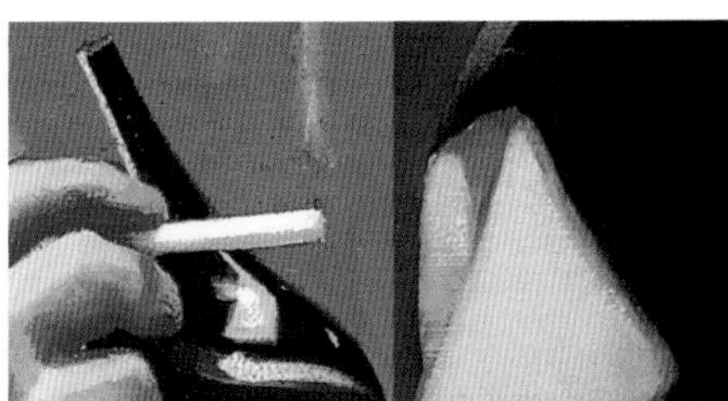

Between Darkness and Dawn

(Following page)

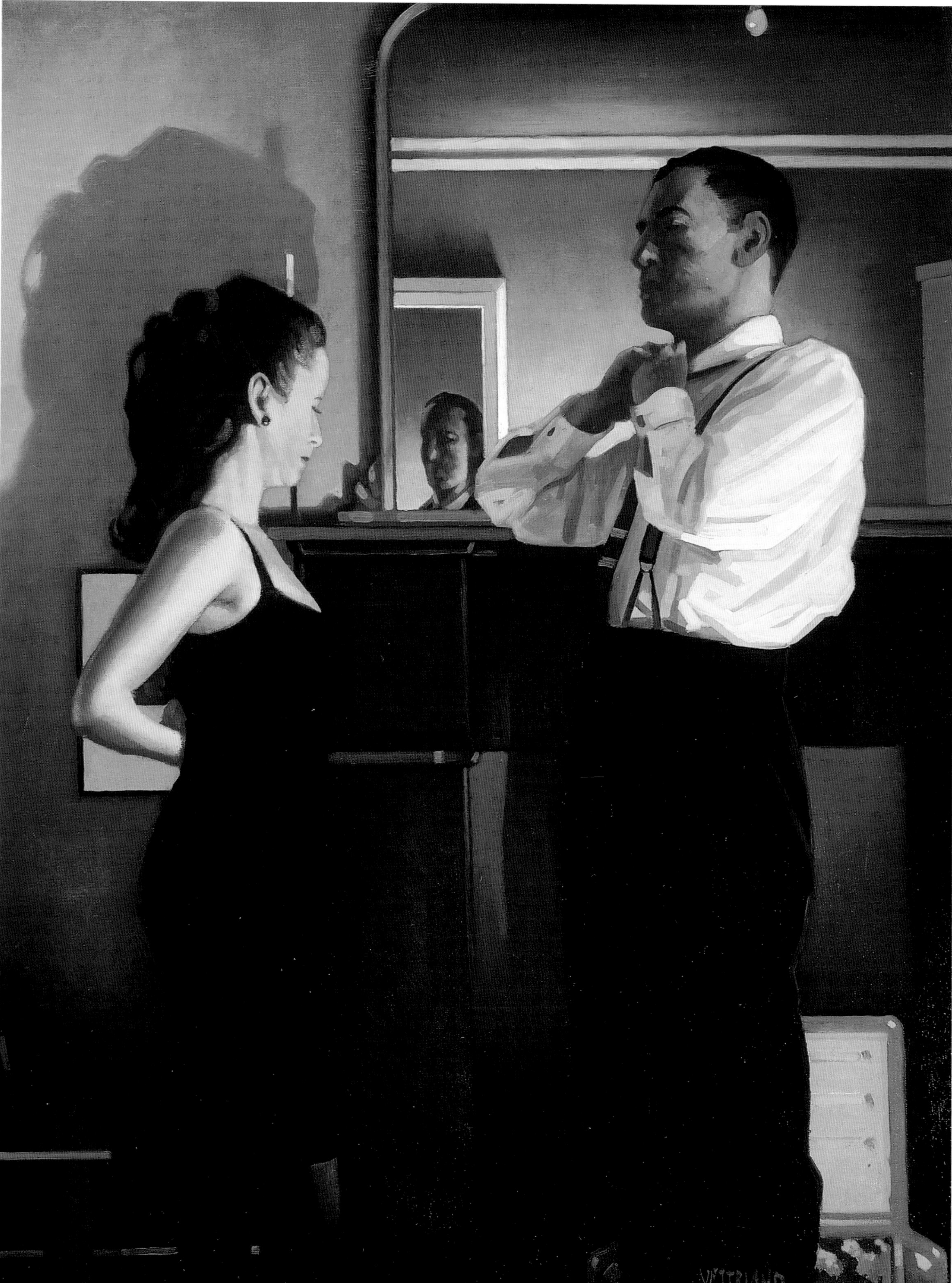
VETTRIANO

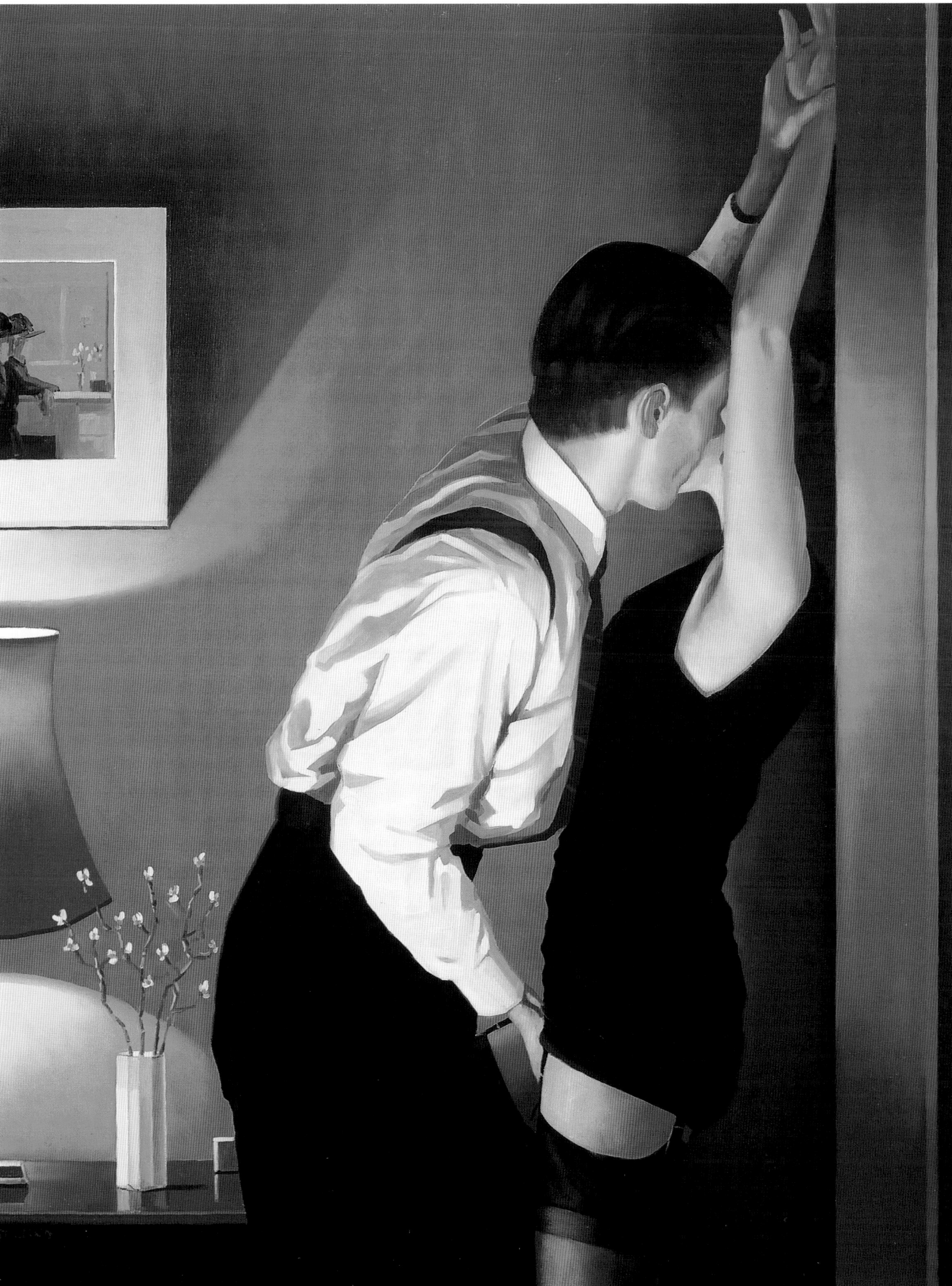

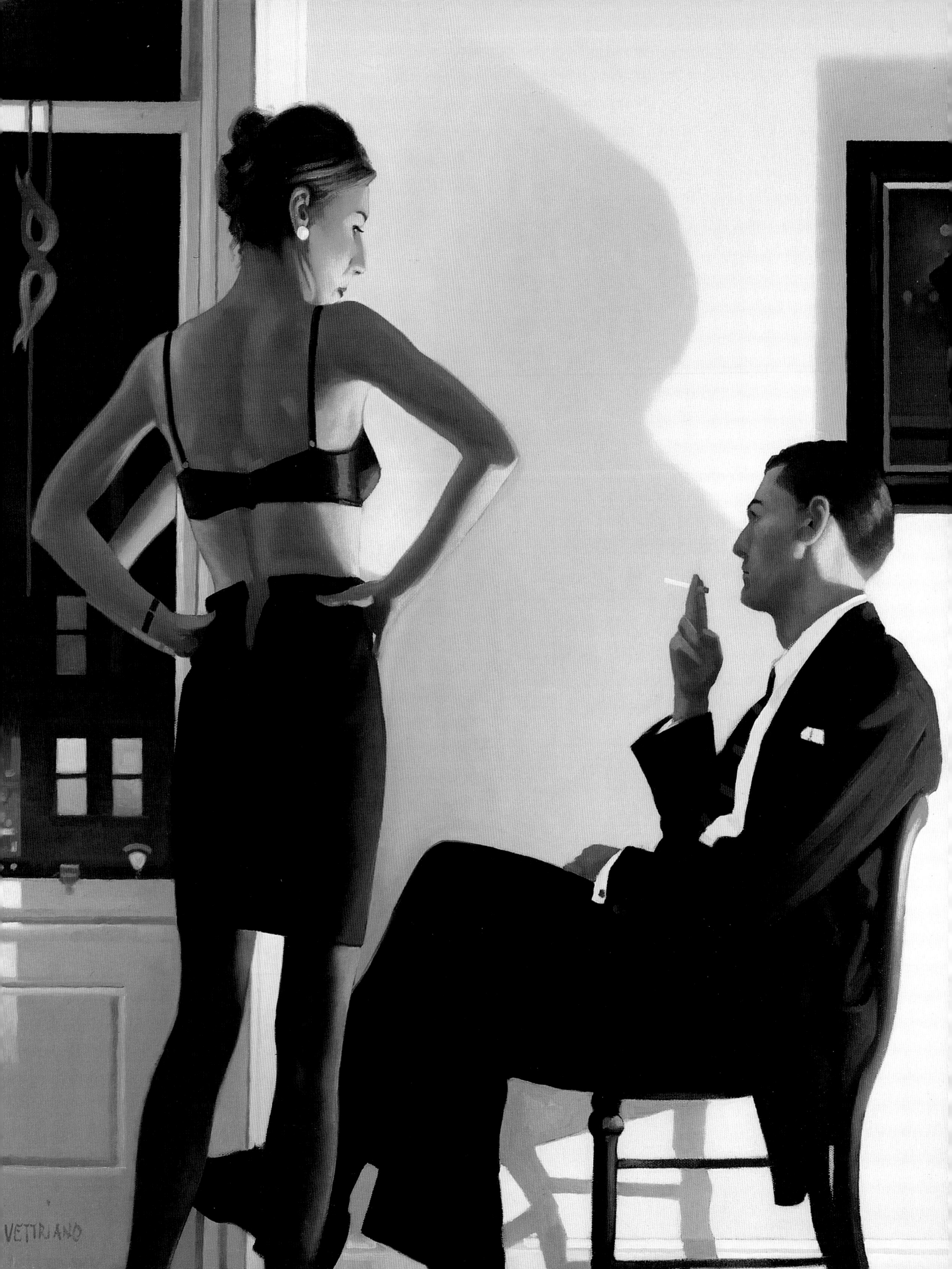
VETTRIANO

The Sailor's Toy

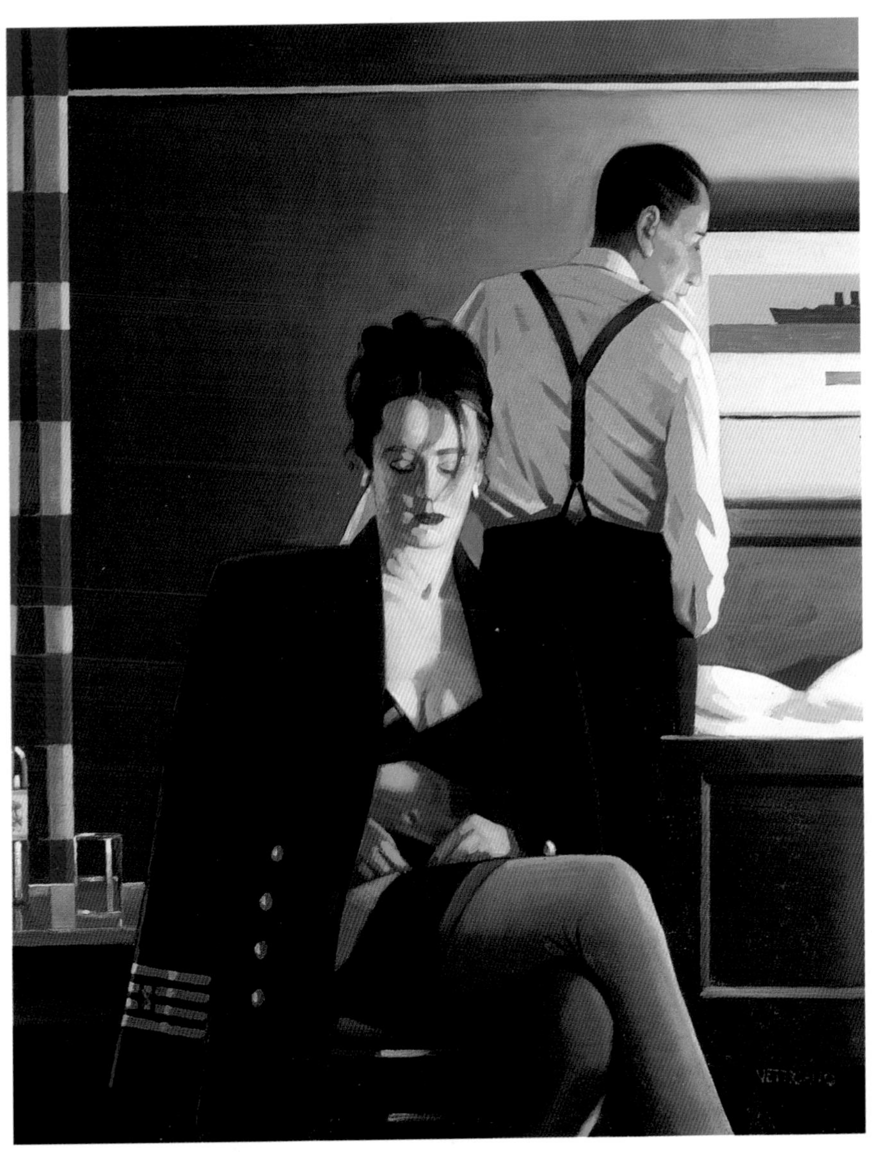

Game On

(Previous page)

Night in The City

Rough Trade

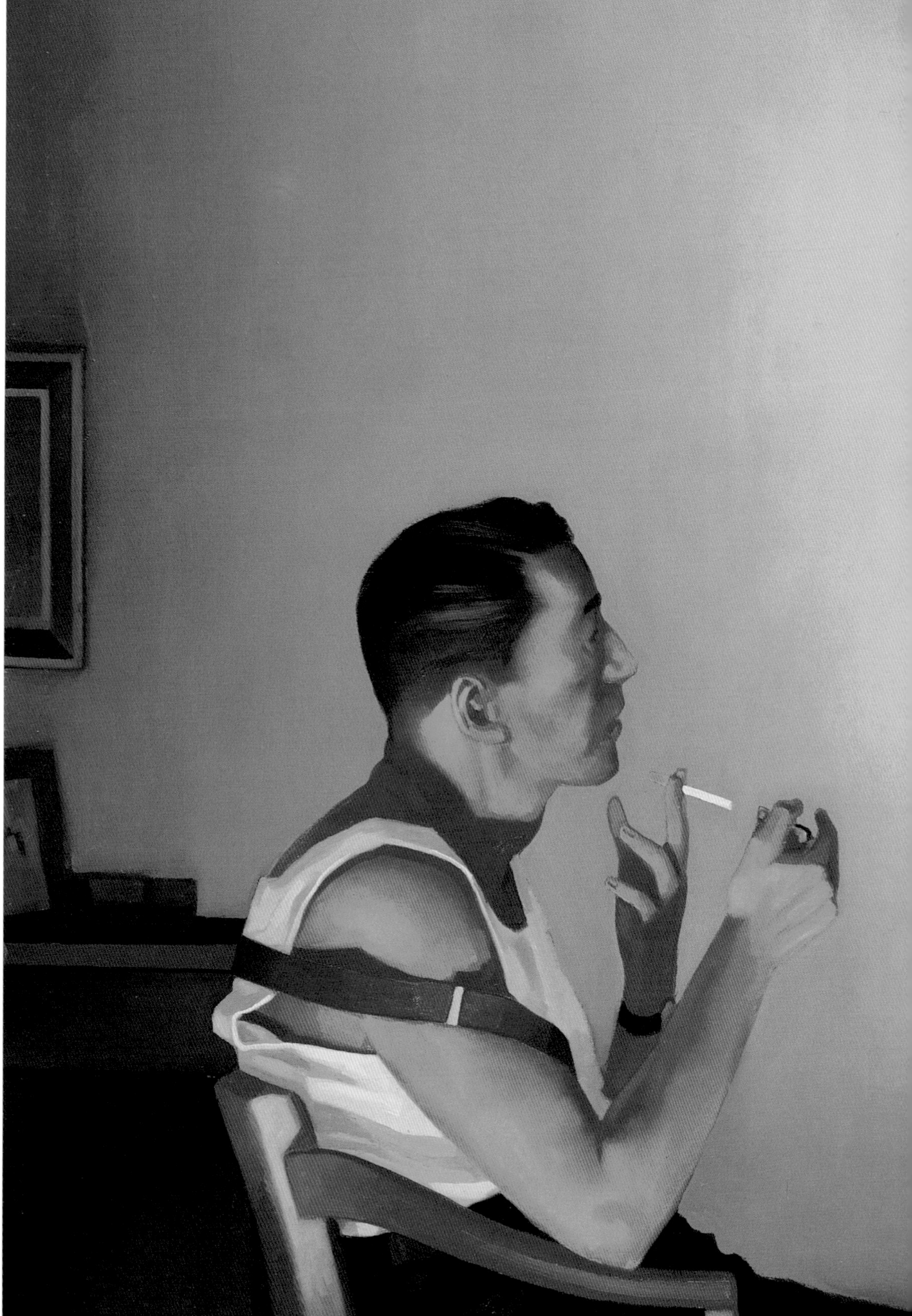

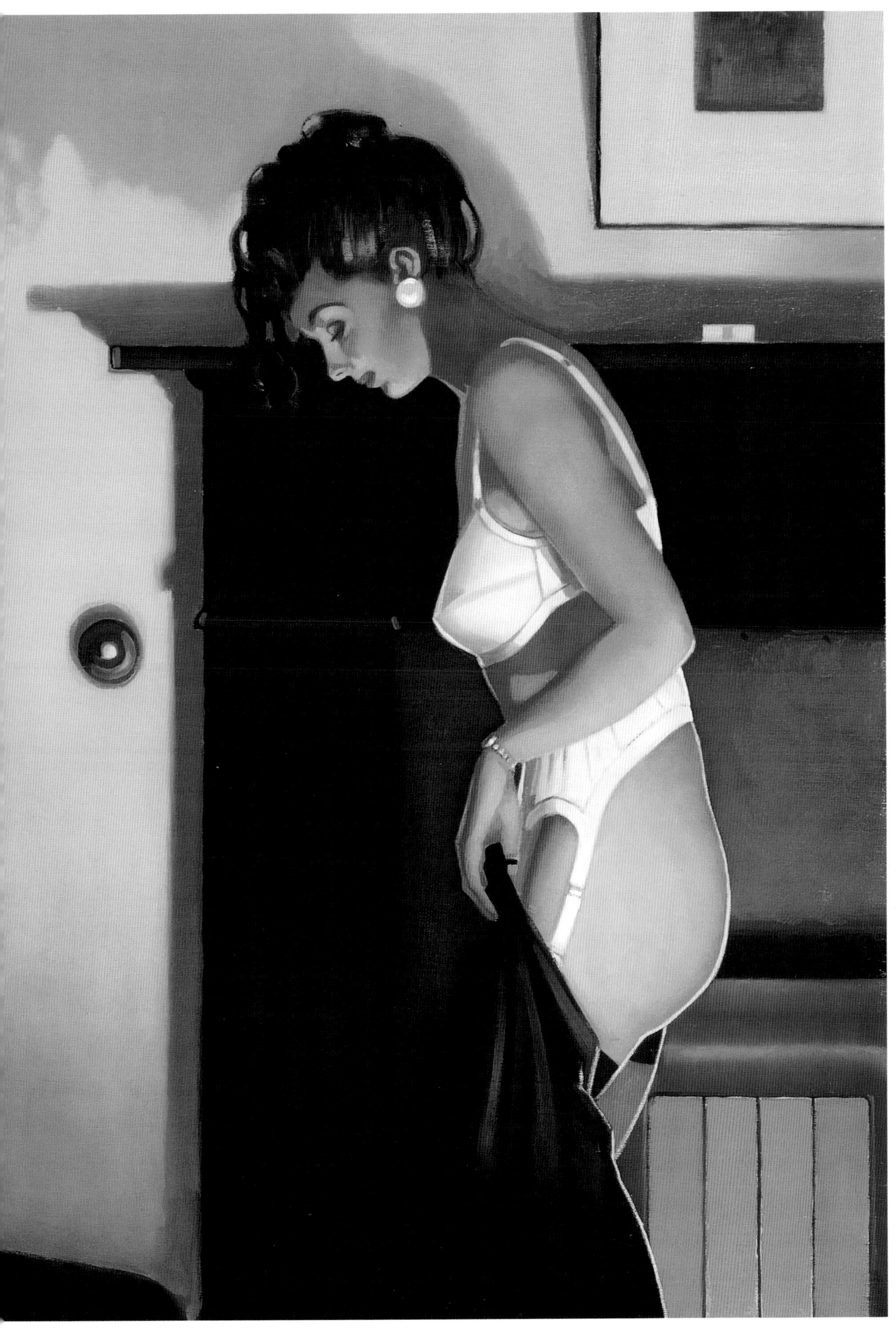

Beautiful Losers

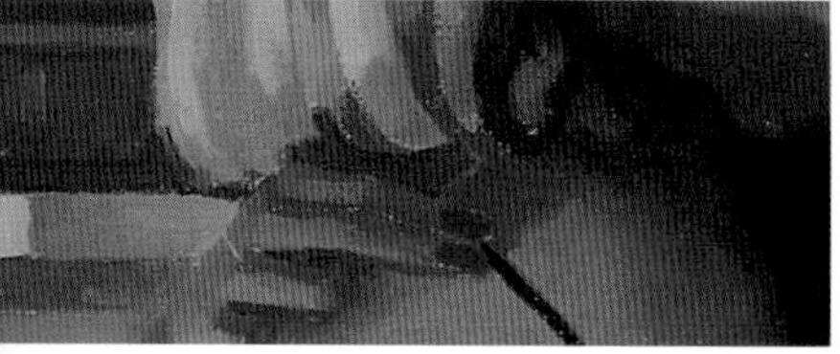

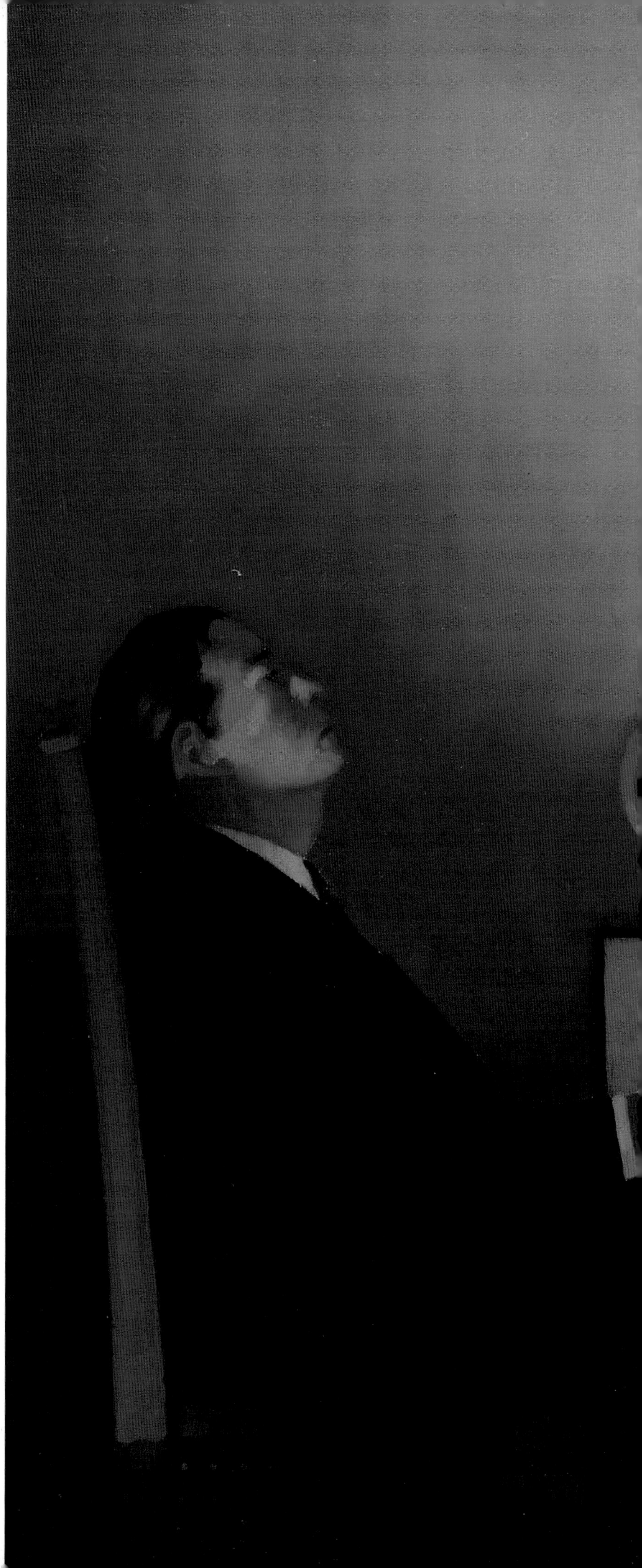

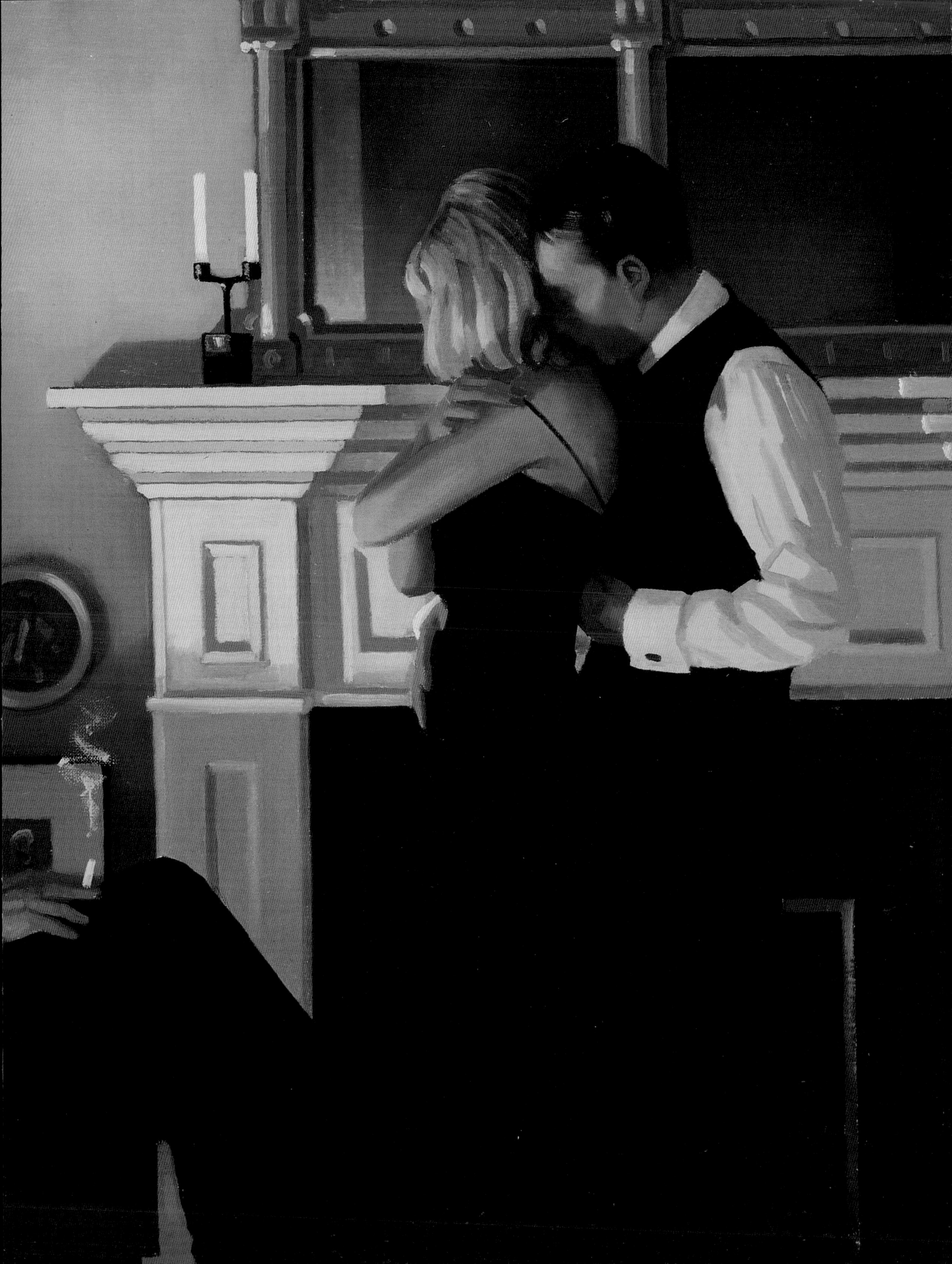

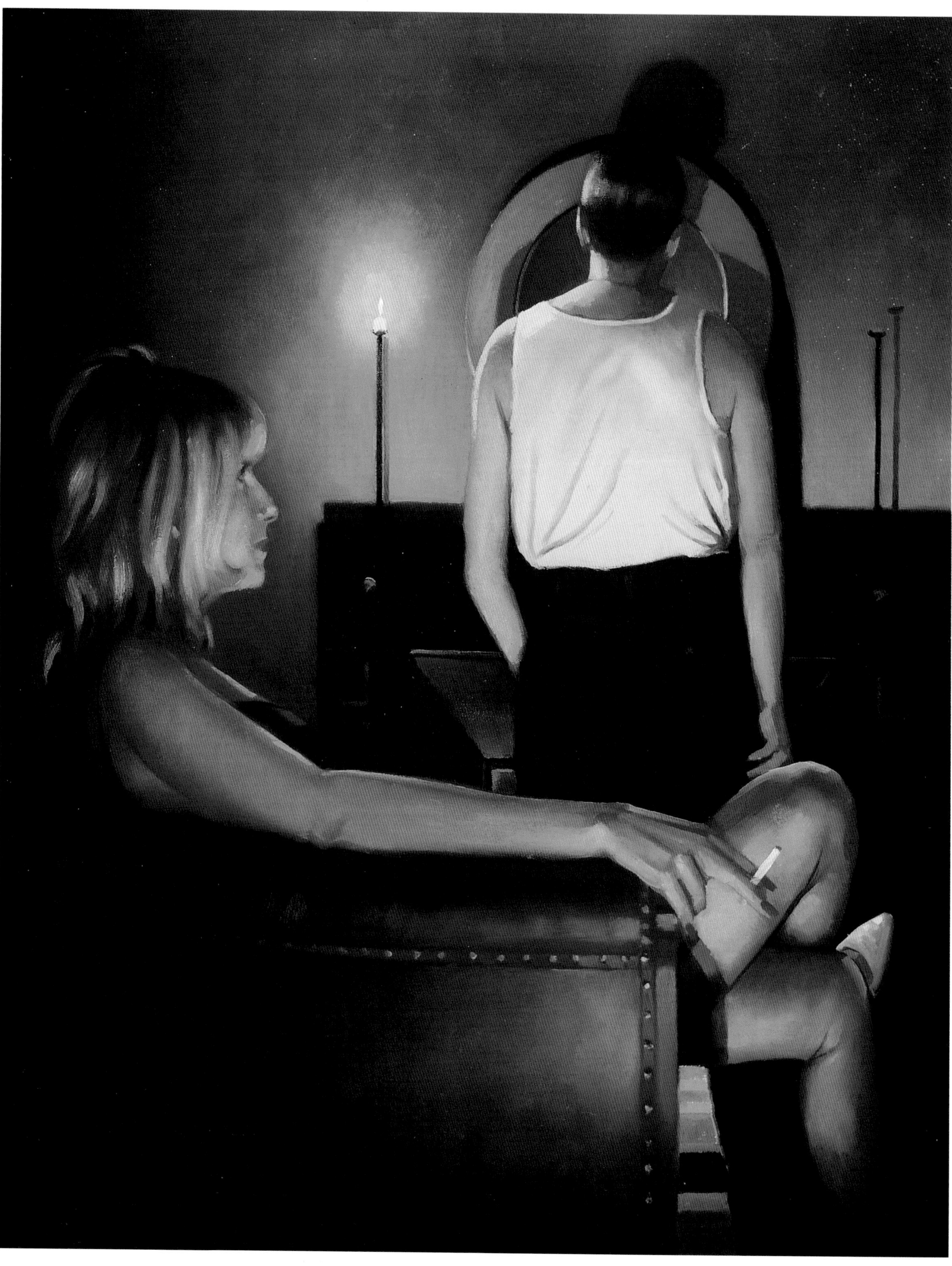

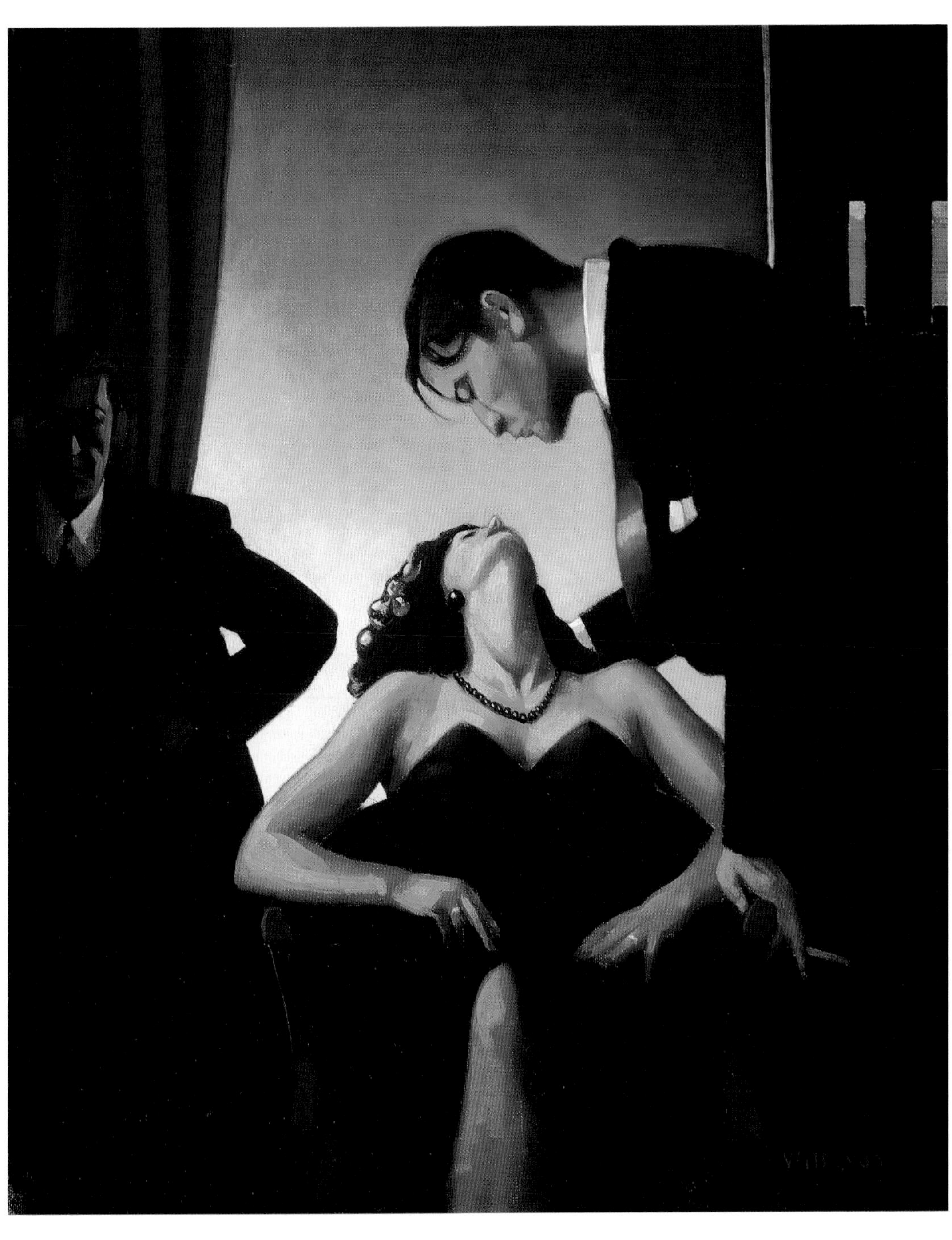

Games of Power

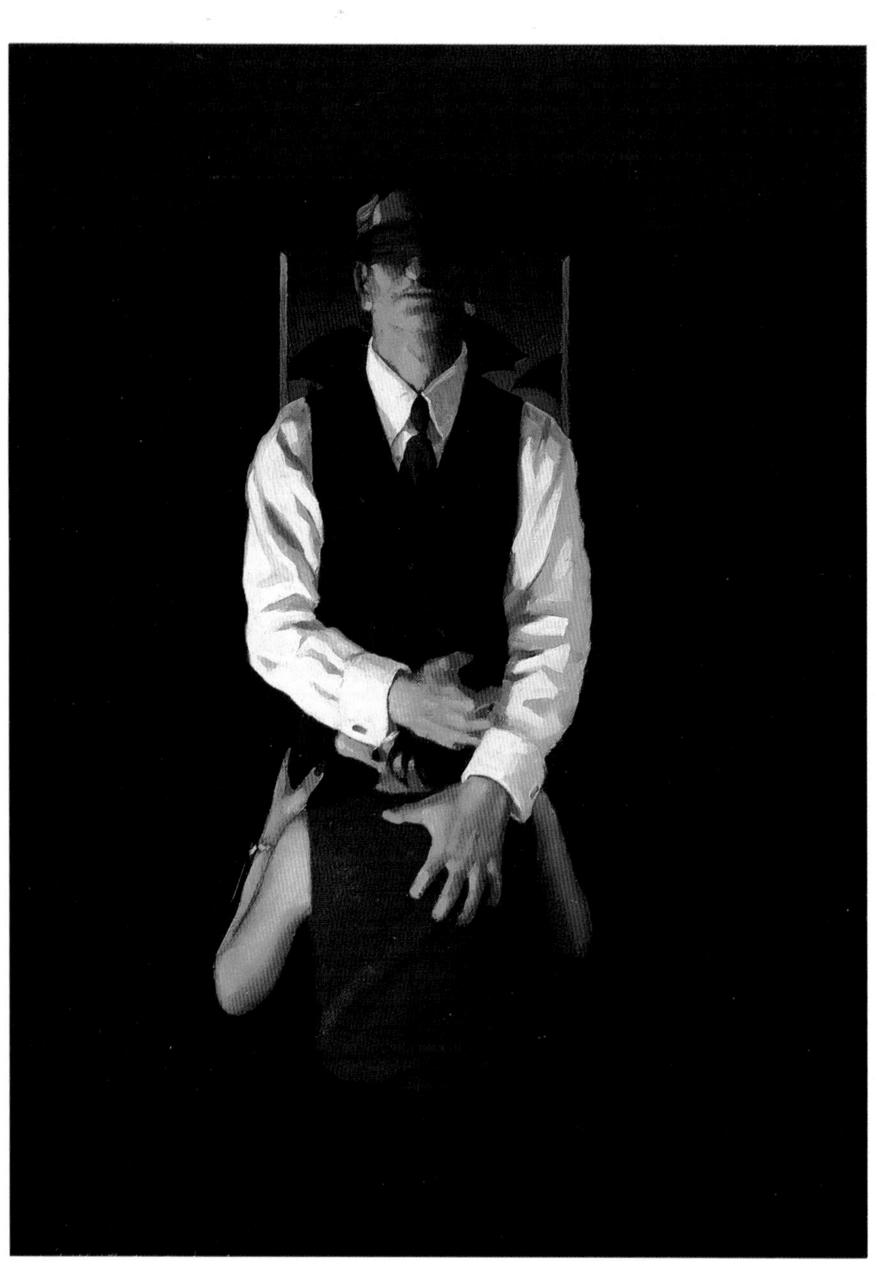

A Strange and Tender Magic

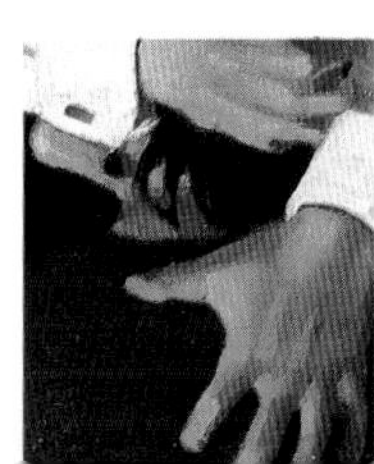

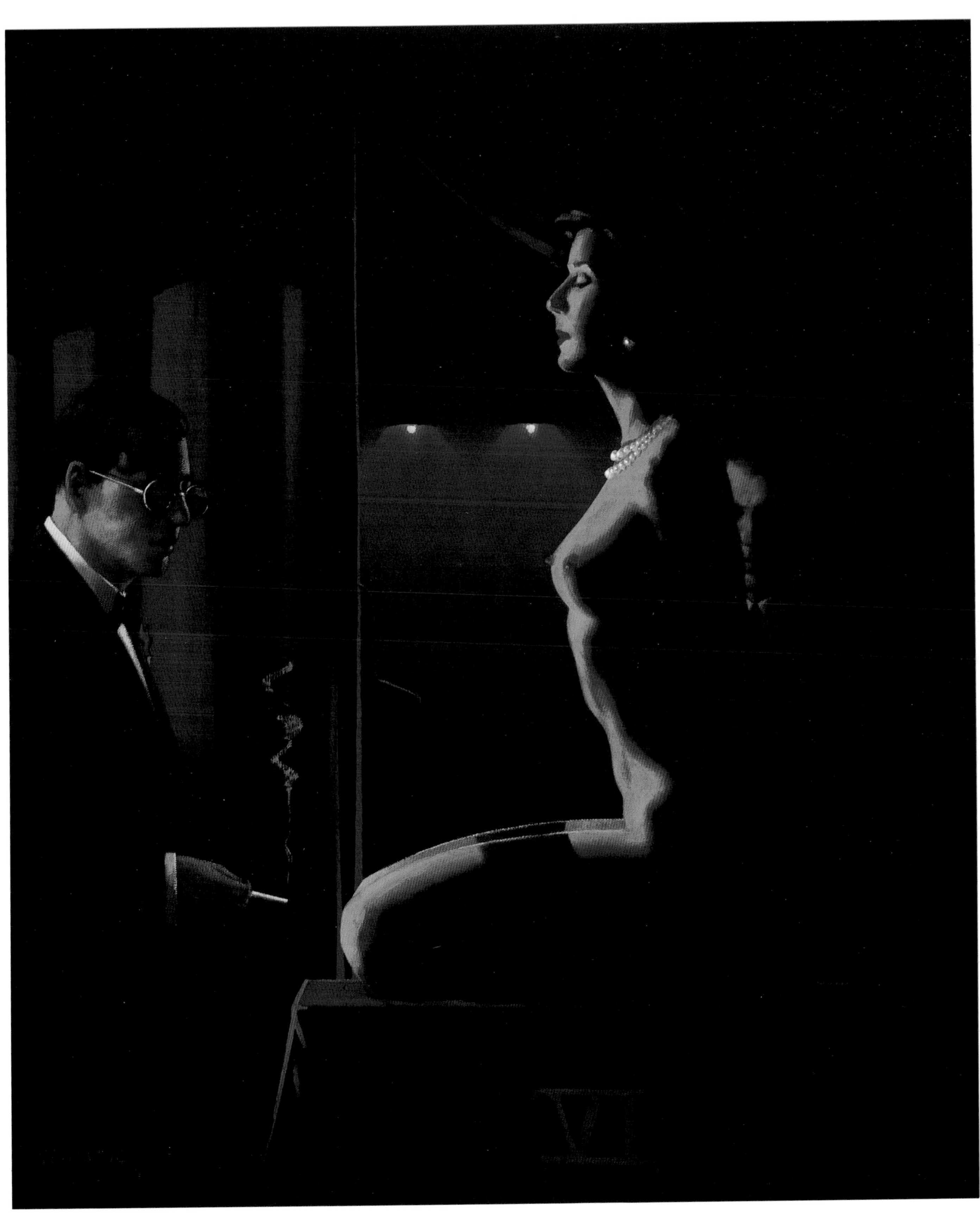

The Assessors

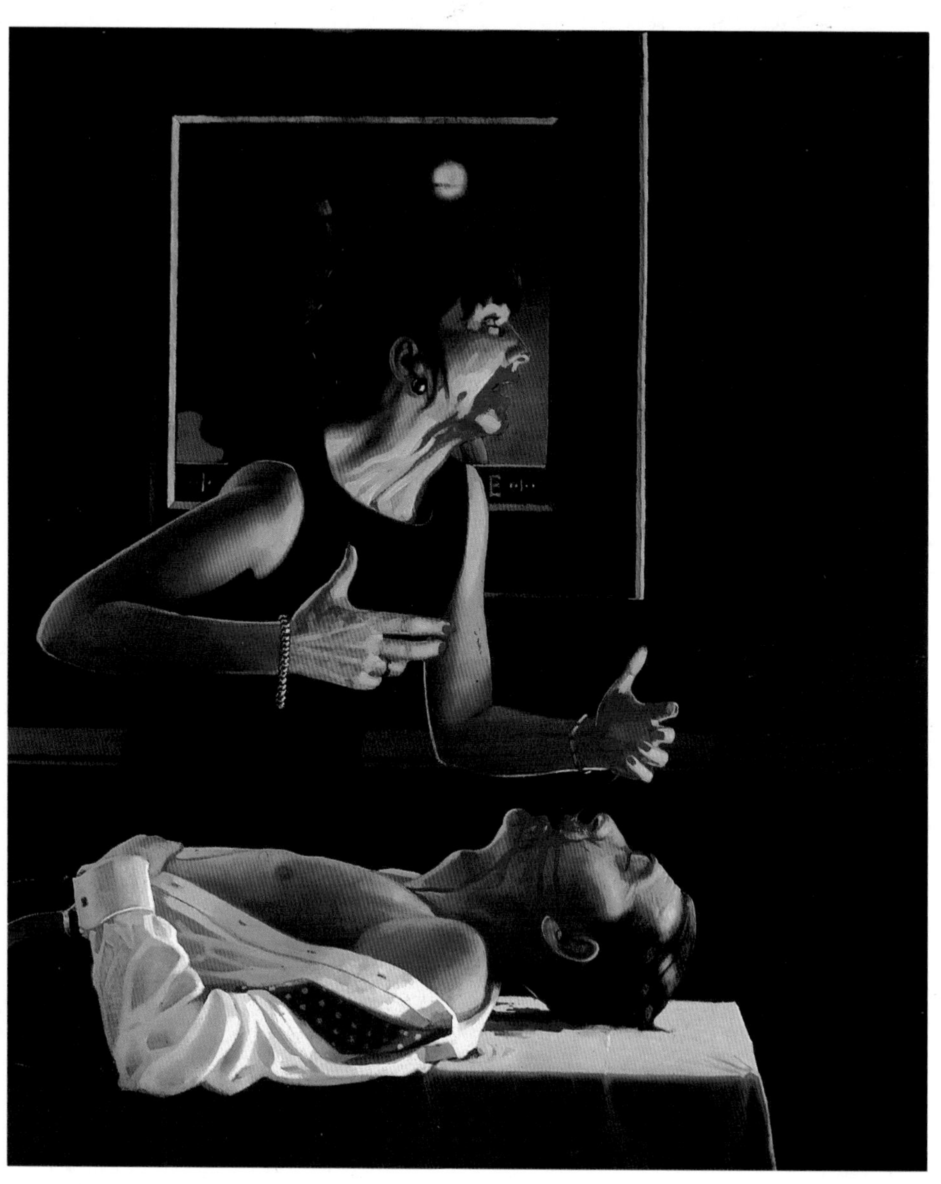

Feeding Frenzy

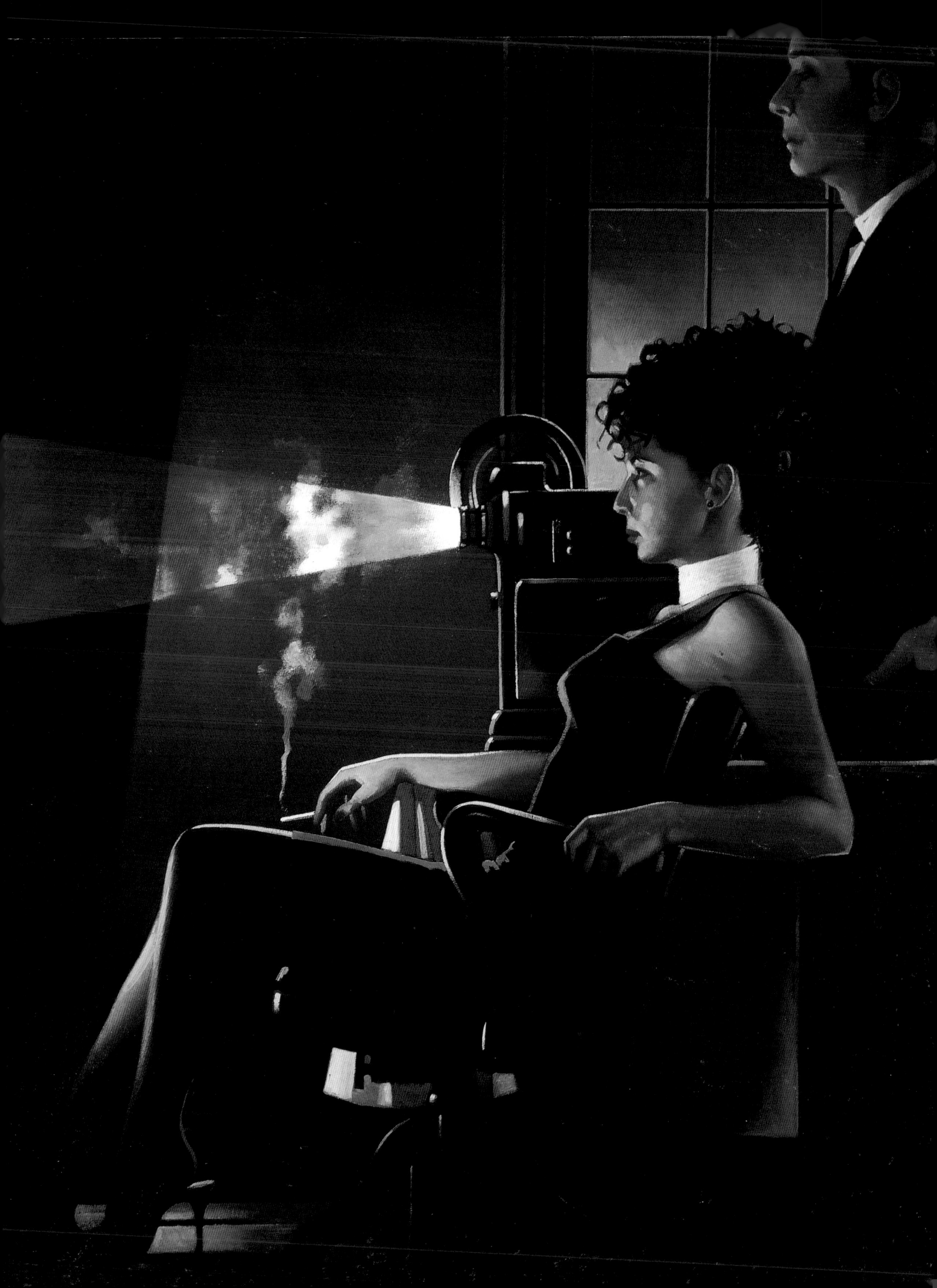

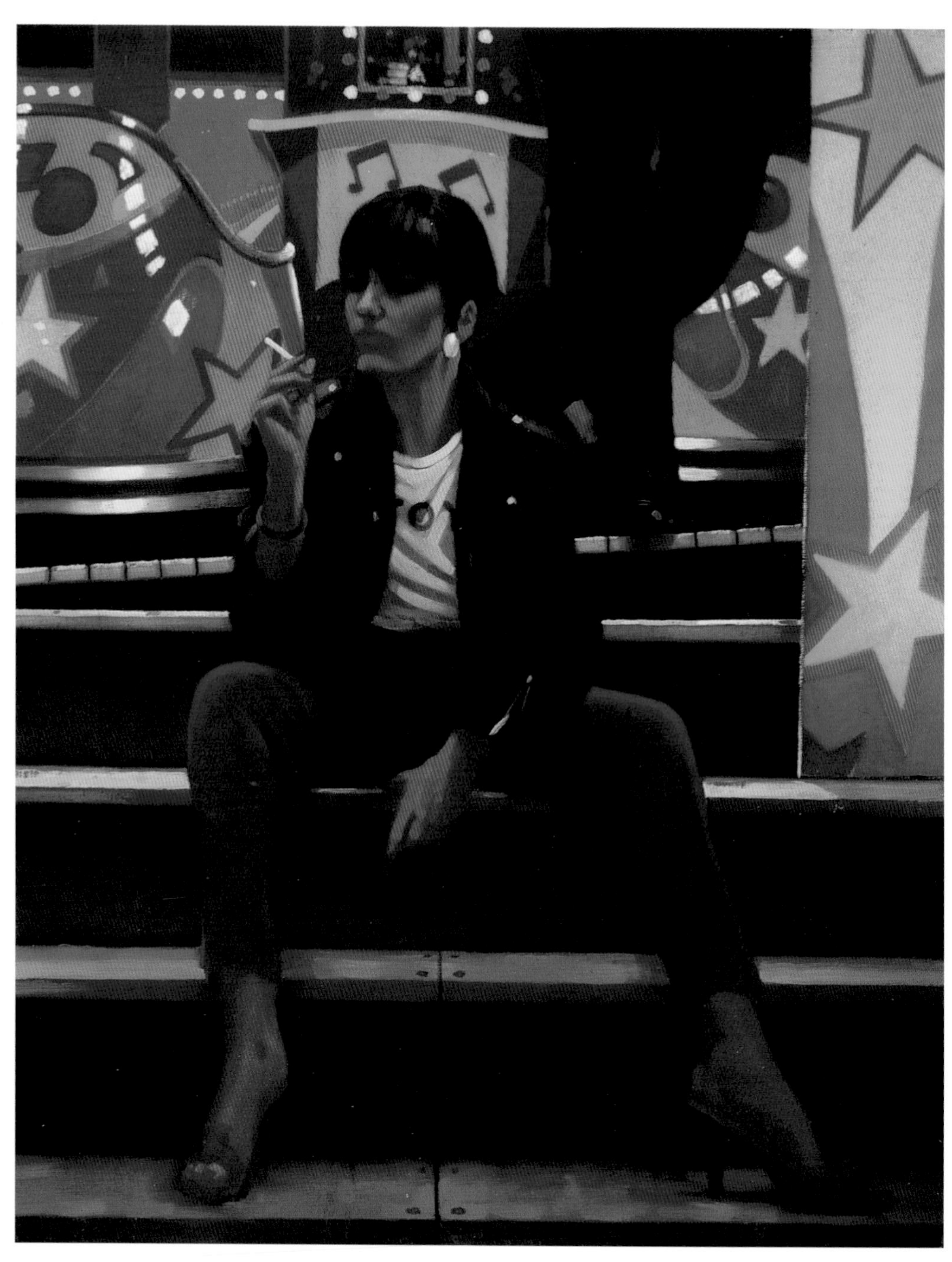

Queen of the Waltzer

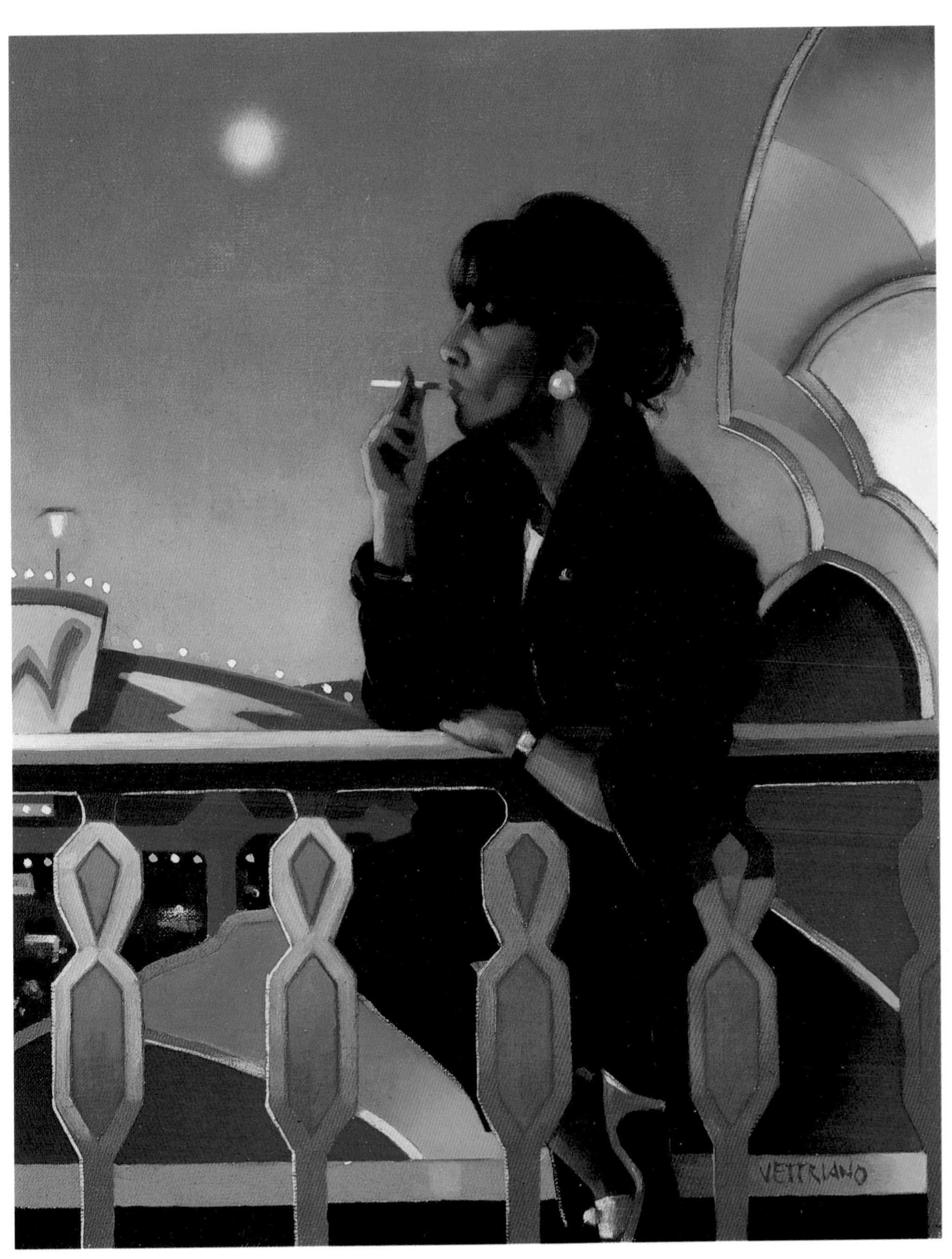

Birdy

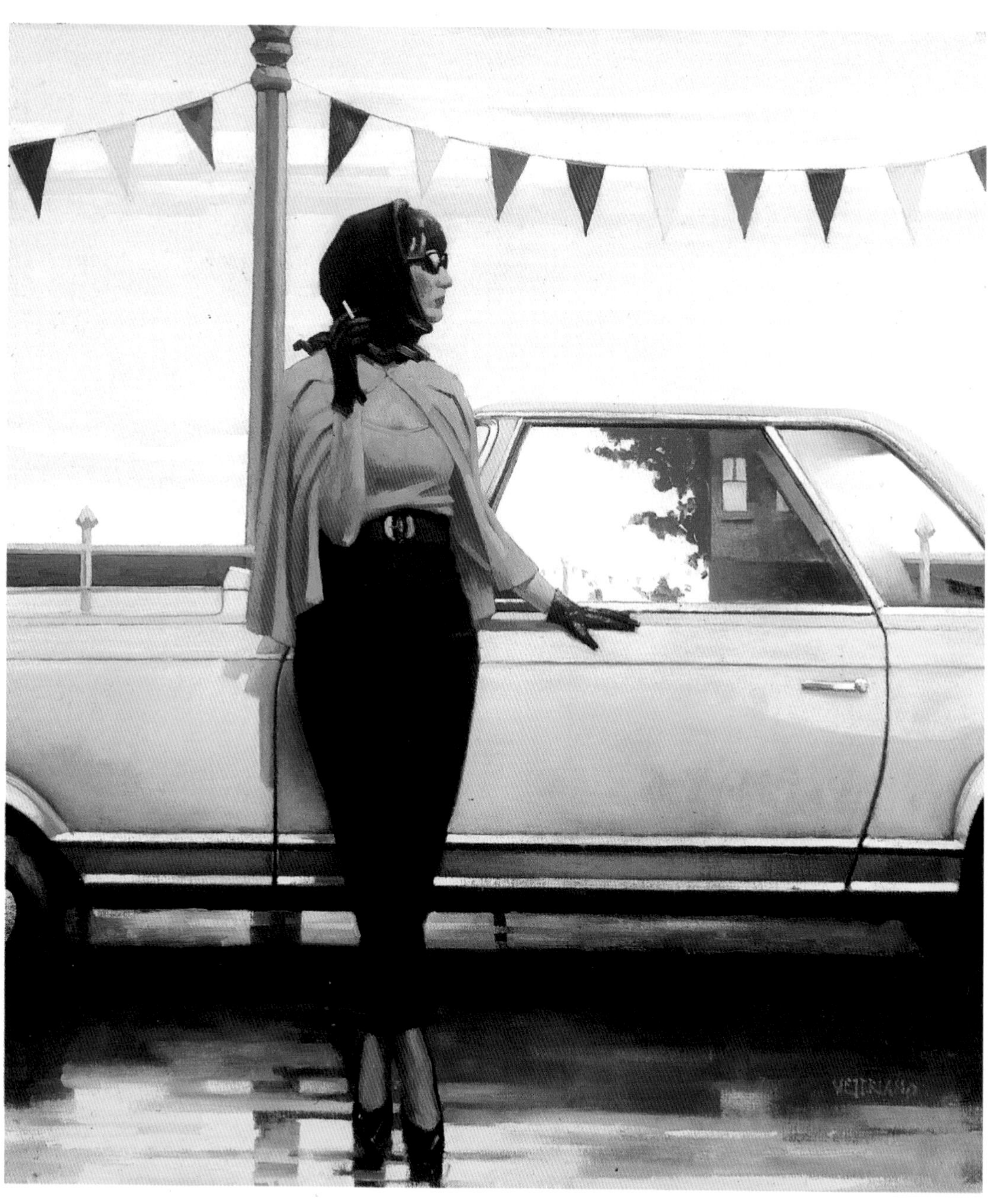

Suddenly One Summer

Lunchtime Lovers

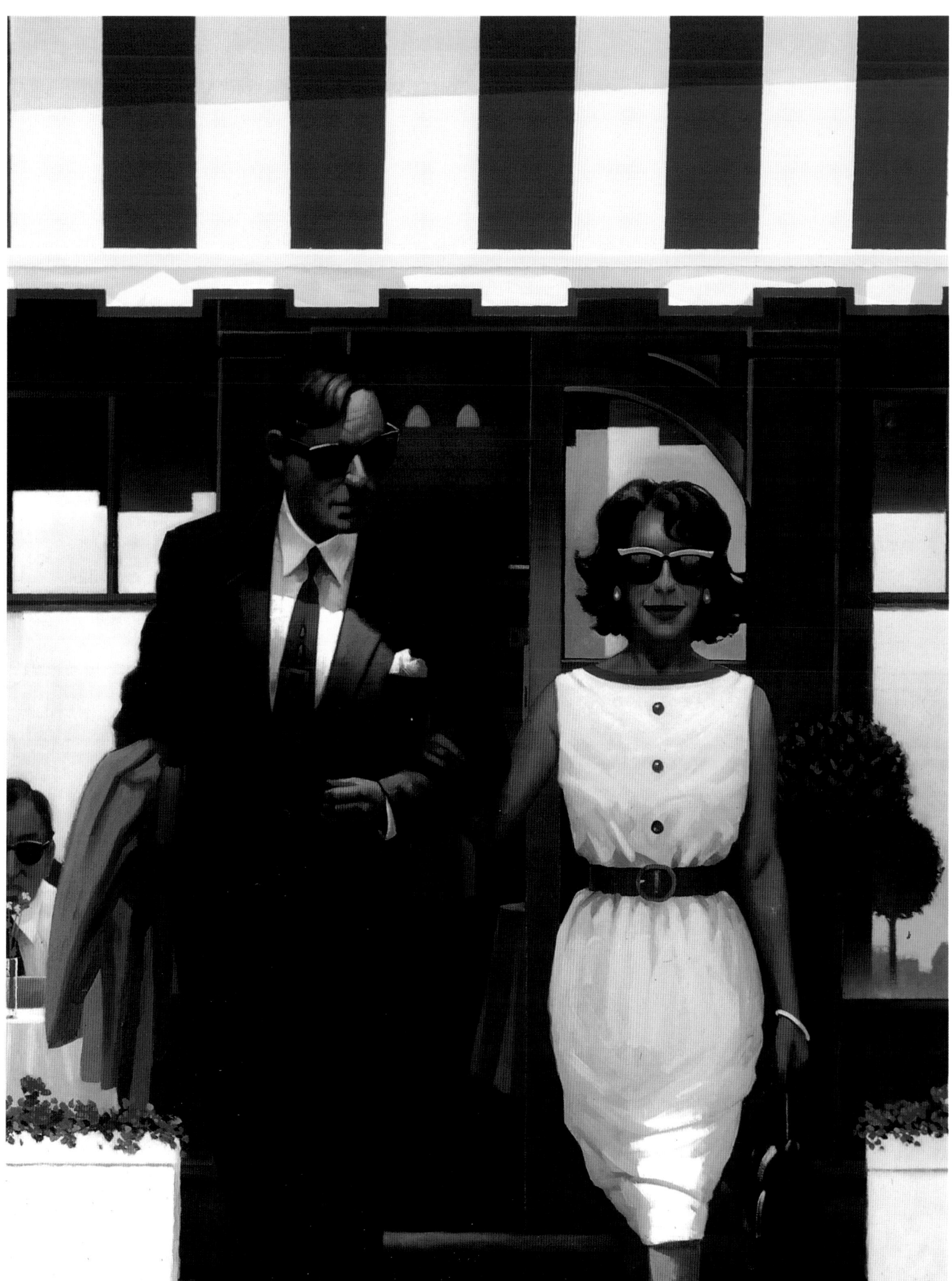

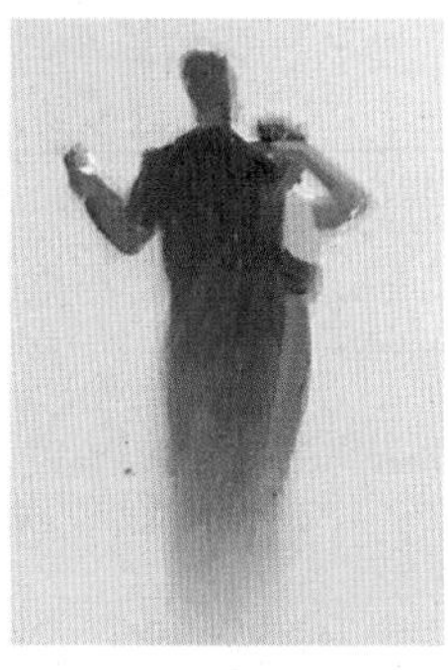

Dance Me To The End of Love

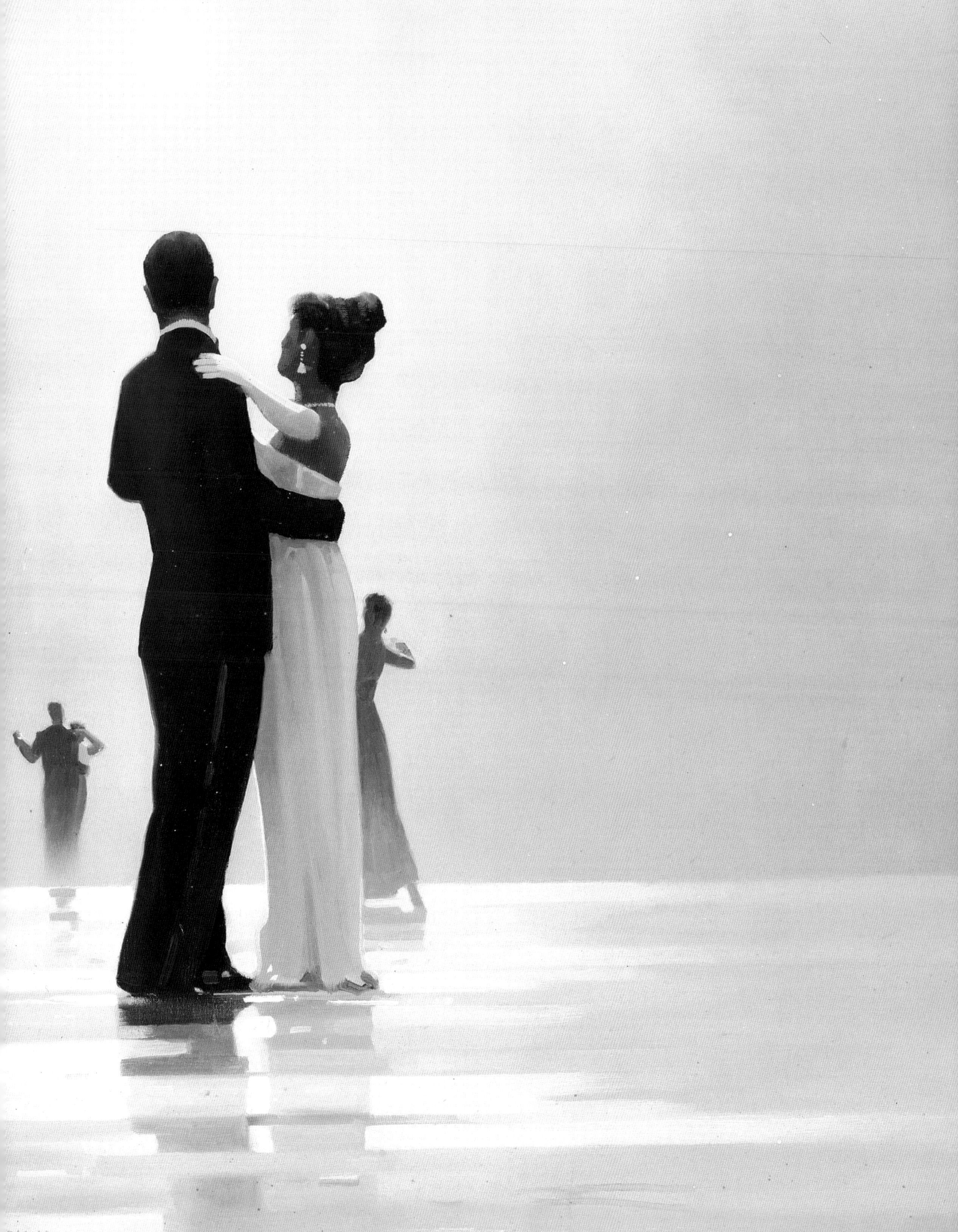

AFTERWORD

JACK VETTRIANO seems to understand perfectly the stylish sexiness and intrigue that you get when high life and low life collide. There's a terrific frisson in many of his paintings; I love the narrative detail you find in so many of them, the way in which you form an impression on first glance that is revised and undermined as you take in the detail. A man straightening his tie as a woman fastens her dress could be a couple getting ready for an evening out; but then you notice the cheap electric fire, the reflection in the mirror of the bare light bulb and another man lurking in the doorway, and an altogether different story constructs itself.

In other paintings, there's a perfect evocation of decadent nightlife: private clubs and gambling and illicit sex. It's that heady mix of drink and sex and fast cars that led me to commission Jack Vettriano to undertake a series of paintings for the Bluebird Club in London.

The other thing I particularly admire – and which seems to me so extraordinary to find in the work of a painter who has no formal training – is Jack Vettriano's appreciation of the quality of light. This is something that's very evident in the Bluebird paintings, but you can see it here, too, whether it's the harsh light from the window in what I take to be his studio, the perfect sunlight at the seaside, or the extraordinarily romantic couples dancing in misty white light, their forms reflected in pools of water.

There's a lot to see and admire here; paintings to please the mind and engage the imagination.

TERENCE CONRAN

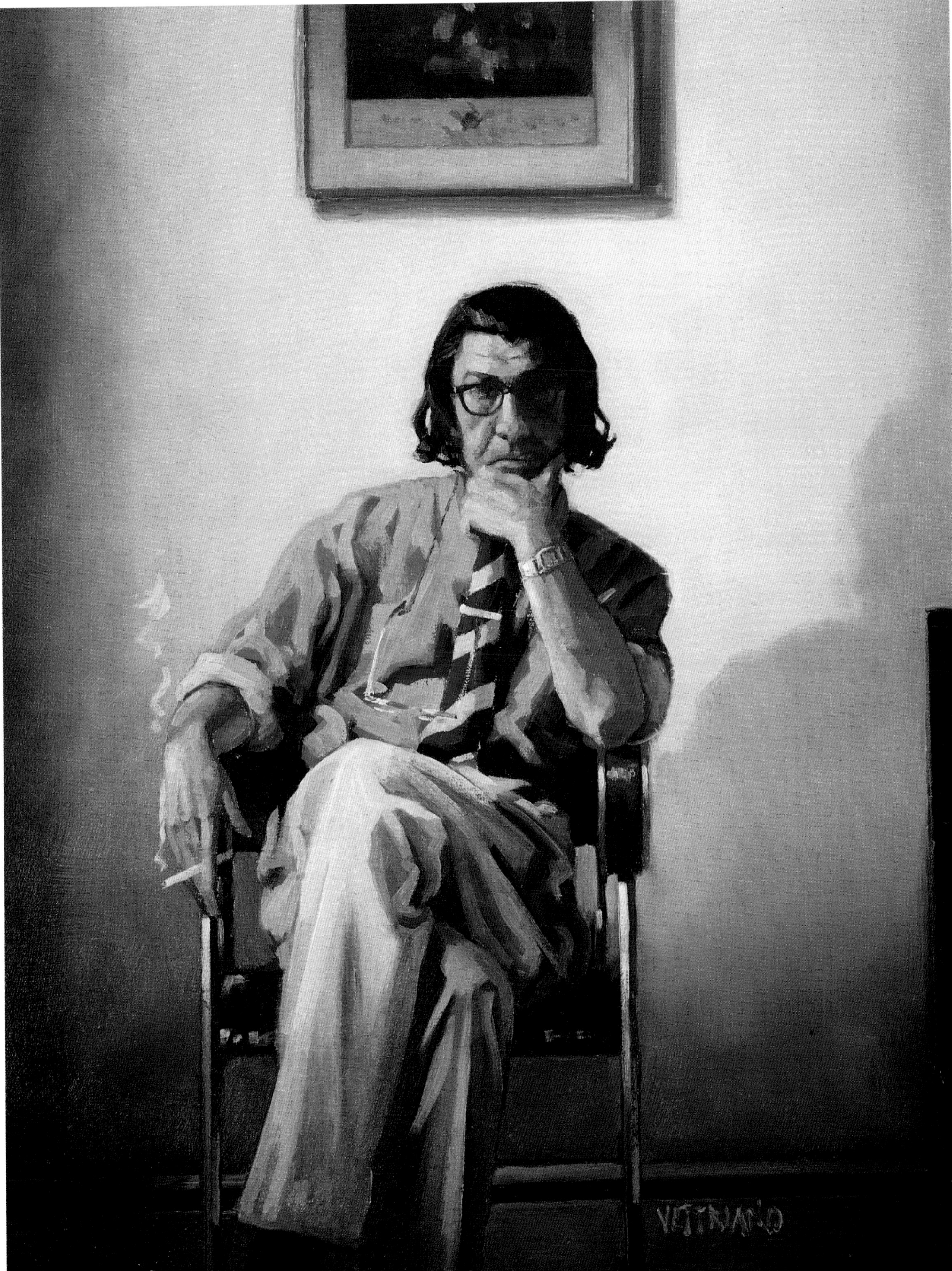
VETTRIANO

Photograph of Jack Vettriano by Lesley Jones.

EXHIBITIONS

1992 **Tales of Love and Other Stories**, Edinburgh Gallery, Edinburgh

1992 **God's Children**, Mall Gallery, London

1993 **Fallen Angels**, Catto Gallery, London

1993 **Summers Remembered**, Corrymella Scott Gallery, Newcastle-upon-Tyne

1994 **Chimes at Midnight**, Portland Gallery, London

1994 **After Midnight**, Everard Read Gallery, Johannesburg

1995 **A Date with Fate**, Edinburgh Festival, Edinburgh

1996 **The Passion and the Pain**, Portland Gallery, London

1996 **Halfway to Paradise**, Portland Gallery, London
The Museum Annex, Hong Kong

1997 **Small Paintings and Studies**, Portland Gallery, London
Edinburgh Festival

1998 **Between Darkness and Dawn**, Portland Gallery, London

1999 **The International 20th Century Arts Fair**, Portland Gallery, London
The Armory, New York

2000 **Lovers and Other Strangers**, Portland Gallery, London

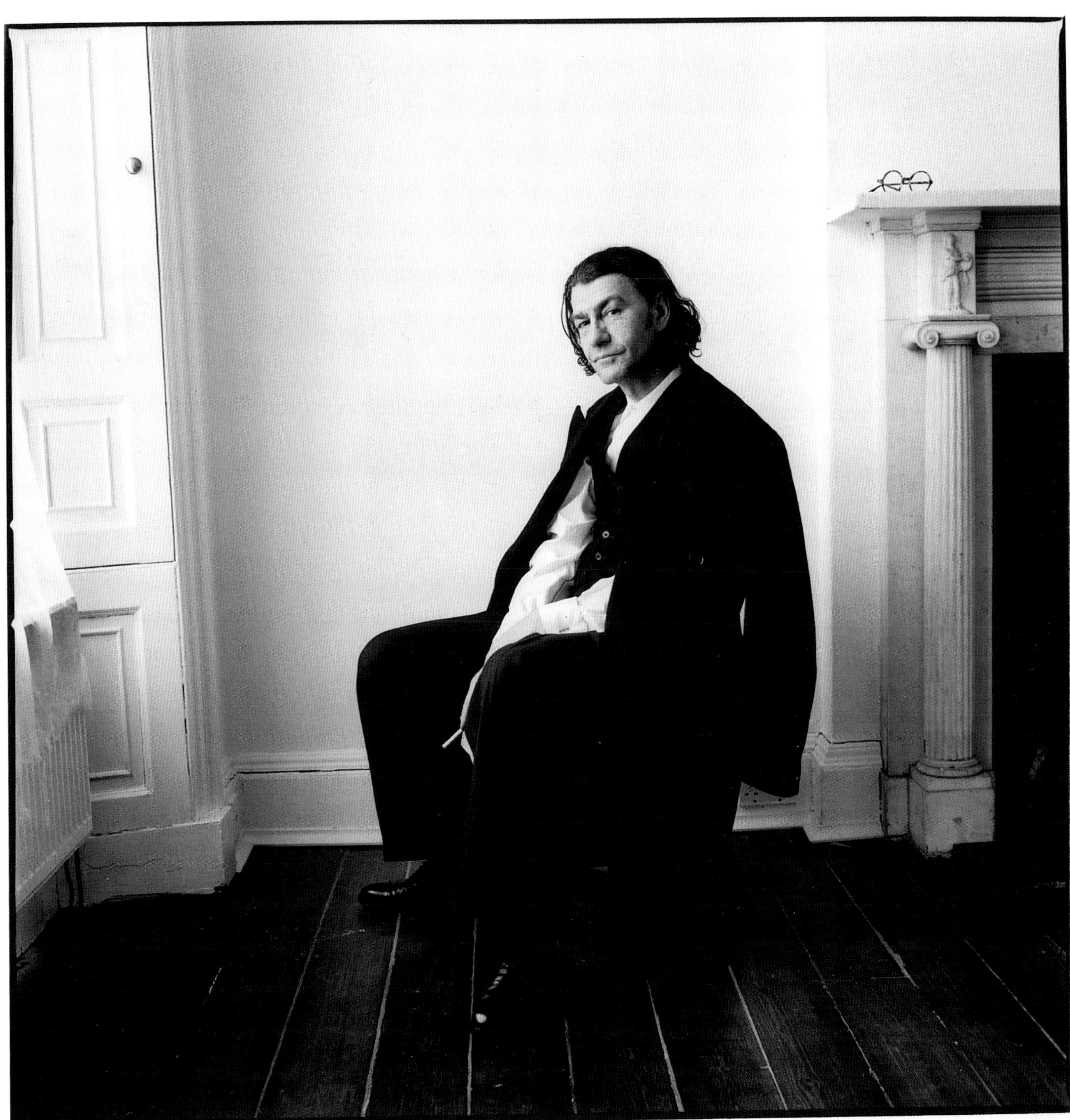

INDEX OF PAINTINGS

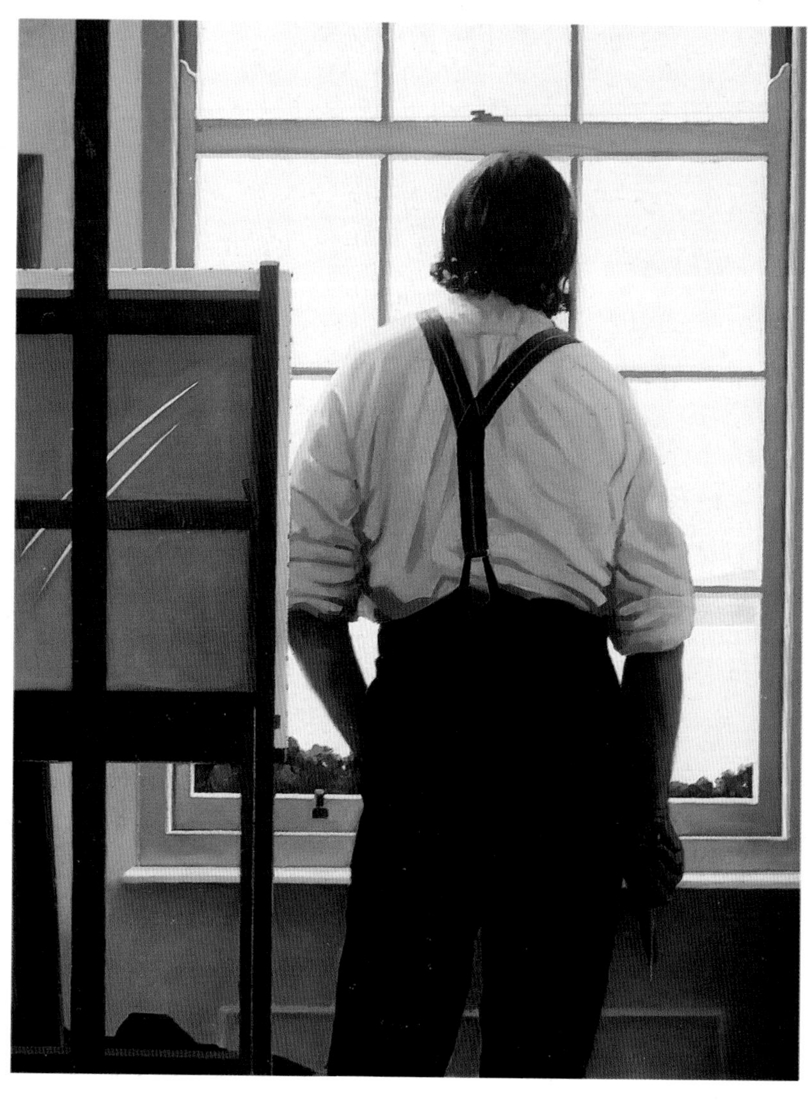